It's another essential resource from CGP!

There's been a seismic shift in GCSE Geography — the latest
Grade 9-1 courses are tougher than ever. But fear not, help is at hand...

This fantastic CGP book covers everything you'll need for
the new Edexcel B course, with no-nonsense explanations,
easy-to-follow diagrams and cracking case studies.

There's also useful advice on fieldwork, geographical skills and the new
decision-making exercise — so you'll be in peak condition for the exams.

CGP — still the best! ☺

Our sole aim here at CGP is to produce the highest quality books —
carefully written, immaculately presented and dangerously close to being funny.

Then we work our socks off to get them out to you
— at the cheapest possible prices.

Contents

Component 3:
People and Environment Issues —
Making Geographical Decisions

Published by CGP

Editors:
Claire Boulter, David Maliphant, Chris McGarry, Claire Plowman, Hannah Roscoe, David Ryan.

Contributors:
Paddy Gannon, Barbara Melbourne.

Proofreading:
Susan Alexander, Karen Wells.

ISBN: 978 1 78294 621 2

With thanks to Ana Pungartnik for the copyright research.

Printed by Elanders Ltd, Newcastle upon Tyne.
Clipart from Corel®

Based on the classic CGP style created by Richard Parsons.

Structure of the Course

'Know thy enemy', 'forewarned is forearmed'... There are many boring quotes that just mean <u>being prepared is a good thing</u>. <u>Don't</u> stumble <u>blindly</u> into a GCSE course — find out what you're facing.

You'll have to do Three Exams

GCSE Edexcel Geography B is divided into <u>three components</u>: <u>Global Geographical Issues</u>, <u>UK Geographical Issues</u> and <u>People and Environment Issues — Making Geographical Decisions</u>.

You'll have to do <u>three</u> exams — <u>one</u> on each of the three components. <u>Geographical skills</u> will be assessed in <u>all three</u> exams, but <u>fieldwork</u> (see p. 84) will only be assessed in <u>Paper 2</u>. <u>All</u> your <u>exams</u> will take place at the <u>end of the course</u>.

Paper 1: Global Geographical Issues

Paper 1 is divided into <u>three sections</u>.
- <u>Section A</u> covers <u>Hazardous Earth</u>.
- <u>Section B</u> covers <u>Development Dynamics</u>.
- <u>Section C</u> covers <u>Challenges of an Urbanising World</u>.

1 hour 30 minutes	94 marks in total	37.5% of your final mark

Paper 2: UK Geographical Issues

Paper 2 is divided into <u>three sections</u>.
- <u>Section A</u> covers <u>The UK's Evolving Physical Landscape</u>.
- <u>Section B</u> covers <u>The UK's Evolving Human Landscape</u>.
- <u>Section C</u> is split into two parts (C1 and C2). Both parts cover <u>Geographical Investigations</u>:
  — C1 covers <u>physical geography fieldwork</u> (<u>Coastal Change and Conflict</u> and <u>River Processes and Pressures</u>).
  — C2 covers <u>human geography fieldwork</u> (<u>Dynamic Urban Areas</u> and <u>Changing Rural Areas</u>).

1 hour 30 minutes	94 marks in total	37.5% of your final mark

You need to <u>answer all the questions</u> in Sections A and B.
In Section C, make sure you <u>only</u> answer questions on the fieldwork <u>you carried out</u>.

Paper 3: People and Environment Issues — Making Geographical Decisions

In the exam, you'll get a <u>Resource Booklet</u> with lots of information about a geographical <u>issue</u>. All the questions on Paper 3 will be based on <u>these resources</u>.

Paper 3 is split into <u>four sections</u>.
- <u>Section A</u> covers <u>People and the Biosphere</u>.
- <u>Section B</u> covers <u>Forests Under Threat</u>.
- <u>Section C</u> covers <u>Consuming Energy Resources</u>.
- <u>Section D</u> is a <u>decision-making exercise</u>, where you will have to use the sources you have been given and your own knowledge to come to a <u>justified decision</u> about the <u>issue</u>.

1 hour 30 minutes	64 marks in total	25% of your final mark

There's more about how to answer the question in Section D on <u>page 116</u>.

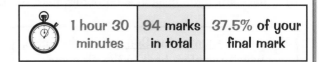

I'm all over those spelling marks.

In <u>each exam</u>, there will be one question which has <u>4 extra marks</u> available for <u>spelling</u>, <u>punctuation</u> and <u>grammar</u> as well as the use of <u>specialist terminology</u> (see p.117). These marks are <u>included</u> in the <u>total marks</u> given for each paper.

May the course be with you...

I know... you just want to get started on some lovely Geography and you're dying to get out your freshly ironed map. Well, have no fear — it's non-stop Geography from here. But it's worthwhile knowing this stuff so you're not the person who doesn't realise there's a third exam — there's a fine line between being relaxed and sabotaging yourself...

Global Atmospheric Circulation

Let's kick things off with a load of <u>hot air</u>. Specifically, air that moves in <u>loops</u> around the <u>Earth</u>...

Winds *Transfer Heat* from the Equator to the Poles

1) The <u>Sun</u> heats the Earth's surface <u>unevenly</u> — <u>insolation</u> (the <u>solar radiation</u> that reaches the Earth's surface) is <u>greater</u> at the equator than the poles.

2) The differences in <u>temperature</u> cause differences in <u>air pressure</u> (see below).

3) Winds blow <u>FROM</u> the areas of <u>high</u> pressure <u>TO</u> the areas of <u>low pressure</u>, transferring heat <u>away</u> from the equator.

4) Winds are part of <u>global atmospheric circulation</u> loops (called <u>cells</u>). These loops have <u>warm rising air</u> which creates a <u>low pressure belt</u>, and <u>cool falling air</u> which creates a <u>high pressure belt</u>.

5) There are <u>three cells</u> in each hemisphere — the <u>Hadley</u>, <u>Ferrel</u> and <u>Polar</u> cells.

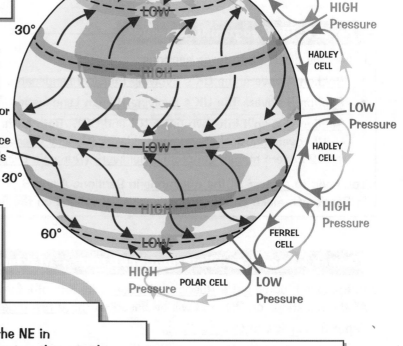

1) At the <u>equator</u> the <u>Sun warms</u> the Earth, which transfers heat to the air above, causing it to <u>rise</u>. This creates a <u>low pressure belt</u>. As the air rises, it <u>cools</u> and <u>condenses</u> forming <u>clouds</u> and <u>rain</u>.

2) The cool, dry air <u>moves out</u> to 30° north and south of the equator.

3) At <u>30° north and south</u> of the equator, the <u>cool air sinks</u>, creating a <u>high pressure belt</u> with <u>cloudless skies</u> and <u>very low rainfall</u>.

4) The cool air reaches the ground surface and moves as surface winds either <u>back to the equator</u> or <u>towards the poles</u>:
- Surface winds blowing towards the <u>equator</u> are called <u>trade winds</u>.
- Trade winds blow from the SE in the southern hemisphere and from the NE in the northern hemisphere. At the equator, these <u>trade winds meet</u> and are heated by the sun. This causes them to rise and form <u>clouds</u>.
- Surface winds blowing towards the <u>poles</u> are called <u>westerlies</u>. They blow from the NW in the southern hemisphere and from the SW in the northern hemisphere.

5) At <u>60° north and south of the equator</u>, the warmer surface winds meet colder air from the poles. The warmer air is less dense than the cold air so it is forced to <u>rise</u>, creating <u>low pressure</u> and <u>frontal rain</u> (rain that forms where the <u>warm</u> and <u>cold</u> air masses <u>meet</u>).

6) Some of the air <u>moves back</u> towards the equator, and the rest moves towards the <u>poles</u>.

7) At the <u>poles</u> the <u>cool air sinks</u>, creating <u>high pressure</u>. The high pressure air is drawn back towards the equator as <u>surface winds</u>.

Global Atmospheric Circulation

Heat is also Transferred by Ocean Currents

1) Ocean currents are large scale movements of water that <u>transfer</u> heat energy from <u>warmer</u> to <u>cooler</u> regions.

2) <u>Surface currents</u> are caused by <u>winds</u> and help transfer heat <u>away</u> from the Equator, e.g. the <u>Gulf Stream</u> brings warm water from the <u>Caribbean</u> and keeps <u>Western Europe</u> warmer than it would otherwise be.

3) There are also <u>deep ocean currents</u> driven by differences in <u>water density</u>.

4) When water <u>freezes</u> at the poles, the surrounding water gets <u>saltier</u>, increasing its <u>density</u>.

5) As it gets denser, it <u>sinks</u>, causing <u>warmer</u> water to flow in at the surface — creating a current.

6) This <u>warmer</u> water is <u>cooled</u> and <u>sinks</u>, continuing the <u>cycle</u>.

7) This cycle of cooling and sinking moves water in a big <u>loop</u> round the Earth — this is known as the <u>thermohaline circulation</u>.

~ deep cold currents   ~ shallow warm currents

There are Different Climate Zones Around the World

The <u>pressure belts</u> caused by <u>global atmospheric circulation</u> (see previous page) cause <u>variations</u> in <u>climate</u>.

Arid (Dry)

<u>Sinking air</u> from the <u>Hadley</u> and <u>Ferrel cells</u> meeting causes <u>high pressure</u> and <u>prevents rainfall</u>. Rainfall is very low for all or most of the year. Temperatures are <u>hot</u> or <u>warm</u>.

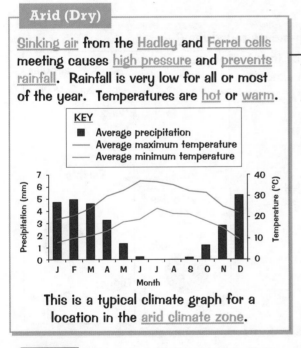

KEY
■ Average precipitation
— Average maximum temperature
— Average minimum temperature

This is a typical climate graph for a location in the <u>arid climate zone</u>.

Polar

<u>Sinking air</u> from the <u>Polar cells</u> creates an area of <u>high pressure</u> at the poles. <u>Temperatures</u> are <u>low</u> all year round and there's <u>very little rainfall</u>.

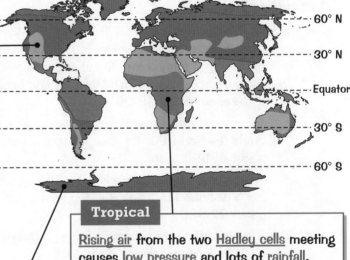

Tropical

<u>Rising air</u> from the two <u>Hadley cells</u> meeting causes <u>low pressure</u> and lots of <u>rainfall</u>. Temperatures are <u>hot</u> all the time and <u>rainfall</u> is <u>high</u>.

This is a typical climate graph for a location in the <u>tropical climate zone</u>.

Climate graphs show the average precipitation and temperatures for a certain area. Rainfall is shown on a bar chart and temperature is shown on a line graph.

Global circulation — Phileas Fogg knew a thing or two about that...

Make sure you understand how circulation cells and ocean currents redistribute heat energy around the Earth and the effect this has on the climate. There's a bit to learn on the diagram on page 2, so keep going back 'til you've got it all.

Natural Climate Change

Climate change <u>isn't</u> a new phenomenon — it's been happening for <u>millions of years</u>. Believe it or not, there are a couple of <u>natural causes</u> of climate change and there's also plenty of <u>evidence</u> we can use to <u>study</u> past climate.

The Earth's Climate is Always Changing

<u>Climate change</u> is any significant <u>change</u> in the <u>Earth's climate</u> over a <u>long period</u>. The climate <u>constantly changes</u>, it always has, and it always will.

1) The <u>Quaternary period</u> is the most recent geological time period, spanning from about <u>2.6 million years ago</u> to the present day.

2) In the period <u>before</u> the Quaternary, the Earth's climate was <u>warmer</u> and quite <u>stable</u>. Then things <u>changed</u> a lot.

The Quaternary period includes the whole of human history.

3) During the Quaternary, <u>global temperature</u> has shifted between cold <u>glacial periods</u> that last for around 100 000 years, and warmer <u>interglacial periods</u> that usually last for around 10 000 years.

4) The <u>last</u> glacial period <u>ended</u> around 15 000 years ago. Since then the climate has been <u>warming</u>.

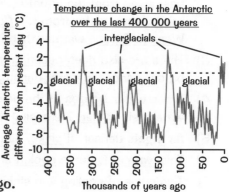

Temperature change in the Antarctic over the last 400 000 years

There are Natural Causes of Climate Change

① Orbital Changes

1) <u>Orbital changes</u> are <u>variations</u> in the <u>way</u> the <u>Earth</u> moves round the <u>Sun</u>.

- <u>Stretch</u> (also called <u>eccentricity</u>) — the path of the Earth's <u>orbit</u> around the Sun changes from an almost perfect <u>circle</u> to an <u>ellipse</u> (an oval) and back again about every 96 000 years.

- <u>Tilt</u> — the Earth's axis is <u>tilted</u> at an <u>angle</u> as it orbits the Sun. This tilt changes over a cycle of about 41 000 years.

- <u>Wobble</u> (also called <u>precession</u>) — the <u>axis</u> of the Earth wobbles like a <u>spinning top</u> on a cycle of about 22 000 years.

2) These cycles affect the amount of <u>solar radiation</u> (energy) the Earth receives. If the Earth receives <u>more energy</u>, it gets <u>warmer</u>.

3) Orbital changes may have caused the <u>glacial</u> and <u>interglacial cycles</u> of the <u>Quaternary period</u>.

elliptical orbit · circular orbit · Sun

axis wobbles in a circle · axis · axis

Earth's axis · Bigger tilt · Smaller tilt

② Volcanic Activity

1) Major <u>volcanic eruptions</u> eject large quantities of material, e.g. ash, into the atmosphere.

2) Some of these particles <u>reflect</u> the <u>Sun's rays</u> back out to space, so the Earth's surface <u>cools</u>.

3) Volcanic activity may cause <u>short-term changes</u> in climate, e.g. the eruption of <u>Mount Tambora</u> in Indonesia in 1815 led to the '<u>Year Without a Summer</u>' in 1816.

③ Solar Output

1) The Sun's <u>output</u> of <u>energy</u> isn't constant — it <u>changes</u> in short cycles of about 11 years, and possibly also in <u>longer cycles</u> of several hundred years.

2) Periods when solar output is <u>reduced</u> may cause the Earth's climate to become <u>cooler</u>.

3) The <u>Maunder Minimum</u> was a period of reduced solar activity between <u>1645</u> and <u>1715</u> which coincided with the <u>Little Ice Age</u> (see p.5).

Natural Climate Change

(4) Asteroid Collisions

1) Asteroids hitting the Earth's surface can throw up huge amounts of dust into the atmosphere.

2) These particles prevent the Sun's energy from reaching the Earth's surface so global temperatures fall (possibly for several years).

3) Some scientists believe that an asteroid collision caused a period of global cooling (the Younger Dryas) around 12 000 years ago.

Evidence for Natural Climate Change Comes from Many Sources

Scientists can work out how the climate has changed over time using a range of methods. For example:

Tree Rings

1) Most trees produce one ring within their trunks every year.

2) The thickness of the ring depends on the climate when the ring was formed — when it's warmer the rings are thicker.

3) Scientists take cores through tree trunks then date each ring by counting them back from when the core was taken. By looking at the thickness of the rings, they can see what the climate was like each year.

Ice Cores

1) Ice sheets are made up of layers of ice — one layer is formed each year.

2) Scientists drill into ice sheets to get long cores of ice.

3) By analysing the gases (e.g. carbon dioxide) trapped in the layers of ice, they can tell what the temperature was each year.

4) One ice core (the Vostok Ice Core) from Antarctica shows the temperature changes over the last 400 000 years (see graph on p.4).

Historical Records

1) Since the 1850s global temperatures have been measured accurately using thermometers. This gives a reliable but short-term record of temperature change.

2) Historical records (e.g. diaries and paintings) can extend the record of climate change a bit further back.

3) For example, historical diaries can show what the climate was like in the past, e.g. by giving the number of days of rain or snow and the dates of harvests (an early harvest suggests warm weather).

4) Paintings of fairs and markets on frozen rivers show that winters in Europe were regularly much colder 500 years ago than they are now.

These Sources have been used to Reconstruct the UK's Past Climate

MEDIEVAL WARM PERIOD
- The Medieval Warm Period was a period of warming between 900 and 1300.
- Harvest records show that England was warm enough to grow large amounts of grapes.
- Tree ring data suggests this was also the case during Roman times, when temperatures were almost 1.0 °C warmer than today.

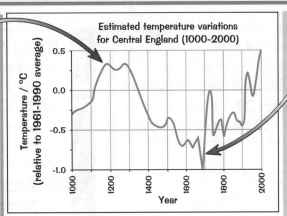
Estimated temperature variations for Central England (1000-2000)

The Inuit are an indigenous people from parts of Canada, Greenland and Alaska.

LITTLE ICE AGE
- The Little Ice Age was a period of cooling that followed the Medieval Warm Period.
- Paintings from the 17th century show the London Frost Fairs, which took place on a frozen River Thames.
- Historical records talk about arctic ice reaching as far south as Scotland and sightings of Inuits.

Greensleeves — my favourite historical record...

Tree rings and paintings aren't obvious sources of evidence for climate change, but make sure you know what they show.

Climate Change — Human Activity

Climate may have been changing long before humans roamed the Earth, but in the last 150 years or so human activities have begun to change it too. It's pretty bad, but what's worse is that you have to know all about it.

The Natural Greenhouse Effect is Essential for Keeping Our Planet Warm

1) The temperature of the Earth is a balance between the heat it gets from the Sun and the heat it loses to space.

2) The incoming energy from the Sun is short-wave radiation. The outgoing energy from the Earth is long-wave radiation.

3) Gases in the atmosphere naturally act like an insulating layer — they let short-wave radiation in, but trap long-wave radiation, helping to keep the Earth at the right temperature.

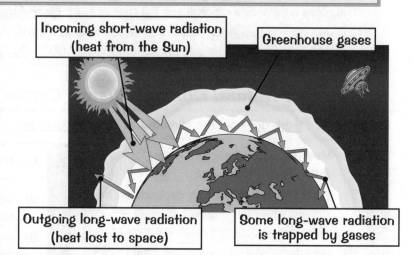

Incoming short-wave radiation (heat from the Sun)

Greenhouse gases

Outgoing long-wave radiation (heat lost to space)

Some long-wave radiation is trapped by gases

4) This is called the greenhouse effect ('cos it's a bit like a greenhouse trapping heat).

5) Gases that trap heat are called greenhouse gases — they include carbon dioxide (CO_2) and methane (CH_4).

6) Some greenhouse gases are stronger than others, e.g. methane absorbs more heat than carbon dioxide.

7) Different greenhouse gases stay in the atmosphere for different lengths of time. For example, methane usually stays in the atmosphere for around 10 years after it has been emitted.

8) The longer the gases stay in the atmosphere, the more they'll contribute to warming.

Human Activities are Making the Greenhouse Effect Stronger

1) The rate of the recent rise in global temperature (global warming) is unheard of.

2) There's a scientific consensus (general agreement) that human activities are causing global warming by making the greenhouse effect stronger. This is called the enhanced greenhouse effect.

3) Too much greenhouse gas in the atmosphere means too much energy is trapped and the planet warms up.

4) Humans are increasing the concentration of greenhouse gases:

Farming

How very dare you!

1) Farming of livestock produces a lot of methane — cows love to fart...

2) Rice paddies contribute to global warming, because flooded fields emit methane.

3) Trees absorb and store CO_2. When land is cleared of trees for agriculture it stops the absorption of CO_2, which leaves more CO_2 in the atmosphere.

Industry

1) Most industry uses a lot of energy.

2) Some industrial processes also release greenhouse gases, e.g. cement is made from limestone, which contains carbon. When cement is produced, lots of CO_2 is released into the atmosphere.

3) Industrial waste may end up in landfill sites where it decays, releasing methane.

Energy

CO_2 is released into the atmosphere when fossil fuels like coal, oil and natural gas are burnt, e.g. in power stations.

Transport

1) Most cars, lorries, ships and planes run on fossil fuels, which release greenhouse gases when burnt.

2) Car ownership is rapidly increasing in countries which are developing, e.g. China.

3) This means there are more cars on the roads (especially in urban areas).

4) This increases congestion. As a result, car engines are running for longer, so the amount of greenhouse gases released increases.

Climate Change — Human Activity

There is Some Evidence that Human Activity is causing Climate Change

Scientists have identified several factors which support the idea that humans are causing global warming.

Declining Arctic Ice

1) Sea ice forms around the poles in winter when ocean temperatures fall below -1.8 °C and melts during the summer when it's warmer.

2) The extent of arctic sea ice in winter has decreased by more than 3% each decade over the past 35 years.

Sea Level Rise and Warming Oceans

Since 1901 sea levels have risen by almost 0.2 m. Scientists have highlighted two factors behind this rise:

- **EUSTATIC SEA LEVEL RISE**

  Warmer temperatures are causing glaciers to shrink and ice sheets to melt. The melting of ice on land, especially from the Greenland and Antarctic ice sheets, means that water stored on land as ice returns to the oceans. This causes sea levels to rise.

- **THERMAL EXPANSION**

  Water in the oceans expands as it gets warmer — this is called thermal expansion. Scientists think this accounts for about half of the measured rise in sea levels.

Global Temperature Rise

Temperatures have increased by nearly 1 °C since 1880 and are expected to rise by 0.3-4.8 °C between 2005 and 2100. The top ten warmest years since records began have all been since the year 2000.

Extreme Weather Events

1) Since 1950 there has been a higher frequency of heat waves in many areas and fewer cold weather extremes.

2) In the UK, more rainfall records were broken in 2010-2014 than in any decade on record, even after only half a decade. 2013 was one of the wettest years on record and December 2015 was the wettest month ever recorded in the UK.

Climate Change Could have Serious Impacts on People

Changes in climate are already having an impact on people, but there could be more serious consequences in the future:

1) In some places deaths due to heat have increased — but deaths due to cold have decreased.

2) Some areas could become so hot and dry that they're difficult or impossible to inhabit. Low-lying coastal areas could be lost to the sea or flood so often that they also become impossible to inhabit. This could lead to migration and overcrowding in other areas.

3) Climate change is affecting farming in different ways around the world:
   - Globally, some crops have suffered from climate change (e.g. maize crops have got smaller due to warming in recent years).
   - But some farmers in high-latitude countries (countries further from the equator) are finding that crops benefit from warmer conditions.

4) Lower crop yields could increase malnutrition, ill health and death from starvation, particularly in lower latitudes (nearer the equator).

5) Climate change means the weather is getting more extreme. This means more money has to be spent on predicting extreme weather events, reducing their impacts and rebuilding after them.

Flooding is becoming more common in the UK

Don't blame it on the sunshine — it's mostly our fault...

Well, that was a cheerful read — a whole load of ways that humans might be affected by climate change.

1) Outline two human activities that are enhancing the greenhouse effect. [4]

EXAM QUESTION

Climate Change Projections

It's time to earn that black belt in climate change. You should now be an expert in the causes and evidence for climate change, so it's high time you had a gander at how to go about predicting future climate change.

Data about Climate Change can be used to Make Predictions

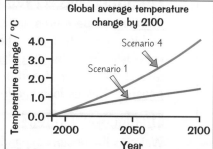

1) Physical processes, e.g. atmospheric circulation and the effect of volcanic eruptions on the climate, can be modelled on computers.

2) Human activity, e.g. growth of industry or development of clean energy, can also be modelled using data that's been collected about greenhouse gas emissions.

3) Scientists can use these models to work out how the climate would be affected under certain scenarios, e.g. what would happen if there was a volcanic eruption in 20 years' time and there were still high levels of greenhouse gas emissions.

4) The Intergovernmental Panel on Climate Change (IPCC) is an international group of scientists that uses models to predict how the climate might change and the consequences of any changes.

5) The IPCC have chosen four "Representative Concentration Pathways" (RCPs) — possible scenarios covering the best to the worst possible outcomes.

6) The IPCC uses projection graphs to show the predicted changes in temperature and sea level by 2100.

7) Lines for the best and worst scenarios are plotted on the graphs. All other outcomes fall between these lines.

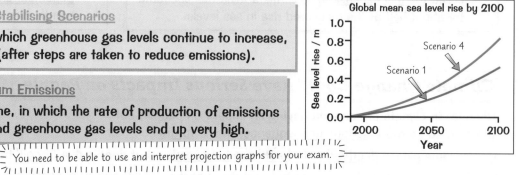

SCENARIO 1 — Minimum Emissions
This is the best outcome, in which levels of greenhouse gases peak, then reduce (i.e. greenhouse gas emissions are significantly reduced).

SCENARIOS 2 & 3 — Stabilising Scenarios
These are scenarios in which greenhouse gas levels continue to increase, but eventually level off (after steps are taken to reduce emissions).

SCENARIO 4 — Maximum Emissions
This is the worst outcome, in which the rate of production of emissions continues to increase and greenhouse gas levels end up very high.

You need to be able to use and interpret projection graphs for your exam.

There is Lots of Uncertainty about Future Climate Change

It's difficult to predict the impacts of changes in climate because there's so much uncertainty.

1) EMISSIONS — we don't actually know how emissions will change, i.e. which scenario is most accurate.
   • Predictions have to take into account things like population increase and economic development.
   • It's hard to know how global population will change in the future (i.e. whether it'll keep growing at the rate it is today) or how much development will take place in the future.

2) COMPLEXITY — we don't know what exact climate changes each scenario will cause.
   • There are lots of natural processes that we don't fully understand, which makes it difficult to predict what will change. We don't know how these natural factors could have an impact on climate change.

3) MANAGEMENT — we don't know what attempts there will be to manage the amount of greenhouse gases in the atmosphere, or how successful they'll be.

All this talk of climate change has got me hot and bothered...
Predicting climate change and its impacts isn't an exact science — no one's going to know what will really happen until it... um... happens. Now take a minute to compose yourself before you get caught up in tropical cyclones...

Tropical Cyclones

Tropical cyclones are <u>intense low pressure</u> weather systems with <u>heavy rain</u> and <u>strong winds</u> that spiral around the <u>centre</u>. They have a couple of other names (<u>hurricanes</u> and <u>typhoons</u>), but they're all the <u>same thing</u>.

Tropical Cyclones Develop over Warm Water

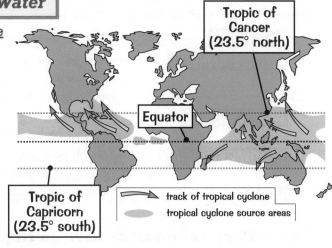

1) Tropical cyclones develop when the <u>sea temperature</u> is <u>26.5 °C</u> or higher and when the <u>wind shear</u> (the difference in windspeed) between <u>higher</u> and <u>lower</u> parts of the atmosphere is <u>low</u>.

2) The source area of most tropical cyclones is between <u>5°</u> and <u>30°</u> north and south of the equator — any further from the equator and the water <u>isn't warm enough</u>.

3) The majority of cyclones occur when sea temperatures are <u>highest</u> — in the <u>northern</u> hemisphere this is <u>June</u> to <u>November</u>. In the <u>southern</u> hemisphere, <u>November</u> to <u>April</u>.

4) <u>Warm</u>, <u>moist</u> air <u>rises</u> and <u>condensation</u> occurs. This releases huge amounts of <u>energy</u>, which makes the storms <u>powerful</u>. The <u>rising air</u> creates an area of <u>low pressure</u>, which increases <u>surface winds</u>.

5) The Earth's <u>rotation</u> deflects the paths of the winds, which causes the cyclone to <u>spin</u>.

6) Tropical cyclones <u>move towards the west</u> because of the <u>easterly winds</u> near the equator (see p.2).

7) When cyclones travel further away from the equator, their path may start to <u>curve</u> to the <u>east</u> as they get caught in the <u>mid-latitude westerlies</u>.

8) Cyclones <u>intensify</u> (<u>get stronger</u>) due to <u>energy</u> from the warm <u>water</u>.

9) They <u>dissipate</u> (<u>lose strength</u>) when they move over <u>land</u> or <u>cooler water</u> because the energy supply from the warm water is <u>cut off</u>. Changes in <u>windspeed</u>, e.g. from meeting other <u>weather systems</u>, can also cause a cyclone to dissipate.

10) <u>Climate change</u> may cause tropical cyclone source areas to <u>change</u>. If sea temperatures <u>rise</u>, more of the world's oceans could be <u>above 26.5 °C</u>. This means <u>more</u> places in the world may <u>experience</u> tropical cyclones.

Learn the Features and Structure of A Tropical Cyclone

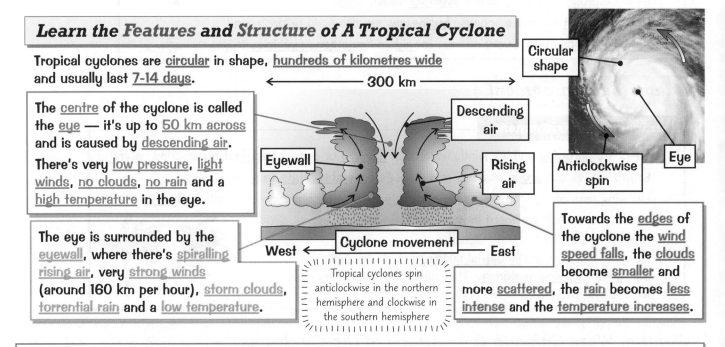

Tropical cyclones are <u>circular</u> in shape, <u>hundreds of kilometres wide</u> and usually last <u>7-14 days</u>.

The <u>centre</u> of the cyclone is called the <u>eye</u> — it's up to <u>50 km across</u> and is caused by <u>descending air</u>. There's very <u>low pressure</u>, <u>light winds</u>, <u>no clouds</u>, <u>no rain</u> and a <u>high temperature</u> in the eye.

The eye is surrounded by the <u>eyewall</u>, where there's <u>spiralling rising air</u>, very <u>strong winds</u> (around 160 km per hour), <u>storm clouds</u>, <u>torrential rain</u> and a <u>low temperature</u>.

Tropical cyclones spin anticlockwise in the northern hemisphere and clockwise in the southern hemisphere

Towards the <u>edges</u> of the cyclone the <u>wind speed falls</u>, the <u>clouds</u> become <u>smaller</u> and more <u>scattered</u>, the <u>rain</u> becomes <u>less intense</u> and the <u>temperature increases</u>.

Forget warm water, you're in hot water when one of these turns up...

Make sure you know how and where tropical cyclones develop as well as a few of their characteristics.

Tropical Cyclones — Impacts

Tropical cyclones try really hard to have an <u>impact</u>. Unfortunately, no-one ever appreciates their effort...

Tropical Cyclones *cause Physical Hazards*

When a tropical cyclone hits <u>land</u>, it causes <u>physical hazards</u>:

- **HIGH WINDS** — <u>windspeeds</u> in a tropical cyclone can reach <u>250 km/h</u>.
- **INTENSE RAINFALL** — tropical cyclones can release <u>trillions</u> of <u>litres</u> of water per day as rain. The rain gets <u>heavier</u> as you get <u>closer</u> to the <u>eye</u> of the cyclone.
- **STORM SURGES** — a <u>storm surge</u> is a large rise in <u>sea level</u> caused by <u>low pressure</u> and <u>high winds</u>.
- **COASTAL FLOODING** — <u>flooding</u> happens as a result of <u>storm surges</u> and <u>strong winds</u> driving <u>large waves</u> onto the shore.
- **LANDSLIDES** — <u>heavy rain</u> makes hills <u>unstable</u>, causing <u>landslides</u>.

These Physical Hazards have an Impact on People...

Impacts on People

- People may <u>drown</u> in the <u>strong currents</u> created by <u>floodwater</u> and <u>storm surges</u>.
- <u>Windspeeds</u> in tropical cyclones can be strong enough to completely <u>destroy</u> buildings, which means people are left <u>homeless</u>.
- <u>High winds</u> and <u>floodwater</u> can carry large amounts of <u>debris</u>, which can <u>kill</u> or <u>injure people</u>.
- <u>Electricity supplies</u> are cut off because cables are damaged or swept away by floodwater.
- Flooding causes <u>sewage</u> overflows which <u>contaminate water supplies</u>.
- The <u>shortage</u> of <u>clean water</u> and <u>lack</u> of proper <u>sanitation</u> makes it easier for <u>diseases</u> to spread.
- In <u>poorer countries</u> there's often a <u>shortage</u> of <u>food</u> because <u>crops</u> are damaged and <u>livestock</u> killed.
- <u>Unemployment</u> increases because <u>businesses</u> are damaged or destroyed.
- <u>Damaged roads</u> make it very difficult for <u>aid</u> and <u>emergency vehicles</u> to get through.

...and the Environment

Impacts on Environments

- Trees are <u>uprooted</u> by high winds which can <u>damage</u> or completely <u>destroy</u> wooded habitats.
- Storm surges can <u>erode</u> beaches and damage <u>coastal habitats</u> (e.g. coral reefs).
- Flooding caused by storm surges can <u>pollute</u> freshwater environments with <u>saltwater</u>.
- Landslides deposit <u>sediment</u> in rivers and lakes, which can <u>kill</u> fish and other <u>wildlife</u>.
- Flooding can damage <u>industrial buildings</u> on the coast, e.g. <u>oil</u> or <u>chemical factories</u>. This causes harmful chemicals to leak into the environment and cause pollution.

Weather Wars Episode II — Attack of the Cyclones...

Tropical cyclones pretty much wreak havoc in the areas they hit — boats get tossed into trees, hills go for a slide and the winds are so strong you can't stand upright... you want to get out of there faster than Superman in a kryptonite mine.

Tropical Cyclones — Preparation and Responses

I think I'm <u>psychic</u> — I just knew this page was going to be about <u>preparation</u> and <u>responses</u> to tropical cyclones.

Some Countries are More Vulnerable than Others

Countries can be <u>vulnerable</u> to the <u>impacts</u> of tropical cyclones for different reasons.

1 Physical Vulnerability

1) <u>Low-lying coastlines</u> are vulnerable to <u>storm surge flooding</u> as well as <u>large waves</u> caused by the <u>high winds</u>.

2) Areas in the <u>path</u> of tropical cyclones are <u>hit more frequently</u>.

3) <u>Steep hillsides</u> may increase the risk of <u>landslides</u>.

2 Economic Vulnerability

<u>Poorer countries</u> are <u>economically</u> vulnerable because:

1) Many people <u>depend</u> on <u>agriculture</u> which is often <u>badly affected</u> — this leads to a loss of <u>livelihoods</u>.

2) People may not have <u>insurance</u> to cover the costs of <u>repairing</u> damage caused by cyclones.

However, the <u>economic impact</u> is often greater in <u>richer countries</u> as the <u>buildings</u> and <u>infrastructure</u> (roads, rail, bridges etc.) damaged are worth <u>a lot</u> of money.

3 Social Vulnerability

<u>Poorer countries</u> are often more <u>socially</u> vulnerable because:

1) Buildings are <u>poorer quality</u> so more easily damaged.

2) <u>Health care</u> isn't as good so they <u>struggle</u> to treat all the <u>casualties</u>.

3) There is <u>little money</u> for <u>flood defences</u> or <u>training emergency teams</u>.

4) It's <u>harder</u> to <u>rescue</u> people because of <u>poor infrastructure</u>.

There are Many Strategies to Prepare for and Respond to Tropical Cyclones

Forecasting

1) <u>When</u> and <u>where</u> tropical cyclones will hit land can be <u>predicted</u>.

2) Scientists can use <u>weather forecasting</u> and <u>satellite technology</u> to <u>monitor</u> cyclones. <u>Computer models</u> are then used to <u>calculate</u> a <u>predicted path</u> for the cyclone.

3) The cyclone's <u>magnitude</u> can be monitored by measuring its <u>windspeeds</u>.

4) Predicting where and when a tropical cyclone is going to happen <u>gives people time</u> to <u>evacuate</u> and <u>protect</u> their <u>homes</u> and <u>businesses</u>, e.g. by <u>boarding up windows</u>.

> Tropical cyclones are classified using the Saffir-Simpson Scale, which is based on windspeed. Category 5 is the strongest (winds over 250 km/h) and 1 is the weakest (winds of 120-150 km/h).

Evacuation

1) <u>Warning strategies</u> are used to <u>alert</u> people to a tropical cyclone. An alert will give people enough time to <u>leave their homes</u> and get to a <u>safe place</u>.

2) Governments can plan <u>evacuation routes</u> to <u>get people away from storms quickly</u>. In Florida, evacuation routes are <u>signposted</u> all along the coast.

3) <u>Successful evacuations</u> can reduce the number of <u>deaths</u> and <u>injuries</u>.

4) <u>Emergency services</u> can <u>train</u> and <u>prepare</u> for disasters, e.g. by practising rescuing people from flooded areas with helicopters. This <u>reduces</u> the number of <u>people killed</u>.

Defences

1) <u>Defences</u> (e.g. <u>sea walls</u>) can be built along the coast to prevent damage from <u>storm surges</u>. Buildings can also be designed to <u>withstand</u> a storm surge, e.g. they can be <u>put on stilts</u> so they're safe from <u>floodwater</u>.

2) This will reduce the number of <u>buildings destroyed</u>, so <u>fewer people</u> will be <u>killed</u>, <u>injured</u>, <u>made homeless</u> and <u>made unemployed</u>.

Lack of revision makes you vulnerable to exam stress...

Check you're clear on these strategies for preparing and responding to cyclones, then try this exam question.

1) Outline how warning strategies can help to prepare people for a tropical cyclone. [2]

Tropical Cyclones — Examples

And now it's time for some <u>examples</u>. I worry I spoil you, but I think you deserve a treat.

A Cyclone's Impact is Linked to Preparation and Responses

The <u>impacts</u> of tropical cyclones depend on how a country <u>prepares</u> for and <u>responds</u> to the event. <u>Wealthier</u>, more <u>developed</u> countries, e.g. the USA, tend to be <u>better prepared</u>, so they can respond <u>quickly</u>.

1) Tropical cyclone in a <u>developed</u> country:

<u>Name</u>: Hurricane Katrina
<u>Magnitude</u>: Category 3 at landfall
<u>Place</u>: South east USA
<u>Date</u>: 29th August, 2005

2) Tropical cyclone in a <u>developing</u> country:

<u>Name</u>: Cyclone Nargis
<u>Magnitude</u>: Category 4 at landfall
<u>Place</u>: Irrawaddy delta, Myanmar
<u>Date</u>: 2nd May, 2008

Forecasting	• The USA has a sophisticated <u>monitoring system</u> to <u>predict</u> if (and where) a hurricane will hit. • The <u>National Hurricane Centre</u> (<u>NHC</u>) in Florida tracks and predicts hurricanes using <u>satellite images</u> and <u>planes</u> that collect weather data on approaching storms.	• Myanmar doesn't have a <u>dedicated monitoring centre</u> for tropical cyclones. • Myanmar doesn't have a <u>radar network</u> that can predict the <u>height</u> of <u>storm surges</u> and <u>waves</u> caused by cyclones.
Warning & Evacuation	• The NHC issued a <u>hurricane warning</u> on <u>26th August</u> for Louisiana, Mississippi and Alabama. It continued to <u>track</u> the hurricane, <u>updating</u> the <u>government</u> on where and when it would hit. • Mississippi and Louisiana declared <u>states of emergency</u> and <u>70-80%</u> of New Orleans residents were <u>evacuated</u> before the hurricane reached land. This <u>reduced</u> the number of people <u>killed</u> because lots of people had left the areas where the hurricane hit.	• Indian weather agencies <u>warned</u> the government of Myanmar that Cyclone Nargis was likely to hit the country <u>48 hours before</u> it did. • <u>Warnings</u> were issued on the <u>TV</u> and <u>radio</u>, but they <u>didn't reach</u> people in poor rural communities. This meant more people were <u>killed</u> because they didn't know <u>what to do</u> or <u>where to evacuate to</u>. • There were no <u>emergency preparation plans</u>, no <u>evacuation plans</u> and the country didn't have an <u>early warning system</u>.
Defences	• The city of <u>New Orleans</u> was very badly damaged — <u>flood defences</u> (e.g. embankments) that were supposed to protect the city <u>failed</u>. • This caused widespread <u>flooding</u> (over <u>80%</u> of the city was <u>underwater</u>).	• <u>Mangrove forests</u> protect the coast from flooding, but loads had been <u>chopped down</u> in the decade before Nargis hit, <u>reducing</u> the <u>natural protection</u>.
Impacts on the Environment	• <u>Coastal habitats</u> such as sea turtle breeding beaches were <u>damaged</u>. • Some <u>coastal conservation areas</u> were destroyed, e.g. around <u>half</u> of <u>Breton National Wildlife Refuge</u> in Louisiana was <u>washed away</u>. • <u>Flooding</u> damaged oil refineries in Louisiana, causing massive <u>oil spills</u>.	• The <u>Irrawaddy delta</u> in Myanmar was the <u>hardest hit</u> area — a large proportion of it is <u>only just above sea level</u> and 14 000 km² of land was <u>flooded</u>. • <u>38 000 hectares</u> of mangrove forests were <u>destroyed</u>. • The flooding caused <u>erosion</u> and <u>salination</u> (increased <u>salt content</u>) of the land.
Impacts on People	• More than <u>1800 people</u> were <u>killed</u>. • <u>300 000 houses</u> were <u>destroyed</u> and <u>hundreds of thousands</u> of people were made <u>homeless</u>. • <u>3 million people</u> were left <u>without electricity</u>. • Roads were <u>damaged</u> and some <u>bridges collapsed</u>. • <u>230 000 jobs</u> were <u>lost</u> from damaged businesses.	• More than <u>140 000 people</u> were <u>killed</u>. • <u>450 000 houses</u> were <u>destroyed</u> and <u>350 000</u> were <u>damaged</u>. • Around <u>65%</u> of rice paddies in the Irrawaddy delta were <u>damaged</u>, which led to a loss of <u>livelihoods</u>. • A lot of people suffered from <u>diseases</u> caused by <u>poor sanitary conditions</u> and <u>contaminated water</u>.

Katrina and Nargis — a couple of mean girls...

Be prepared for some sort of comparison question on examples of tropical cyclones in your exam — examiners seem to really like them. Right, now you can give yourself a pat on the back and take a well-earned biscuit break*.

* Save me one, please.

Structure of the Earth

Welcome, geographer, to <u>plate tectonics</u> — it's the bit everyone looks forward too. It's a <u>hazardous</u> topic though — <u>earthquakes</u> and <u>volcanoes</u> are on the agenda, so keep your arms and legs in at all times.

The Earth has a Layered Structure

1) At the <u>centre</u> of the Earth is the <u>core</u>:

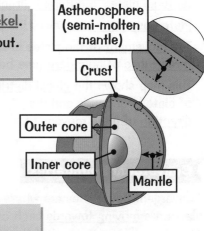

- The core is a ball of <u>solid</u> (inner) and <u>liquid</u> (outer) <u>iron</u> and <u>nickel</u>.
- At the <u>centre</u>, it's <u>very dense</u>. It becomes <u>less dense</u> further out.
- The <u>temperature</u> inside the core ranges from <u>4400-6000 °C</u>.

2) Around the core is the <u>mantle</u>:

- The mantle is made up of <u>silicon-based rocks</u>.
- The part of the mantle <u>nearest the core</u> is <u>quite rigid</u>.
- The <u>layer above</u> this, called the <u>asthenosphere</u>, is <u>semi-molten</u> (it can flow).
- And the <u>very, very top bit</u> of the mantle is <u>rigid</u>.
- The temperature of the mantle is between <u>1000</u> and <u>3700 °C</u>. It's <u>hotter</u> towards the core and <u>cooler</u> towards the Earth's surface.

3) The solid <u>outer layer</u> of the Earth is called the <u>crust</u>:

- The crust is also made up of <u>silicon-based rocks</u>.
- There are <u>two</u> types of crust — <u>continental</u> and <u>oceanic</u>.
  - Continental crust is <u>thicker</u> and <u>less dense</u>.
  - Oceanic crust is <u>thinner</u> and <u>more dense</u>.

Ooh la la

4) The crust is <u>divided</u> into <u>slabs</u> called <u>tectonic plates</u>.

Tectonic Plates Move due to Convection Currents in the Mantle

1) The tectonic plates <u>float</u> on the mantle.
2) <u>Radioactive decay</u> of some elements in the <u>mantle</u> and <u>core</u>, e.g. uranium, generates <u>a lot of heat</u>.
3) When <u>lower parts</u> of the <u>asthenosphere</u> <u>heat up</u> they become <u>less dense</u> and slowly <u>rise</u>.
4) As they move towards the <u>top</u> of the asthenosphere they <u>cool down</u>, become <u>more dense</u>, then slowly <u>sink</u>.
5) These <u>circular movements</u> of semi-molten rock are called <u>CONVECTION CURRENTS</u>.
6) Convection currents in the asthenosphere <u>create drag</u> on the <u>base</u> of the <u>tectonic plates</u> (which are solid and rigid) — and this causes them to <u>move</u>.

tectonic plates are moved by the moving mantle

Tectonic plate

Asthenosphere

Rising hot material

Sinking cool material

Wash tectonic plates by hand — they won't fit in the dishwasher...

Yes, I know this page isn't terribly exciting, but you need to understand the Earth's structure and what tectonic plates are or you'll really get your knickers in a twist later on. Only carry on when your knickers are secure...

Plate Boundaries

The places where tectonic plates <u>meet</u> are called <u>boundaries</u>. I like to think they have a cup of tea, a slice or two of cake and a natter about what's going on in the world. But in reality it's <u>not</u> so <u>civilised</u>...

There are Three Types of Plate Boundary

1) <u>Convection currents</u> in the mantle move <u>tectonic plates</u> in <u>different directions</u>.

2) <u>Plate boundaries</u> are where the plates <u>meet</u>.

3) The <u>movement</u> of the plates creates <u>three types</u> of <u>boundary</u> (see below).

4) This map shows the <u>global distribution</u> of plate boundaries and the <u>direction</u> of plate movement.

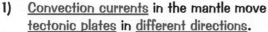

—— divergent plate boundary   ------ conservative plate boundary
—— convergent plate boundary   → direction of plate movement

1 Convergent Boundaries

Convergent boundaries are where two plates are <u>moving towards</u> each other, e.g. along the west coast of South America.

Where an <u>oceanic plate</u> meets a <u>continental plate</u>, the denser <u>oceanic</u> plate is <u>forced down</u> into the mantle and <u>destroyed</u>. This often creates <u>volcanoes</u> and <u>ocean trenches</u> (very deep sections of the ocean floor where the oceanic plate goes down).

Where <u>two continental plates</u> meet, the plates <u>collide</u>, and the ground is <u>folded</u> and <u>forced upwards</u> to create <u>mountain ranges</u>.

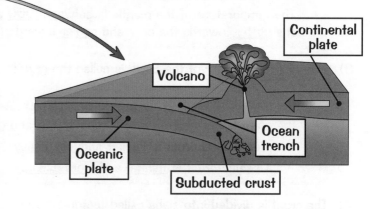

Continental plate

Volcano

Ocean trench

Oceanic plate

Subducted crust

2 Divergent Boundaries

Divergent boundaries are where two plates are <u>moving away</u> from each other, e.g. at the mid-Atlantic ridge. <u>Magma</u> (molten rock) <u>rises</u> from the mantle to fill the gap and <u>cools</u>, <u>creating new crust</u>.

Plate

Plate

Magma rises

3 Conservative Boundaries

Conservative boundaries are where two plates are <u>moving sideways</u> past each other, or are moving in the <u>same direction</u> but at <u>different speeds</u>, e.g. along the west coast of the USA. Crust <u>isn't created</u> or <u>destroyed</u>.

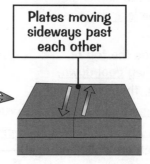

Plates moving sideways past each other

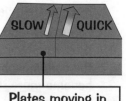

SLOW QUICK

Plates moving in the same direction at different speeds

Giant plates whacking into each other — smashing stuff...

Make sure you've got your head round the different types of plate boundary, then try this exam question:

1) Describe what a convergent plate boundary is.   [3]

Volcanic Hazards

Volcanoes usually look like mountains... until they explode and throw molten rock everywhere. Honestly, they've got such a temper. Though I'd probably be in a bad mood if I was sitting on a load of magma...

Volcanoes are Found at Convergent and Divergent Plate Boundaries

1) At convergent plate boundaries the oceanic plate goes under the continental plate because it's more dense.

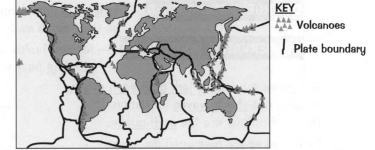

KEY
▲▲▲ Volcanoes
| Plate boundary

- The oceanic plate moves down into the mantle, where it's melted and destroyed.
- A pool of magma forms.
- The magma rises through cracks in the crust called vents.
- The magma erupts onto the surface (where it's called lava) forming a volcano.

2) At divergent boundaries the magma rises up into the gap created by the plates moving apart, forming a volcano.

3) When a volcano erupts, it emits lava and gases. Some volcanoes emit lots of ash, which can cover land, block out the sun and form pyroclastic flows (super-heated currents of gas, ash and rock).

Hotspots are Found Away From Plate Boundaries

Some volcanoes form in the middle of tectonic plates over hotspots:

1) They occur where a plume of hot magma from the mantle moves towards the surface, causing an unusually large flow of heat from the mantle to the crust.

2) Sometimes the magma can break through the crust and reach the surface. When this happens, there is an eruption and a volcano forms.

3) Hotspots remain stationary over time, but the crust moves above them. This can create chains of volcanic islands, e.g. Hawaii is a chain of volcanic islands in the middle of the Pacific plate.

There are Different Types of Volcano

1) Composite volcanoes (E.g. Mount Fuji in Japan)

- Occur at convergent plate boundaries (see p.14).
- Subducted oceanic crust contains lots of water. The water reacts with magma and creates gases, which cause the subducted crust to erupt.
- They have explosive eruptions that start with ashy explosions that deposit a layer of ash.
- They erupt andesitic lava that has a high silica content which makes it thick and sticky. The lava can't flow far so forms a steep-sided cone.

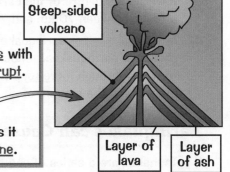

Steep-sided volcano

Layer of lava | Layer of ash

2) Shield volcanoes (E.g. Mauna Loa on the Hawaiian islands)

- Occur at hotspots or divergent plate boundaries (see p.14).
- They are not very explosive and are made up of only lava.
- They erupt basaltic lava, which has low silica content and is runny. It flows quickly and spreads over a wide area, forming a low, gentle-sided volcano.

Low, flat volcano | Runny lava | Layers of lava

Studying volcanoes — what a blast...

There are different types of volcanoes, but they've all got one thing in common — throwing up lava without bothering to rush to the toilet. Make the lava types stick in your head by linking them to shield and composite volcanoes.

Earthquake Hazards

Where plates meet, earthquakes can occur. If only the waiter would carry them more carefully.

Earthquakes *Occur at All Three* Types of *Plate Boundary*

1) Earthquakes are caused by the tension that builds up at all three types of plate boundary:

- **CONVERGENT BOUNDARIES** — tension builds up when one plate gets stuck as it's moving down past the other into the mantle.
- **DIVERGENT BOUNDARIES** — tension builds along cracks within the plates as they move away from each other.
- **CONSERVATIVE BOUNDARIES** — tension builds up when plates that are grinding past each other get stuck.

2) The plates eventually jerk past each other, sending out shock waves (vibrations). These vibrations are the earthquake.

3) Earthquakes are measured using the moment magnitude scale, which measures the energy released by an earthquake. You may still see some references to the Richter scale (which also measures the energy released) but it's no longer used by scientists.

KEY
- Earthquakes
- Plate margin

Earthquakes *Occur at Various Depths*

1) The focus of an earthquake is the point in the Earth where the earthquake starts. This can be at the Earth's surface, or anywhere up to 700 km below the surface.

2) Shallow-focus earthquakes are caused by tectonic plates moving at or near the surface. They have a focus between 0 km and 70 km below the Earth's surface.

3) Deep-focus earthquakes are caused by crust that has previously been subducted into the mantle (e.g. at convergent plate boundaries) moving towards the centre of the Earth, heating up or decomposing. They have a focus between 70 km and 700 km below the Earth's surface.

4) In general, deeper earthquakes do less damage at the surface than shallower earthquakes. Shock waves from deeper earthquakes have to travel through more rock to reach the surface, which reduces their power (and the amount of shaking) when they reach the surface.

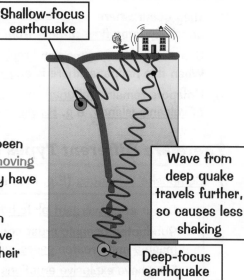

Shallow-focus earthquake

Wave from deep quake travels further, so causes less shaking

Deep-focus earthquake

Earthquakes can *Cause Tsunamis*

1) Tsunamis are a series of enormous waves caused when huge amounts of water get displaced.

2) Underwater earthquakes cause the seabed to move, which displaces water. Waves spread out from the epicentre of the earthquake (the point on the Earth's surface that's straight above the focus).

3) The depth of an earthquake affects the size of a tsunami — shallow-focus earthquakes displace more water because they're closer to the Earth's surface. This increases the size of a tsunami.

4) The waves travel very fast in deep water so they can hit the shore without much warning. This means they can cause a high death toll.

Tension, jerks, shock waves — sounds like my dance moves...

I'd better say this now... don't be put off by maps like the one at the top of the page — you won't ever have to draw them. But you might need to use one you're given in the exam to answer a question...

1) Using the map above, describe the global distribution of earthquakes.   [2]

Management of Tectonic Hazards

Plenty of people live in areas affected by tectonic hazards, so they need ways to manage them...

There are Methods for Predicting Tectonic Hazards

Earthquakes

1) Earthquakes cannot be reliably predicted, but scientists can still monitor certain signs that could indicate that an earthquake is likely.

2) Lasers can be used to detect the movement of tectonic plates before an earthquake.

3) Vibrations in the Earth's crust can be monitored using seismometers. If vibrations increase, it could mean there's going to be an earthquake.

4) Scientists can measure gases (e.g. radon) that escape from cracks in the crust just before an earthquake.

5) Rocks will crack and expand because of the increased pressure just before an earthquake.

Volcanoes

1) Volcanic eruptions can be predicted if the volcano is well-monitored to look for the tell-tale signs that come before a volcanic eruption.

2) Things such as tiny earthquakes and changes in the shape of the volcano (e.g. bulges in the land where magma has built up under it) all mean an eruption is likely.

3) Thermal imaging cameras can be used to detect changes in temperature around the volcano. Temperatures increase before an eruption.

4) Scientists can analyse the gases escaping from a volcano. Volcanoes emit lots of sulfurous gases before an eruption.

Long-Term Planning helps to Prepare a Country for Tectonic Hazards

Wealthier, more developed countries can plan for tectonic hazards to help reduce the impacts:

1) Emergency services can train and prepare for disasters, e.g. by practising rescuing people from collapsed buildings or setting up shelters. This will reduce the number of people killed.

2) Buildings can be designed to withstand earthquakes, e.g. by using strong materials like reinforced concrete or building special foundations that absorb an earthquake's energy.

3) People can be educated so that they know what to do if an earthquake or eruption happens.

4) Governments can plan evacuation routes to get people out of dangerous areas quickly and safely in case of an earthquake or volcanic eruption. This reduces the number of people killed or injured by things like fires, pyroclastic flows or mudflows.

5) Emergency supplies like blankets, clean water and food can be stockpiled. If a natural hazard is predicted the stockpiles can be moved close to areas likely to be affected.

Short-Term Relief is Needed After a Disaster

Short-term relief deals with the immediate impacts of a tectonic hazard.
Well-prepared countries are better able to:

1) Provide food and drink and shelter to evacuated people.

2) Treat people who have been injured (e.g. from falling debris) to prevent more deaths.

3) Recover dead bodies to prevent the spread of disease.

4) Rescue people who have been trapped (e.g. in collapsed buildings) or cut off by damage to roads or bridges.

5) Provide temporary supplies of gas, electricity and communications systems if regular supplies have been damaged.

My long-term planning suggestion — put a big cork in it...

Being able to predict and plan for tectonic hazards can save lives. As a general rule of thumb, the more wealthy and developed a country is, the better its long-term planning and ability to provide short-term relief will be.

Tectonic Hazards — Examples

And you thought I'd forgotten all about the <u>real-world examples</u>. Shame on you.

Some Countries are More Prepared than Others

1) <u>Preparedness</u> for tectonic hazards is <u>different</u> in countries of contrasting <u>wealth</u> and <u>development</u>.
2) <u>Japan</u> (a <u>developed</u> country) and <u>Pakistan</u> (a <u>developing</u> country) have a long history of <u>earthquakes</u>, and both countries have <u>different levels</u> of <u>preparedness</u>.

	Japan	Pakistan
Prediction	• The <u>Japan Meteorological Agency</u> (<u>JMA</u>) and <u>local governments</u> monitor <u>seismic activity</u> all over the country. • If an earthquake is <u>detected</u>, people are <u>warned immediately</u>.	• Up until recently, there wasn't <u>extensive monitoring</u> of <u>seismic activity</u> in Pakistan. • This means earthquakes could strike <u>without warning</u>.
Preparation	• <u>Strict building laws</u> help prevent major damage during an earthquake. • Buildings are <u>reinforced</u> with <u>steel frames</u> to prevent them from <u>collapsing</u>. • <u>High-rise</u> buildings have <u>deep foundations</u> with <u>shock absorbers</u> to reduce <u>vibrations</u> and <u>shaking</u> in the building. • Japan has <u>early warning systems</u> to <u>alert</u> residents to <u>earthquakes</u> and <u>tsunamis</u>. • High-speed '<u>bullet</u>' trains automatically <u>brake</u> in the event of an earthquake to stop them <u>derailing</u>. • <u>Automatic alarms</u> stop <u>mechanical equipment</u> to alert <u>workers</u> and prevent <u>injuries</u>.	• As a <u>developing country</u>, Pakistan doesn't have <u>access</u> to the same <u>building materials</u> or <u>technologies</u> as Japan. • Many buildings are constructed using <u>wood</u> and <u>cement</u>, which are <u>easily destroyed</u> during earthquakes. • Up until recently, <u>building laws</u> didn't include measures of <u>protection</u> against <u>earthquake damage</u>. Even now, they're often <u>ignored</u> when constructing new buildings. • <u>Poor communication networks</u> make it difficult to <u>alert</u> the population.
Long-Term Planning	• Japan's population is <u>educated</u> on being <u>prepared</u> for earthquakes, e.g. <u>Disaster Prevention Day</u> is an annual nationwide <u>drill</u> to practise <u>evacuations</u> in the event of an earthquake. • <u>Schools</u> carry out drills to teach <u>children</u> what to do if there's an earthquake. • People living in <u>coastal communities</u> practise getting to <u>higher ground</u> or <u>emergency bunkers</u> in the event of a <u>tsunami</u>.	• There are lots of <u>poor</u>, <u>remote settlements</u> in Pakistan that have no <u>education programme</u> for teaching people <u>what to do</u> if there's an earthquake. • Planning <u>evacuations</u> is difficult because there are <u>very few roads</u> and <u>poor communications</u>. 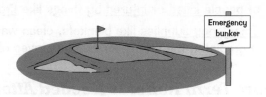 

Recent Earthquakes have tested their Preparedness

Japan

1) On <u>11th March 2011</u>, a powerful earthquake struck <u>north-east Japan</u>.
2) It measured <u>9.0</u> on the moment magnitude scale and triggered a <u>tsunami</u> that <u>overwhelmed</u> the <u>coast</u> and <u>inland areas</u>.
3) <u>Japanese scientists</u> had predicted a <u>smaller</u> earthquake to hit the <u>north</u> of the country, but an earthquake of this <u>magnitude</u> was <u>unexpected</u>.

Pakistan

1) On <u>8th October 2005</u>, <u>Kashmir</u>, Pakistan was struck by a major earthquake.
2) It measured <u>7.6</u> on the moment magnitude scale, causing <u>landslides</u>, <u>rockfalls</u> and <u>huge amounts of destruction</u>.
3) Although scientists <u>monitor</u> seismic activity in the area, the earthquake was <u>unpredicted</u>.

Tectonic Hazards — Examples

Both Earthquakes had Major Impacts

The <u>primary impacts</u> of an earthquake are the <u>immediate impacts</u> of the ground shaking.

Primary Impacts

- <u>Thousands</u> of <u>buildings</u> were <u>damaged</u>.
- The earthquake caused severe <u>liquefaction</u> (where <u>waterlogged</u> soil <u>behaves</u> like a <u>liquid</u>). This caused many buildings to <u>tilt</u> and <u>sink</u> into the ground.

- The Pakistan earthquake caused around <u>80 000 deaths</u>, mostly from <u>collapsed buildings</u>.
- <u>Tens of thousands</u> of people were <u>injured</u>.
- <u>Hundreds of thousands</u> of buildings were <u>damaged or destroyed</u>, including whole villages.
- Around <u>3 million people</u> were made <u>homeless</u>.
- <u>Water pipelines</u> and <u>electricity lines</u> were <u>broken</u>, cutting off supply.

The <u>secondary impacts</u> happen later on, often as a result of the primary impacts, e.g. <u>landslides</u> and <u>tsunamis</u>.

Secondary Impacts

- The earthquake triggered a <u>tsunami</u> which killed <u>thousands</u> of people.
- <u>Hundreds of thousands</u> of <u>buildings</u> were <u>completely destroyed</u>. Over <u>230 000</u> people were made <u>homeless</u>.
- The <u>tsunami</u> cut off the <u>power supplies</u> to the <u>Fukushima nuclear power plant</u>, causing a <u>meltdown</u>.
- <u>Road</u> and <u>rail networks</u> suffered <u>severe damage</u>, e.g. <u>325 km</u> of <u>railway tracks</u> were <u>washed away</u>.

- <u>Landslides</u> buried <u>buildings</u> and <u>people</u>. They also <u>blocked access roads</u> and cut off <u>telephone lines</u>.
- <u>Diarrhoea</u> and <u>other diseases</u> spread due to lack of <u>clean water</u>.
- <u>Freezing winter conditions</u> shortly after the earthquake caused <u>more casualties</u> and meant <u>rescue</u> and <u>rebuilding</u> operations were <u>difficult</u>.

Short-Term Relief was Slow to Reach People in Pakistan

Short-Term Relief

- <u>International aid</u> and <u>search and rescue teams</u> were brought in.
- <u>Rescue workers</u> and <u>soldiers</u> were sent to help deal with the <u>aftermath</u>.
- <u>Transport</u> and <u>communications</u> were <u>restored</u> a couple of weeks after the earthquake.
- <u>Power supplies</u> were restored in the weeks following the earthquake.

- The <u>Pakistani army</u> was initially <u>slow to respond</u> to the disaster.
- Help from <u>India</u> was <u>refused</u> because of <u>political tensions</u> between Pakistan and India.
- Help <u>didn't reach</u> many areas for <u>days</u> or <u>weeks</u>, and many people had to be rescued <u>by hand</u> without any <u>equipment</u> or help from <u>emergency services</u>.
- <u>Tents</u>, <u>blankets</u> and <u>medical supplies</u> were distributed, although it took up to a <u>month</u> for them to reach most areas.

Long-Term Planning in Japan was Very Effective

Effects of Long-Term Planning

- The <u>Japanese authorities</u> gave an <u>advance warning</u> of the earthquake and the tsunami, which gave people time to <u>evacuate</u> and get to <u>higher ground</u>.
- Despite <u>very strong shaking</u> in <u>Tokyo</u>, <u>not a single building</u> collapsed thanks to <u>buildings designed</u> to prevent earthquake damage.
- <u>Nobody</u> died on the bullet train network because of the <u>automatic braking systems</u>.

- <u>Fault lines</u> in the <u>Himalayas</u> were <u>poorly monitored</u>, which meant the Pakistan earthquake was <u>unpredicted</u>.
- The absence of <u>building laws</u> meant buildings <u>weren't reinforced</u> and were <u>extremely vulnerable</u> to <u>damage</u> from earthquake shaking.
- Most buildings had been constructed using <u>poor quality materials</u>, e.g. <u>cement</u> made from <u>sand</u> which <u>crumbled</u> during the earthquake.

Mo' money, fewer problems in responding to a tectonic hazard...

Whether you use these examples or the ones you were taught in class, this stuff is just absolutely begging for an exam question along the lines of "Compare and contrast the responses to tectonic hazards... etc.". It makes sense to learn it...

Revision Summary

Well, you just survived a very hazardous section. There may have been a lot of pages about disasters, but get a load of these questions down you and there won't be any kind of disaster in the exam. I know it looks like there's a lot of stuff here, but you'll be surprised how much you just learned.
Try them out a few at a time, then check the answers on the pages. Once you can answer them all standing on your head and juggling five balls, move on to the next section.

Global Atmospheric Circulation (p.2-3) ☑

1) How does global atmospheric circulation lead to high and low pressure belts?
2) Describe how ocean currents transfer heat around the Earth.
3) How do high and low pressure belts create climatic zones?

Climate Change (p.4-8) ☑

4) Describe how climate has changed from the beginning of the Quaternary period to the present day.
5) Describe how asteroid collisions might cause climate change.
6) List three other natural causes of climate change.
7) Why are ice cores a useful source of information about past climate?
8) What is the greenhouse effect?
9) Name two greenhouse gases.
10) Give four ways that human activities increase the concentration of greenhouse gases in the atmosphere.
11) Give three pieces of evidence for human activity causing climate change.
12) Give two possible future impacts of climate change on people.
13) Explain why it is difficult to predict the impacts of climate change.

Tropical Cyclones (p.9-12) ☑

14) What conditions are required for a tropical cyclone to develop?
15) What can cause a tropical cyclone to dissipate?
16) Describe two impacts of tropical cyclones on people.
17) Explain why some countries are more vulnerable to tropical cyclones than others.
18) Give three strategies that are used to prepare for and respond to tropical cyclones.
19) For two countries that you have studied, describe the differences in their approaches to warning and evacuation in response to a tropical cyclone.

Tectonic Plates (p.13-14) ☑

20) Describe the layered structure of the Earth.
21) Why do tectonic plates move?
22) Name the type of plate boundary where two plates of continental crust are moving towards each other.
23) Name the type of plate boundary where two plates are moving sideways against each other.

Tectonic Hazards (p.15-19) ☑

24) How do volcanoes form at convergent plate boundaries?
25) What is a hotspot?
26) Describe the features of composite and shield volcanoes.
27) What causes earthquakes?
28) Describe how tsunamis are caused.
29) Describe how scientists can try to predict earthquakes.
30) For one developed and one developing country that you have studied:
    a) Compare the level of preparation for tectonic hazards.
    b) Compare the secondary impacts of tectonic hazards that occurred in each of the countries.
    c) Compare the effectiveness of the long-term planning for tectonic hazards in each of the countries.

Measuring Development

This topic is a little <u>tricky</u> — but take a <u>deep breath</u> and <u>believe in yourself</u> and you'll be <u>just fine</u>.

Development *is when a Country is Improving*

When a country <u>develops</u> it basically gets <u>better</u> for the people living there.
There are <u>different aspects</u> to development:

- <u>Economic</u> — progress in <u>economic growth</u>, e.g. how <u>wealthy</u> a country is, its level of <u>industrialisation</u> and use of <u>technology</u>.
- <u>Social</u> — improvement in people's <u>standard of living</u>, e.g. <u>better health care</u> and access to <u>clean water</u>.
- <u>Political</u> — having a <u>stable</u> political system with <u>institutions</u> that can <u>meet the needs</u> of society.

I make this development about 25 m.

There Are Loads of Measures of Development

1) Development is <u>pretty hard to measure</u> because it <u>includes so many things</u>. But you can <u>compare</u> the development of different countries using 'measures of development'.

Name	What it is	A measure of...	As a country develops, it gets...
<u>Gross Domestic Product (GDP)</u>	The <u>total value</u> of <u>goods</u> and <u>services</u> a <u>country produces</u> in a <u>year</u>. It's often given in US$.	Wealth	Higher
<u>GDP per capita</u>	The GDP <u>divided</u> by the <u>population</u> of a <u>country</u>. It's often given in <u>US$</u> and is sometimes called <u>GDP per head</u>.	Wealth	Higher
<u>Gross National Income (GNI) and GNI per capita</u>	The <u>total value</u> of <u>goods</u> and <u>services</u> produced by a <u>country</u> in a <u>year</u>, including income from <u>overseas</u>. It's often given in <u>US$</u>. GNI per capita is the GNI <u>divided</u> by the <u>population</u> of a <u>country</u>.	Wealth	Higher
<u>Birth rate</u>	The number of <u>live babies born per thousand</u> of the population <u>per year</u>.	Women's rights	Lower
<u>Death rate</u>	The number of <u>deaths per thousand</u> of the population <u>per year</u>.	Health	Lower
<u>Fertility rate</u>	The average number of <u>births per woman</u>.	Women's rights	Lower
<u>Infant mortality rate</u>	The number of <u>babies</u> who <u>die under 1 year old</u>, <u>per thousand babies born</u>.	Health care	Lower
<u>Maternal mortality rate</u>	The number of <u>women</u> who <u>die</u> due to <u>pregnancy</u> related problems <u>per hundred thousand</u> live births.	Health care	Lower
<u>Doctors per 1000 of population</u>	The number of <u>working doctors per thousand</u> of the population.	Access to health care	Higher
<u>Gini coefficient</u>	A measure of <u>economic inequality</u>. Countries are given a score between <u>0</u> (<u>equal</u>) and <u>1</u> (total <u>inequality</u>).	Inequality	Lower
<u>Gender Inequality Index</u>	A number that's calculated using data on e.g. <u>women's education</u>, access to <u>jobs</u>, <u>political rights</u> and <u>health</u> during <u>pregnancy</u>. The <u>higher</u> the score, the <u>more inequality</u>.	Women's rights	Lower
<u>Human Development Index (HDI)</u>	This is a number that's calculated using <u>life expectancy</u>, <u>education level</u> (e.g. average number of years of schooling) and <u>income per head</u>. Every country has an HDI value between <u>0</u> (<u>least developed</u>) and <u>1</u> (<u>most developed</u>).	Lots of things	Higher
<u>Corruption Perceptions Index (CPI)</u>	A measure of the level of <u>corruption</u> that is believed to exist in the public sector on a scale of <u>1-100</u>. The <u>lower</u> the score, the <u>more corruption</u>.	Corruption	Higher

2) <u>Single</u> indicators can be <u>misleading</u> if they are used <u>on their own</u> because, as a country develops, some aspects <u>develop before others</u>. So it might seem that a country's <u>more developed</u> than it <u>actually is</u>.

3) Using a composite indicator of development, where <u>more than one measure</u> is used (i.e. wealth and something else) avoids these problems. The <u>Human Development Index</u> is a composite indicator.

Measuring Development

Development affects Fertility and Mortality Rates

1) Countries can be <u>classified</u> based on their <u>level of development</u>.

2) <u>Developed</u> countries, e.g. the UK, have <u>very high</u> human development. <u>Emerging</u> countries, e.g. India, have <u>medium</u> to <u>high</u> human development. <u>Developing</u> countries, e.g. Chad, have <u>low</u> human development.

3) A country's level of development (particularly its <u>birth</u> and <u>death rates</u>) affects the <u>growth</u> and <u>age structure</u> of its population.

	Chad	India	UK
Human Development Index (2014)	0.392	0.609	0.907
Fertility rate (per woman)	4.45	2.5	1.9
Birth rate (per 1000)	36.1	19.3	12.1
Death rate (per 1000)	14	7.3	9.4
Maternal mortality rate (per 100 000 live births)	856	174	9
Infant mortality rate (per 1000 babies born)	87	40.5	4.3

Developing Countries

1) Developing countries have <u>higher fertility</u> and <u>birth rates</u> because there's <u>no</u> use of <u>contraception</u>. People also have <u>lots of children</u> because <u>poor health care</u> means that many infants <u>die</u>.

2) The <u>death rate</u> is also <u>high</u> due to <u>poor health care</u>, and <u>life expectancy</u> is <u>low</u> (few people reach old age).

3) This means that there are <u>lots more children</u> than older people — population pyramids for developing countries have a very <u>wide base</u>, which rapidly <u>narrows</u>.

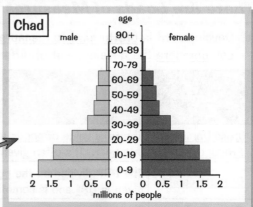

Emerging Countries

1) Emerging countries see their <u>fertility rates fall</u> rapidly as women have a more <u>equal</u> place in society and a <u>better education</u>.

2) The use of <u>contraception increases</u> and more women <u>work</u> instead of having children.

3) <u>Health care improves</u> so <u>life expectancy increases</u>.

4) This means that there are more people of <u>working age</u> and there is a <u>lower proportion</u> of <u>children</u> — the <u>base</u> of the pyramid starts to <u>narrow</u> and the <u>top</u> starts to <u>widen</u>.

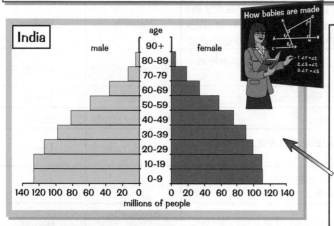

Developed Countries

1) In developed countries <u>fertility rates</u> are <u>low</u> because people want <u>possessions</u> and a <u>high quality of life</u>, and may have <u>dependent elderly relatives</u>, so there is <u>less money available</u> for having children.

2) <u>Health care</u> is <u>good</u>, so the <u>death rate</u> is <u>low</u> and <u>life expectancy</u> is <u>high</u>.

3) This means there are lots <u>more older people</u> and the proportion of <u>children decreases</u> — the top of the pyramid <u>widens</u> further and the <u>base</u> gets <u>narrower</u>, so the <u>middle bulges</u> out.

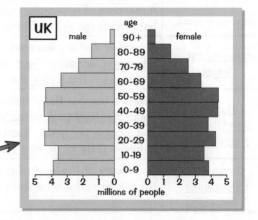

Population pyramids — I thought they were only found at the circus...

You need to know the different ways of measuring development as well as how development affects a country's population structure — take a look at the lovely pyramids on this page. What's that... You think they're odd... Hmph.

Causes of Global Inequalities

You need to know the <u>reasons why</u> there are <u>global inequalities</u> — i.e. why <u>countries differ</u> in how <u>developed</u> they are. Not as exciting as tropical cyclones or volcanoes, I know, but still <u>important stuff</u>.

Lots of Factors can Affect How Developed a Country is

Climate

1) If a country has a poor climate (<u>really hot</u> or <u>really cold</u> or <u>really dry</u>) not much will grow. This <u>reduces</u> the amount of <u>food produced</u>, which can lead to <u>malnutrition</u>. People who are malnourished have a <u>low quality of life</u>.

2) People also have <u>fewer crops to sell</u>, so <u>less money</u> to <u>spend</u> on <u>goods and services</u>. This also <u>reduces</u> their <u>quality of life</u>.

Topography (shape of land)

1) If the land in a country is <u>steep</u>, then it <u>won't</u> produce a lot of <u>food</u>. This has the same effect as a <u>poor climate</u> (see left).

2) <u>Steep land</u> can also make it difficult to develop <u>infrastructure</u>, e.g. roads, power lines etc. This can <u>limit trade</u> and make it hard to provide <u>basic services</u>.

Education

1) Educating people produces a more <u>skilled workforce</u>, meaning that the country can produce more <u>goods</u> and offer more <u>services</u> (e.g. ICT). This can bring <u>money</u> into the country through <u>trade</u> or <u>investment</u>.

2) Educated people also <u>earn more</u>, so they pay more <u>taxes</u>. This provides <u>money</u> that the country can spend on <u>development</u>.

Health

1) In some poorer countries, <u>lack of clean water</u> and <u>poor health care</u> mean that many people suffer from <u>diseases</u> such as <u>malaria</u> and <u>cholera</u>.

2) People who are ill <u>can't work</u>, so they're not contributing to the <u>economy</u>. They may also need <u>expensive medicine</u> or <u>health care</u>.

3) Lack of economic <u>contribution</u> and increased <u>spending</u> on health care means that there's <u>less money</u> available to spend on <u>development</u>.

Colonialism

1) Countries that were <u>colonised</u> (<u>ruled by a foreign country</u>) are often at a <u>lower</u> level of development when they gain <u>independence</u> than they <u>would be</u> if they had <u>not been colonised</u>.

2) <u>European countries</u> colonised much of Africa in the 19th century. They controlled the economies of their colonies, <u>removed raw materials</u> and <u>slaves</u>, and sold back expensive <u>manufactured goods</u>. This was <u>bad</u> for African development as it made parts of Africa <u>dependent</u> on Europe, and led to <u>famine</u> and <u>malnutrition</u>.

Neo-colonialism

1) After colonies gained their <u>independence</u>, <u>richer</u> countries <u>continued</u> to <u>control</u> them <u>indirectly</u>.

2) For example, some transnational corporations (TNCs) <u>exploit</u> the <u>cheap labour</u> and <u>raw materials</u> of <u>poorer</u> countries (see p. 26).

3) <u>International organisations</u> sometimes offer <u>conditional loans</u>, which mean <u>poorer</u> countries have to <u>develop</u> in the way their <u>donors want</u> them to.

Democratic governments are chosen by the people but authoritarian governments tell people what to do.

Economic and Political

1) <u>Authoritarian</u> governments can put development policies in place <u>without worrying</u> about anyone <u>stopping</u> them — this can be very <u>good</u> for economic <u>development</u>, e.g. the rapid growth of China, but things can also go really <u>wrong</u>, e.g. Cuba's economic crash. Development under <u>democratic</u> governments is usually <u>less extreme</u> — different <u>interest groups</u> prevent either <u>huge growth</u> or <u>economic collapse</u>.

2) <u>Corrupt</u> governments can <u>hinder</u> development, e.g. by <u>taking money</u> that's intended for building <u>new infrastructure</u> or <u>improving facilities</u> for people.

3) Countries with good <u>international relations</u> are more likely to get good <u>trade agreements</u>. They can also get <u>loans</u> from international organisations to invest in <u>development projects</u>.

We don't need no education — unless we want to develop...

So, there are loads of things that can hinder a country's development. Make sure you learn 'em all.

1) Explain one way that colonialism can affect a country's development after it gains independence. [2]

Consequences of Global Inequalities

Countries really do have a tough time trying to <u>develop</u>. And things don't look great if you can't make it off the <u>bottom</u> of the pile either. <u>Inequalities</u> affect all of us though — just some more than others...

Uneven Development Leads to Inequalities Between Countries

<u>Wealth</u> is not spread <u>evenly</u> across all <u>countries</u> in the world. People in the <u>richest 20%</u> of the world's countries (the <u>5th quintile</u>) have <u>70.1%</u> of the world's wealth (GDP per capita), whereas people in the <u>poorest 20%</u> (the <u>1st quintile</u>) have just <u>1.0%</u> of the world's wealth.

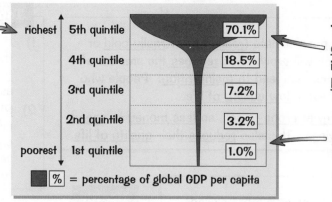

The <u>UK</u> is in the <u>5th quintile</u>. Other countries in the 5th quintile include <u>Norway</u> and <u>Japan</u>.

<u>Chad</u> is in the <u>1st quintile</u>. Other countries in the 1st quintile include <u>Malawi</u> and <u>Cambodia</u>.

Global Inequalities have Social and Political Consequences

<u>Differences</u> in <u>wealth</u> can make things <u>difficult</u> for <u>poorer people</u> and developing <u>countries</u>:

Education

1) <u>Poorer</u> countries <u>can't afford</u> to invest as much in <u>education</u> as <u>richer</u> countries.

2) <u>Poorer</u> people may not be able to afford <u>school fees</u> or <u>children</u> may have to <u>work</u> to support their families instead of attending <u>school</u>.

3) Lack of <u>education</u> means people can't get <u>better-paid</u>, <u>skilled jobs</u> in the future, so the <u>cycle</u> of <u>poverty</u> continues.

Health

1) People in <u>developing</u> countries are at <u>higher risk</u> for many <u>diseases</u> than people in developed countries leading to <u>lower life expectancies</u>.

2) <u>Infant mortality</u> is also much <u>higher</u> in developing countries.

3) Poorer people find it harder to get <u>quality health care</u> and <u>healthy food</u>.

Politics

1) Inequalities can increase <u>political instability</u>, <u>crime</u> and <u>discontent</u> in <u>poorer</u> countries.

2) This means <u>civil wars</u> are <u>more likely</u> in <u>developing</u> countries. Conflict can increase inequality — poverty <u>increases</u> as money is spent on fighting rather than <u>development</u>.

3) Developing countries are often <u>dependent</u> on <u>richer</u> countries. This means they have <u>less influence</u> over regional and global <u>decisions</u>.

Global Inequalities also Cause Environmental Problems

1) <u>Economic development</u> leads to <u>more consumption</u> of food, water and energy as people get <u>wealthier</u>. This puts <u>pressure</u> on <u>scarce resources</u> and can threaten <u>ecosystems</u>, e.g. as more land is built on.

2) <u>Industrialisation</u> leads to increased <u>air</u>, <u>water</u> and <u>land pollution</u>. The release of <u>greenhouse gases</u> enhances the greenhouse effect, contributing to <u>climate change</u>. <u>Waste</u> is dumped in <u>landfill sites</u> and <u>untreated sewage</u>, <u>chemical waste</u> and <u>runoff</u> from farmland ends up in <u>rivers</u> and <u>lakes</u>.

3) Many <u>developed</u> countries have <u>factories</u> in <u>developing</u> countries or <u>buy goods</u> that are <u>produced</u> there. This means that <u>local pollution</u> levels are often <u>much higher</u> in <u>developing</u> countries.

4) <u>Poorer people</u> can also be <u>trapped</u> in a cycle of <u>environmental damage</u>, e.g. if they <u>can't afford fuel</u> they have to <u>collect firewood</u> from their local environment which can lead to <u>deforestation</u>.

Global inequalities — they're why the Earth's tilted on its axis...

... or so I heard, anyway. The consequences of inequality may not be cheerful reading but that won't stop the examiners grilling you on it. So re-read this page 'til you know it inside-out, back-to-front and sideways. OK, onwards.

Theories of Development

Rostow and Frank came up with theories about how countries develop (or don't develop, in Frank's case).

Rostow's Theory shows Five Stages of Economic Development

1) Rostow's modernisation theory predicts how a country's level of economic development changes over time — it describes how a country's economy changes from relying mostly on primary industry (e.g. agriculture), through secondary industry (e.g. manufacturing goods) to tertiary and quaternary industry (e.g. services and research).

2) At the same time, people's standard of living improves.

3) Stage 1 is the lowest level of development and Stage 5 is the highest.

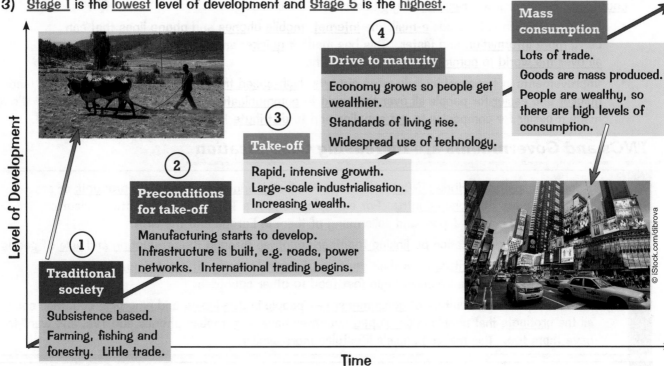

5 Mass consumption
Lots of trade.
Goods are mass produced.
People are wealthy, so there are high levels of consumption.

4 Drive to maturity
Economy grows so people get wealthier.
Standards of living rise.
Widespread use of technology.

3 Take-off
Rapid, intensive growth.
Large-scale industrialisation.
Increasing wealth.

2 Preconditions for take-off
Manufacturing starts to develop. Infrastructure is built, e.g. roads, power networks. International trading begins.

1 Traditional society
Subsistence based.
Farming, fishing and forestry. Little trade.

Level of Development (vertical axis) / *Time* (horizontal axis)

© iStock.com/dibrova

Frank's Dependency Theory says Poor Countries Rely On Rich Countries

1) Frank's dependency theory was developed as an alternative to Rostow's model to explain why some countries are more developed than others.

2) The theory suggests that some poorer, weaker countries (the periphery) remain poor because they are dependent on the core countries (those that are richer and more powerful).

3) It argues that the exploitation that started during the colonial period has continued — this is neo-colonialism (see p. 23). The richer, former colonial countries continue to dominate the trading system even though the colonised countries have gained independence — richer countries continue to take advantage of the cheap raw materials and labour available in poorer countries.

4) For example, poorer countries have been encouraged to plant crops for export and produce primary products to sell cheaply to richer countries. This means they need to import manufactured goods at higher cost from richer countries to provide for their own population. This traps them in poverty and makes them dependent on the economy of the core countries.

5) Richer countries may also exploit poor countries by interfering in local politics in poorer countries or loaning them money with high rates of interest, leading to large debts.

6) This means that poor countries remain dependent on richer countries. Some people think that as long as they remain part of the capitalist (free trade, profit-seeking) system, these countries can't develop.

Darling, I'm going to be frank — we've got dependency issues...

I told my mum that I'll need a car so that I can drive to maturity but she wasn't having it. She needs to have a look at Rostow's model or I'll never get to the age of mass consumption. Hang on, maybe she's more clued up than I thought.

Globalisation

Reducing global inequalities is a massive task. Let's start at the very beginning with some globalisation...

Globalisation *is the Process of Countries Becoming More Integrated*

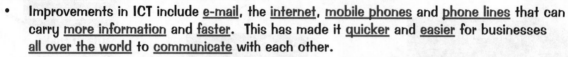

1) Every country has its own political and economic systems as well as its own culture.

2) Globalisation is the process of all the world's systems and cultures becoming more integrated — it's the whole world coming together like a single community.

3) It happens because of the movement of money and people between countries, as well as businesses locating their operations and selling their products in more countries. Here are a few reasons why globalisation is increasing:

- Improvements in ICT include e-mail, the internet, mobile phones and phone lines that can carry more information and faster. This has made it quicker and easier for businesses all over the world to communicate with each other.

- Improvements in transport include more airports, high-speed trains and larger ships. This has made it quicker and easier for people all over the world to communicate with each other face to face. It's also made it easier for companies to get supplies and to distribute their products all over the world.

TNCs *and Governments are Increasing Globalisation*

TNCs

1) Transnational corporations (TNCs) are companies that produce products, sell products or are located in more than one country. For example, Sony is a TNC — it manufactures electronic products in China and Japan, and sells many of them in Europe and the USA.

2) TNCs increase globalisation by linking together countries through the production and sale of goods.

3) They also bring the culture from their country of origin to many different countries, e.g. McDonald's brings Western-style fast food to other countries.

4) TNCs also promote a culture of consumerism — people in developing and emerging countries see all the products that people in developed countries have, e.g. mobile phones and TVs, and want to have them too. This makes people's lifestyles more similar.

Governments

1) Free trade — governments increase globalisation by promoting free trade, e.g. reducing tariffs on goods. This means it's much easier to move goods, money and services between countries.

2) Investment — governments compete with each other to attract investment by TNCs. They think that TNCs will bring jobs, increase income from taxes and promote economic growth in their country.

3) Privatisation — governments hand over services and industries to private companies, e.g. in the UK, some rail services are now run by companies from the Netherlands, Germany and France.

Globalisation Benefits Some Countries More than Others

1) Some countries have benefited from globalisation, e.g. China, India, Brazil. This is because they have, e.g:

- large, cheap workforces
- governments open to foreign investment
- less strict environmental, labour and planning laws
- lots of cheap raw materials
- reasonable infrastructure
- available land

2) However, some people think that globalisation is increasing global inequality.

- Free trade benefits richer countries — TNC profits normally return to their headquarters, which are often in developed countries, and poor countries can struggle to compete, i.e. produce cheaper goods.

- Richer countries benefit from freer movement of labour — skilled workers are attracted by higher wages and better living conditions in richer countries, leading to a 'brain drain' in poorer countries.

Globalisation is going large — with extra barbecue sauce...

Back in my day the internet was only just getting going. Take a moment to imagine it. If you can picture that, you're well on the way to understanding the impacts of globalisation. Hold that thought and go over this page again.

Reducing Global Inequalities

...And when they were <u>up</u> they were <u>up</u>, and when they were <u>down</u> they were <u>down</u>. And when they were <u>top-down</u> maybe they should have been <u>bottom-up</u>. Or something like that. I need a rest already...

Development Strategies *can be* Top-Down *or* Bottom-Up

1) Some people are trying to <u>decrease global inequalities</u> by helping <u>poor</u> countries <u>develop</u>.

2) Development projects can include building <u>schools</u> to <u>improve literacy</u> rates, making <u>dams</u> to provide <u>clean water</u> or providing <u>farming education</u> and <u>equipment</u> to <u>improve agriculture</u>.

3) There are <u>two</u> different approaches to development strategies:

	Top-down approaches	Bottom-up approaches
Type of strategy	A <u>government</u> or <u>large organisation</u>, e.g. an inter-governmental organisation (IGO) (see p. 28) or transnational corporation (TNC) makes <u>decisions</u> about how to increase development and <u>direct</u> the project.	<u>Local people</u> and <u>communities</u> decide on ways to improve things for their own community. <u>Non-governmental organisations</u> (NGOs) are often involved (see p. 28).
Scale and aims	• Often used for <u>large projects</u>, e.g. <u>dams</u> for hydroelectric power (HEP) or <u>irrigation schemes</u>. • These aim to solve <u>large scale</u> problems and improve the lives of <u>lots</u> of people.	• Usually <u>small-scale</u>, e.g. building or maintaining a well in a village. • They often aim to <u>improve</u> the <u>quality of life</u> for the <u>poorest</u> and <u>most vulnerable</u> people in society. *Still or sparkling?*
Funding	• The projects are usually very <u>expensive</u>. • Some projects are <u>funded</u> by <u>TNCs</u> or <u>governments</u> from <u>developed</u> countries who will <u>profit</u> from the <u>development</u>, e.g. by selling the HEP produced. • Other projects may be <u>funded</u> by <u>loans</u> from <u>international organisations</u>, e.g. the World Bank or the International Monetary Fund (IMF). The money may have to be <u>paid back later</u> or the <u>organisation</u> may have <u>conditions</u> for lending the money, e.g. removing trade barriers.	• Projects are usually much <u>cheaper</u>. • Most <u>money</u> comes from <u>charities</u>, which often rely on <u>donations</u> from people in richer countries.
Technology	• The projects are often <u>high-tech</u> and <u>energy intensive</u>. The construction usually involves <u>machinery</u> and <u>technology</u>, which is often operated by <u>skilled workers</u> from <u>developed</u> countries rather than local people. • The <u>recipient</u> country becomes <u>dependent</u> on <u>technology</u> and <u>workers</u> from the <u>donor</u> country for <u>operation</u> and <u>maintenance</u>.	• Projects involve <u>intermediate</u> technology. • <u>Local materials</u> are used and <u>local people</u> are employed. This means people have the <u>materials</u> and <u>skills</u> to <u>maintain</u> the project.

For more on intermediate technology see next page.

Clean drinking water? Bottoms up...

Development is a complicated matter with no easy solutions. There's more on the pros and cons of different approaches on the next page but, for now, learn the differences between the ol' top-down and bottom-up.

EXAM QUESTION

1) Explain one way in which top-down approaches to development differ from bottom-up approaches. [2]

Reducing Global Inequalities

There are <u>lots</u> of different ways to help a country to <u>develop</u>, but none of them are <u>trouble-free</u>...

Approaches to Development *Include NGO-Led Intermediate Technology...*

1) <u>Non-governmental organisations</u> (<u>NGOs</u>) are not-for-profit groups which are <u>independent</u> from governments. They're often charities, e.g. the <u>British Red Cross</u> or <u>Oxfam</u>.

2) <u>NGO-led development projects</u> often involve the use of <u>intermediate technology</u>. This includes tools, machines and systems that are <u>simple to use</u>, <u>affordable</u> to buy or build and cheap to <u>maintain</u>.

Advantages

1) Projects are designed to <u>address</u> the <u>needs</u> of people <u>local</u> to where the projects are carried out.

2) <u>Locally available</u>, <u>cheap</u> materials are used so the community <u>isn't</u> dependent on <u>expensive imports</u>.

3) Projects are <u>labour intensive</u> — they create <u>jobs</u> for <u>local people</u>.

Disadvantages

1) Projects are often <u>small-scale</u>, so they may <u>not</u> benefit <u>everyone</u>.

2) Different organisations may <u>not work together</u>, so projects may be <u>inefficient</u>.

...IGO-Funded *Large Infrastructure...*

<u>Inter-governmental organisations</u> (<u>IGOs</u>), e.g. the World Bank, the International Monetary Fund (IMF) and the United Nations (UN), are made up of the <u>governments</u> of <u>several countries</u>.

Advantages

1) <u>IGOs</u> can afford to fund <u>large infrastructure</u> projects in <u>developing</u> and <u>emerging</u> countries.

2) Projects can improve the country's <u>economy</u>, helping with <u>long-term development</u>, e.g. HEP stations may <u>promote industry</u>, which <u>provides jobs</u> and <u>boosts</u> the <u>economy</u>.

3) Projects can also <u>improve</u> people's <u>quality of life</u>, as people have better access to <u>reliable power</u>, <u>clean water</u> etc.

Disadvantages

1) Large projects are often <u>expensive</u> and the country may have to <u>pay back the money</u> (if it's a loan). This can lead to lots of <u>debt</u>.

2) They <u>may not benefit everyone</u> — e.g. HEP may not supply power to remote areas.

3) If governments are <u>corrupt</u>, they may use the <u>money</u> for their <u>own purposes</u>.

4) Projects tend to be <u>energy intensive</u> — they use <u>scarce resources</u>, <u>release greenhouse gases</u> and lead to <u>loss</u> of <u>ecosystems</u>.

...and Investment *by TNCs*

<u>TNCs</u> are also involved in <u>development</u> through <u>investment</u> in the <u>countries</u> they operate in.

Advantages

1) TNCs provide <u>employment</u> for <u>local</u> people.

2) More <u>companies</u> mean a <u>greater income</u> from <u>taxes</u> for the <u>host</u> country.

3) Some TNCs run programmes to <u>help development</u>.

4) TNCs may also <u>invest</u> in <u>infrastructure</u>, <u>improving</u> <u>roads</u>, <u>basic services</u> and <u>communication links</u> in the area. This may improve the <u>quality of life</u> of local people.

Disadvantages

1) Some <u>profits leave</u> the <u>host</u> country.

2) TNCs can cause <u>environmental problems</u> — <u>developing</u> countries may have <u>less strict environmental regulations</u>, leading to e.g. the dumping of <u>toxic waste</u>.

3) TNCs may <u>move around</u> the country to take advantage of <u>local tax breaks</u>, leaving people <u>jobless</u> as the company moves on.

Right, so that's TNCs, NGOs or IGOs like the IMF or the UN...

I'd say that's TMA — too many acronyms. Still, that's your last lot of theory so get it well and truly learnt.

1) Describe two ways that investment by TNCs can help development. [2]

Development — Case Study

India is an <u>emerging</u> country with a <u>huge population</u> and <u>lots of potential</u>. Time for a whirlwind tour...

India is an Emerging Country in Southern Asia

1) <u>India</u> is a rapidly developing <u>emerging</u> country. It has the <u>second largest</u> population in the world (approx. 1.3 billion) and is <u>still growing</u>.

2) India was a <u>British colony</u> until <u>1947</u>, but now has its own <u>democratically elected</u> government.

3) India has a <u>rich</u> and <u>diverse cultural</u> background. It's renowned for its production of '<u>Bollywood</u>' films, which are exported <u>worldwide</u>.

4) India has a beautiful and <u>varied landscape</u>, including areas of <u>mountains</u>, <u>desert</u>, <u>great plains</u> and a large <u>coastline</u>, making it an attractive <u>tourist destination</u>.

5) The large <u>coastline</u> also allows the development of <u>ports</u>, such as Mumbai, increasing trade.

India's Economy has Changed a lot Since 1990

	1990	2015
GDP ($ trillion)	0.3	2.1
GNI per capita ($)	390	1600

1) India is getting <u>rapidly wealthier</u>.

2) India has a <u>medium</u> level of development (<u>HDI = 0.61</u>). There are <u>large inequalities</u> — some people are <u>very wealthy</u>, but the <u>majority</u> are <u>poor</u>.

3) Economic development has changed the <u>importance</u> of the different <u>economic sectors</u>. <u>Primary</u> and <u>secondary</u> industry (see page 35) employ 69% of the workforce, but contribute <u>less than half</u> of India's GDP. India's <u>tertiary service</u> and high-tech <u>quaternary industries</u> have <u>grown</u> hugely in recent years, now accounting for <u>45%</u> of <u>GDP</u>.

	1990	2015
Exports	Low-value manufactured goods, e.g. clothing, and primary products, e.g. tea	High-value manufactured goods, e.g. machinery
Imports	Manufactured goods, e.g. machinery, chemicals	Crude oil (for transport and industry)

4) These changes have <u>affected</u> what India <u>imports</u> and <u>exports</u>:

Globalisation and Government Policies have Increased Development

Globalisation

1) More than <u>50%</u> of all Indians now own a <u>mobile phone</u>. This has enabled lots of people to start their own <u>small businesses</u>, giving them a <u>larger income</u>.

2) India has 12 major <u>ports</u> and more than 20 international <u>airports</u>. It also has an extensive <u>rail network</u>, carrying <u>8 billion passengers</u> a year and almost <u>3 million tonnes</u> of <u>freight</u> per day. This makes it <u>easier</u> to transport goods, so <u>trade</u> can <u>increase</u>, and <u>TNCs</u> are more <u>likely</u> to <u>invest</u>.

3) Some large TNCs, e.g. Microsoft®, Nokia, Unilever and Coca-Cola®, outsource some <u>manufacturing</u> and <u>IT</u> to India. These bring <u>jobs</u>, greater <u>income</u> from <u>taxes</u> and the latest <u>technology</u> and <u>business</u> practices.

Government Policy

1) In 1991, India received US $2.2 billion in <u>aid</u> from the <u>IMF</u> in exchange for the government <u>changing</u> its <u>economic policies</u>, e.g. by <u>reducing tariffs</u> (extra taxes) on imported goods.

2) In 2009 India made primary education <u>free</u> and <u>compulsory</u> — 96% of children now <u>enrol</u> for school. Having a <u>more educated</u> workforce helps to <u>fuel development</u> — see page 23.

3) The <u>rail network</u> is being upgraded and <u>new roads</u> and <u>airports</u> are being built. These <u>reduce travel time</u> — e.g. the Delhi metro enables thousands of <u>commuters</u> to get to <u>work</u>.

4) India is one of the <u>top locations</u> in the world for FDI (foreign direct investment — <u>foreign</u> companies buy <u>land</u>, <u>buildings</u> or parts of <u>companies</u> in a country). <u>Most investment</u> comes from Singapore, Mauritius, Japan and the USA. India is trying to attract <u>more FDI</u> by <u>relaxing</u> the <u>rules</u> on <u>how much</u> land, property etc. <u>foreign companies</u> can <u>own</u>.

Development — Case Study

Development is Causing Population Change in India

1) Birth rates in India are high. Death rates and infant mortality have fallen, partly due to better health care and health education, e.g. encouraging people to wash their hands. This means that:
   - India's population is rapidly increasing — it grew from about 870 million in 1990, to 1.3 billion in 2015.
   - The majority of the population are young — about 28% are under 14.
   - Life expectancy has increased from 58 in 1990 to 68 in 2014.

2) The fertility rate is starting to fall — it decreased from 4.0 in 1990 to 2.4 in 2014, partly due to growing wealth and better education (see p. 22). So population growth rates are gradually slowing down.

3) As the country gets wealthier, urban areas are growing because of migration and natural increase:
   - In 1990, only 26% of the population lived in urban areas. By 2015 this had risen to 33%.
   - India already has 4 megacities (see p. 33) — New Delhi, Mumbai, Kolkata and Bengaluru, and is expected to have 3 more by 2030.

Some Regions of India are Developing Faster than Others

1) Rapid economic growth has increased inequality within India — the gap between the richest and poorest states has been widening.

2) The growth of manufacturing and services has benefited urban areas more than rural areas. GDP per capita is highest in the south and west states, e.g. Maharashtra, which have the highest urban population.

3) More money gets spent on these areas in order to attract more FDI and TNCs. The wealth generated can then be spent on development projects improving literacy rates and quality of life.

	Maharashtra	Bihar
Urban population (%)	45	11
GDP per capita ($)	2561	682
HDI	0.572	0.367
Literacy rate (%)	83	64

4) More rural states, e.g. Bihar, have higher rates of poverty. This has led to undernourishment and health problems because people can't afford to buy enough food. Many children have to work rather than attend school leading to low literacy rates. Poor health and education leads to a low HDI score. Older people are less likely to migrate to urban areas, instead remaining in rural areas.

Economic Development has Pros and Cons for Different Groups of People

Economic development is good news for some people, but can cause problems for others:

Positive Impacts

1) All age groups have better health:
   - Elderly people are living longer.
   - There is a lower infant mortality rate.
   - There is a lower maternal mortality rate.

2) Some age groups have better education:
   - Higher education has given young graduates access to better jobs, e.g. in technical firms and ICT.
   - Many adults have better literacy.

3) There can be better gender equality:
   - Women have better access to education — literacy rates for Indian women have increased from 34% in 1991 to 59% in 2011.
   - Women have better access to contraception and family planning advice.

Negative Impacts

1) Rapid industrialisation means young working men may have to do dangerous jobs. Working conditions may also be poor due to a lack of regulations put in place by Indian authorities.

2) As young people move to urban areas to find work, there are fewer workers in rural villages. This means:
   - Children in rural areas may get a poor education due to a lack of skilled teachers — nearly 50% of teachers have only completed secondary education.
   - Children may have to work as agricultural labourers to support their families.

3) There is still a lot of gender inequality:
   - It is unsafe for women in many urban areas. E.g. in Delhi, crimes against women increased by 20% from 2014-15.
   - When men leave to find work in cities, women are left to care for and provide for the entire household — balancing a job with housework.

Topic 2 — Development Dynamics

Development — Case Study

Economic Development has Impacts on the Environment

1) <u>Industrialisation</u> leads to higher <u>energy consumption</u>. Increased <u>demand</u> for <u>fossil fuels</u> in industry, homes and vehicles means <u>more greenhouse gases</u> are released, contributing to <u>climate change</u>. India releases almost <u>7%</u> of all global greenhouse gas emissions.

2) More <u>factories</u> and <u>cars</u> mean more <u>air pollution</u>. The pollution is so <u>bad</u> in some cities, e.g. New Delhi, that a thick, toxic <u>smog</u> often forms. <u>Gases</u> such as sulfur dioxide and <u>smoke particles</u> damage people's health and cause <u>breathing problems</u> and <u>lung diseases</u>. More than <u>0.5 million</u> people in India <u>die</u> from diseases related to air pollution each year.

3) <u>Urban sprawl</u> leads to <u>land</u> and <u>water pollution</u> — lack of <u>infrastructure</u> means that about <u>70%</u> of India's sewage flows <u>untreated</u> into <u>rivers</u>. Waste may not be <u>correctly sorted</u> and <u>disposed of</u>, e.g. <u>dangerous contaminated waste</u> from a factory in Kodaikanal was initially <u>dumped</u> instead of being <u>disposed</u> of <u>safely</u>.

India's Global Influence is Increasing

1) India is playing a <u>larger role</u> in <u>regional</u> and <u>global politics</u> as it develops. In recent years the Indian government has <u>improved relations</u> with its immediate <u>neighbours</u> (e.g. joining <u>ASEAN</u>, a <u>political</u> and <u>economic</u> organisation made up of countries in <u>southeast Asia</u>).

2) India is a member of several <u>international organisations</u> — India was one of the founding members of the <u>United Nations</u> (UN), which works towards <u>sustainable development</u>. It is also part of the <u>World Trade Organisation</u> (WTO) and a member of <u>G20</u>, a group of 20 of the world's <u>largest economies</u>.

3) Economic <u>growth</u> has also <u>changed</u> India's <u>relationship</u> with the <u>USA</u> and <u>EU</u>:

<table>
<tr>
<td rowspan="3">India and the USA</td>
<td>

1) India used to have a <u>poor</u> relationship with the <u>USA</u> but this has been <u>improving</u>.

2) The USA expects the economic development of India to <u>increase trade</u>, <u>employment</u> and <u>economic growth</u> in <u>both</u> countries.

3) The <u>USA</u> also sees <u>India</u> as a <u>huge market</u> for <u>renewable</u> and <u>nuclear energy</u> because of the number of <u>increasingly wealthy</u> people and the <u>growth</u> of <u>industry</u>.
</td>
<td rowspan="3">India and the EU</td>
<td>

1) India has had a <u>good</u> relationship with the EU and they became <u>strategic partners</u> in 2004, agreeing to <u>cooperate</u> on certain issues.

2) Negotiations for a <u>free trade</u> agreement began in 2007. The EU is one of India's <u>biggest markets</u> and <u>trading partners</u>.

3) The EU supports <u>health</u> and <u>education</u> programmes in India to promote <u>continued development</u>.
</td>
</tr>
</table>

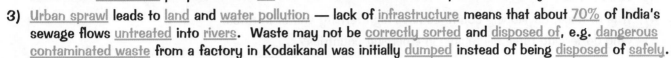

There are Costs and Benefits to Foreign Influences on India

India is increasingly <u>open</u> to the influence of the rest of the <u>world</u> — but <u>not everyone</u> is <u>happy</u> about this.

1) Changing <u>international relations</u> have <u>costs</u> and <u>benefits</u>:

- <u>Costs</u> — there is increasing <u>tension</u> between <u>India</u> and <u>China</u> — both have <u>rapidly growing economies</u>. <u>Developed</u> nations are also concerned about <u>losing economic power</u> as India grows.

- <u>Benefits</u> — improved relations mean India can <u>cooperate</u> with <u>other countries</u> on <u>global issues</u>, e.g. climate change, FDI brings <u>economic benefits</u> to <u>both</u> India and the country of origin, and global trade agreements mean that <u>political actions</u>, e.g. sanctions, are more <u>effective</u>.

2) <u>Foreign investment</u> (<u>TNCs</u>) is bringing <u>wealth</u> and <u>jobs</u> to India but there are <u>problems</u> too:

- TNCs can cause <u>environmental problems</u> — e.g. the concern of local communities about the amount of <u>water</u> being <u>extracted</u> by Coca-Cola® bottling plants led to plants in Kerala and Varanasi being <u>closed</u>.

- Large global <u>retail chains</u> can offer <u>cheap</u> prices on goods — Indian <u>street traders</u> are concerned that this will <u>destroy</u> their <u>livelihoods</u> as people choose to shop in supermarkets instead.

- TNCs could <u>withdraw</u> their <u>business</u> from India at <u>any time</u>, e.g if the <u>economic climate</u> changes.

Ohdia — I can't think of a decent gag for these pages...

Don't worry if you've studied a different country — you can learn that one instead, or use this one. Just make sure you know about the economic changes caused by globalisation, the impacts on people and its changing role in the world.

Revision Summary

Despite the dynamic nature of this section, I suspect that you've developed a serious case of boredom. Well before you move onto doing something that you actually want to do, have a go at these questions. They'll help you check what you know and what you need to work on. The answers can all be found in the content on the pages, so if you can't answer them, take another look through the section.

Measuring Development (p.21-22) ☑

1) Other than economic, give two other types of development.
2) What's the difference between GDP and GDP per capita?
3) What is HDI?
4) True or false: developing countries have high fertility and birth rates.
5) Why do fertility rates fall rapidly in emerging countries?

Causes and Consequences of Global Inequalities (p.23-24) ☑

6) Explain how climate can affect how developed a country is.
7) How can topography affect how developed a country is?
8) What is meant by neo-colonialism?
9) Give two possible social consequences of global inequality.
10) Give one possible political consequence of global inequality.

Theories of Development and Globalisation (p.25-26) ☑

11) List the five stages of economic development according to Rostow's theory.
12) Briefly summarise Frank's dependency theory.
13) What is globalisation?
14) Give one reason why globalisation is increasing.
15) What does TNC stand for?
16) Give two ways in which governments are increasing globalisation.
17) Give one reason why some people think that globalisation increases global inequality.

Reducing Global Inequalities (p.27-28) ☑

18) Explain what is meant by a top-down approach to development.
19) Give one advantage and one disadvantage of the top-down approach.
20) Explain what is meant by a bottom-up approach to development.
21) Give one benefit of using bottom-up development.
22) What is an NGO?
23) What is intermediate technology? What are its advantages?
24) Give one advantage and one disadvantage of IGO-funded large infrastructure.

Development — Case Study (p.29-31) ☑

Answer these questions for an emerging country you have studied:
25) Give one example of the cultural importance of the country.
26) How has the economy of the country changed since 1990?
27) How has globalisation helped increase development in the country?
28) Explain how development has changed the country's population structure.
29) How have some age and gender groups been negatively impacted by development?
30) Give an example of how development has had an impact on the country's environment.
31) How is the country's global influence changing?
32) Give one advantage and one disadvantage of foreign investment in the country.

Urbanisation

Urban areas (towns and cities) are <u>popular places</u> to be and getting <u>ever more so</u> — some <u>faster</u> than others...

Urbanisation is Happening Fastest in Poorer Countries

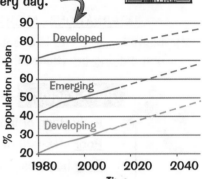

1) <u>Urbanisation</u> is the <u>growth</u> in the <u>proportion</u> of a country's population living in <u>urban areas</u>.

2) It's happening in countries <u>all over the world</u> — more than <u>50%</u> of the world's population currently live in <u>urban areas</u> (<u>3.9 billion</u> people) and this is <u>increasing</u> every day.

3) Urbanisation happened <u>earlier</u> in developed countries (see p. 22), e.g. during the <u>Industrial Revolution</u> (in the 18th and 19th centuries), and <u>most</u> (79%) of the population now <u>already live</u> in <u>urban areas</u>. Developed countries have very <u>slow rates</u> of urban growth.

4) A <u>smaller proportion</u> (35%) of the population in developing countries <u>currently live</u> in urban areas. In general, the <u>fastest rates</u> of urbanisation in the world are in developing countries.

5) The percentage of the population living in urban areas <u>varies</u> in <u>emerging countries</u>. Some, such as <u>Thailand</u>, <u>Nigeria</u> and <u>China</u>, are experiencing <u>rapid urban growth</u>.

6) Urbanisation is predicted to continue at a <u>fast rate</u> in regions that still have <u>large rural populations</u>. By 2050, the <u>majority</u> of people in <u>every global region</u> are predicted to live in <u>urban areas</u>.

The Number of Megacities is Increasing

1) <u>High rates</u> of <u>urbanisation</u> are leading to the growth of <u>megacities</u>. A megacity is an urban area with <u>over 10 million people</u> living there, e.g. Mumbai in India.

2) In 1950 the <u>biggest</u> and most <u>influential</u> cities were largely in <u>developed countries</u>. There were only <u>2</u> megacities — Tokyo and New York.

3) By 2014 there were <u>28</u> megacities and this number is still growing — it's predicted to rise to <u>41</u> by 2030.

4) More than <u>two-thirds</u> of current megacities are in <u>developing</u> and <u>emerging</u> countries, mostly in <u>Asia</u>, e.g. <u>Jakarta</u> in Indonesia, <u>Karachi</u> in Pakistan and <u>Dhaka</u> in Bangladesh.

A Primate City Dominates a Country

1) <u>Urban primacy</u> is when one city <u>dominates</u> the country it is in. These '<u>primate cities</u>' have a <u>much larger population</u> than other cities in the country — usually more than <u>twice</u> as many people as the <u>next biggest city</u>.

2) They <u>influence</u> the country <u>economically</u>:

- <u>Investment</u> — <u>businesses</u> often locate there, attracting investment in <u>infrastructure</u> and <u>services</u>.
- <u>Migration</u> — there are lots of <u>jobs</u> so people move there to find work. Highly-skilled workers are attracted by <u>better opportunities</u>, e.g. <u>higher-paid</u>, more <u>prestigious</u> jobs.
- <u>Transport</u> — <u>international ports</u> and <u>airports</u> are often located there, encouraging <u>further investment</u> and <u>migration</u>.

3) They also have <u>political influences</u>:

<u>Governments</u> and the <u>headquarters</u> of large, powerful <u>businesses</u> are often <u>located</u> there. This can mean that <u>decisions</u> about development <u>favour</u> the <u>city</u> rather than the rest of the <u>country</u>.

Zip wires and bouncy pavements — that would be a mega city...

What better way to start a new section than learning the page and then having a crack at an exam question:

1) Describe how global trends of urbanisation vary between global regions. [2]

Cities — Growth and Decline

The lure of the <u>city lights</u> can be strong, but beware — they won't stay on <u>forever</u> and then it'll be <u>time to go</u>.

Migration is a Result of Push and Pull Factors

1) Migration to <u>cities</u> can be <u>national</u> or <u>international</u>:
   - <u>NATIONAL MIGRATION</u> — when people move to a city <u>in</u> the <u>same</u> country, e.g. <u>rural-urban migration</u> is the <u>movement</u> of people from the <u>countryside</u> to the <u>cities</u>.
   - <u>INTERNATIONAL MIGRATION</u> — when people move from one country to a <u>city</u> in <u>another country</u>.

2) Migration <u>to</u> a city is affected by <u>push factors</u> (things that <u>encourage</u> people to <u>leave</u> an area) and <u>pull factors</u> (things that <u>encourage</u> people to <u>move to</u> the city).

Push Factors
- A <u>shortage</u> of jobs or <u>low</u> wages.
- <u>Poor</u> standard of living.
- <u>Poor</u> healthcare and education.
- <u>War</u> or conflict.
- <u>Natural disasters</u> like earthquakes or floods.
- A <u>poor environment</u> due to pollution or crime.

Pull Factors
- <u>More</u> employment opportunities and <u>higher</u> wages.
- <u>Better</u> standard of living.
- <u>Better</u> health care and education.
- A <u>safe</u> place with little crime or risk of natural disasters.
- A <u>cleaner</u> environment.

Economic Change Leads to Migration

<u>Economic change</u> is causing cities in countries of different levels of development to <u>grow</u> or to <u>decline</u>.

Developing

Cities in <u>developing</u> countries are <u>growing</u>. This is because:
1) <u>Rural</u> areas are very <u>poor</u> — <u>improvements</u> in <u>agriculture</u> mean <u>fewer</u> farm workers are needed. This leads to <u>national migration</u> to cities as people seek <u>better jobs</u>. There are lots of <u>opportunities</u> in the <u>informal sector</u> (see next page) for low-skilled migrants from rural areas.
2) Some cities have <u>good transport links</u> so <u>trade</u> is focused there — providing <u>lots</u> of <u>jobs</u>.
3) Some cities are attracting <u>foreign companies</u> and <u>manufacturing industry</u> is <u>expanding</u>.

Emerging

Some cities in <u>emerging</u> countries are <u>growing</u> and some have <u>stabilising</u> populations.
1) Some cities have become <u>industrial centres</u> — there are lots of <u>manufacturing jobs</u>. Other cities have a <u>rapidly expanding service sector</u>, e.g. the IT industry in India. People <u>move to</u> the cities to work in the <u>new industries</u> and in <u>services</u> supporting them.
2) As countries get <u>wealthier</u> they are <u>investing</u> in flagship projects, e.g. sports stadiums for international events, to attract <u>foreign investment</u>. This creates <u>more jobs</u>, attracting <u>workers</u>.

Developed

Some cities in <u>developed</u> countries have <u>stable</u> populations and others are <u>declining</u>.
1) <u>De-industrialisation</u> has led to the <u>decline</u> of industrial areas (see p. 75) — people moved <u>away</u> to find work elsewhere. Some cities are <u>still declining</u>, e.g. Sunderland, however many cities have been <u>regenerated</u> and are <u>attracting</u> people again, e.g. Bristol.
2) A lot of <u>low-skilled workers</u>, e.g. cleaners and factory-line workers, are <u>attracted</u> to more <u>successful cities</u> in the region. This leads to the <u>decline</u> of the <u>cities</u> they are <u>leaving</u>.

Umm-igration is when you don't know whether you're coming or going...

Urbanisation isn't a random process — it's the result people moving to where there are jobs and away from where there aren't many. Simple. The tricky bit is working out why it's different in different places. Well, just turn over the page...

Urban Economies

Cities in <u>richer</u> and <u>poorer</u> countries are quite <u>different</u>. This is partly because they have different <u>economic</u> <u>structures</u> — people work in <u>different</u> kinds of <u>jobs</u>. First up, you're going to need some <u>definitions</u>...

There are Different Kinds of Work

1) There are <u>two</u> different types of <u>employment</u> — <u>formal</u> and <u>informal</u>.

- <u>Formal</u> employment is <u>officially</u> recognised — workers are <u>protected</u> by the <u>laws</u> of country. There are rules about how many <u>hours</u> people can work, the <u>age</u> of workers and <u>health</u> and <u>safety</u>. Workers pay <u>tax</u> to the <u>government</u> out of the <u>wages</u> they earn.
- <u>Informal</u> employment is <u>unofficial</u> — jobs <u>aren't taxed</u> or <u>regulated</u> by the government. People often work <u>long hours</u> in <u>dangerous</u> conditions for <u>little pay</u>.

2) There are also <u>four</u> different <u>economic sectors</u> — <u>primary</u>, <u>secondary</u>, <u>tertiary</u> and <u>quaternary</u>.

- The <u>primary</u> sector involves collecting <u>raw materials</u>, e.g. <u>farming</u>, <u>fishing</u>, <u>mining</u> and <u>forestry</u>.
- The <u>secondary</u> sector involves turning a <u>product</u> into <u>another product</u> (<u>manufacturing</u>), e.g. making <u>textiles</u>, <u>furniture</u>, <u>chemicals</u>, <u>steel</u> and <u>cars</u>.
- The <u>tertiary</u> sector involves providing a <u>service</u> — anything from <u>financial</u> services, <u>nursing</u> and <u>retail</u> to the <u>police force</u> and <u>transport</u>.
- The <u>quaternary</u> sector is the <u>information economy</u> — e.g. <u>research and development</u>, where scientists and researchers investigate and develop new products (e.g. in the <u>electronics</u> and <u>IT industry</u>), and <u>consultancy</u> (e.g. advising businesses).

Urban Economies Vary By Level of Development

	Developing countries	Emerging countries	Developed countries
Formal and informal employment	<u>Many</u> workers are employed in the informal sector.	Number of workers in the informal sector <u>decreases</u> as the country develops.	<u>Few</u> workers in the informal sector.
Economic sectors	Lots of people work in <u>low-skilled tertiary sector</u> jobs, e.g. on market stalls. <u>Few people</u> work in the <u>secondary</u> sector because there's <u>not enough money</u> to <u>invest</u> in the <u>technology needed</u> for this type of industry, e.g. to build large factories. A <u>small percentage</u> of people work in high-skilled <u>tertiary</u> jobs, e.g. in government offices or IT.	<u>Employment</u> in the <u>secondary sector</u> is <u>high</u>. There are established <u>industrial zones</u> and <u>good infrastructure</u>. There are also lots of <u>low-skilled tertiary</u> jobs, e.g. in retail or tourism. As the <u>industrial economy grows</u> people have <u>more money</u> to spend on services — jobs are created in <u>higher-skilled jobs</u> in the <u>tertiary sector</u>, e.g. in medicine or law. Some cities <u>specialise</u> in certain <u>services</u>, e.g. Hyderabad, India specialises in <u>IT development</u>.	<u>Fewer people</u> work in the <u>secondary sector</u> than in <u>emerging</u> countries. <u>Most people</u> work in the <u>tertiary sector</u> because there's a <u>skilled</u> and <u>educated</u> workforce, and there's a <u>high demand</u> for services like banks and shops. There's some employment in the <u>quaternary sector</u> because the country has lots of <u>highly skilled labour</u> and has <u>money</u> to <u>invest</u> in the <u>technology needed</u>.
Working conditions	Conditions are <u>poor</u>. Pay is <u>low</u>, hours are <u>long</u> and conditions can <u>be dangerous</u>.	Conditions <u>improve</u> and workers' rights <u>increase</u>.	Conditions are <u>good</u>. Pay is <u>high</u>, workers have many <u>rights</u> protected by <u>law</u>.

I prefer smart-casual employment myself...

Have a go at this handy exam-style question to check you've got to grips with this page.

1) Describe the characteristics of urban economies in developing countries. [3]

Urban Change

Urban areas go through a <u>lot</u> of changes as they <u>develop</u>. Changes in the <u>economy</u> mean people <u>move in</u>, then they <u>move out</u>, and then they <u>move in</u> again. In, out, in, out, do the hokey cokey and turn around...

Cities Go Through Different Stages as they Develop

Urbanisation

Urbanisation is the <u>increase</u> in the <u>proportion</u> of the population living in built-up <u>urban areas</u>. Urban areas <u>spread</u> into the <u>surrounding countryside</u> as the population increases.

- Cities in <u>developed</u> countries grew during the <u>Industrial Revolution</u> (1760-1850). Workers lived in <u>small terraced houses</u> around the <u>factories</u> in the <u>city centres</u>.
- When factories <u>relocated</u> to <u>emerging</u> countries in the <u>1970s</u> and <u>80s</u>, slums and <u>apartment blocks</u> sprang up around them to house the <u>workers</u>.

Suburbanisation

Suburbanisation is the movement of people from the <u>middle</u> of the city to the <u>edges</u> — urban areas <u>expand rapidly</u> (<u>sprawl</u>) as <u>housing</u> is <u>built</u> in the <u>outskirts</u>. It began occurring in the <u>early 20th century</u> in many <u>developed</u> counties.

- Urbanisation caused urban areas to become <u>overcrowded</u> and <u>polluted</u>, with <u>little</u> 'natural' space. Suburban areas offered more open <u>green spaces</u> and seemed more <u>family-friendly</u>.
- Improvements in <u>transport networks</u> meant that people could live in the suburbs and <u>commute</u> in to the city to work.

De-industrialisation

1) As countries <u>develop</u>, they experience <u>de-industrialisation</u> (<u>manufacturing</u> moving <u>out</u> of an area). Urban areas are affected by industry moving:
   - out of <u>city centres</u> into <u>rural areas</u> where <u>rents</u> are <u>cheaper</u>.
   - <u>overseas</u> to countries where <u>costs are lower</u> — this is known as <u>global shift</u>.
2) De-industrialisation can lead to <u>de-population</u> as people <u>leave</u> the old industrial areas.
3) The <u>city centre</u> and <u>industrial zones</u> on the <u>edges of cities decline</u> — <u>unemployment increases</u> leading to <u>lower living standards</u> and <u>poverty</u>. Shops, restaurants and other amenities <u>close</u>.

Counter-urbanisation

<u>Counter-urbanisation</u> is the movement of people <u>away</u> from large <u>urban areas</u> to smaller settlements and <u>rural areas</u>. In many <u>developed</u> countries this process began in the <u>1970s</u> and <u>80s</u>.

- People think they'll have a <u>higher quality of life</u> in <u>rural</u> areas and house prices are often <u>lower</u>.
- Increased <u>car ownership</u> and improved <u>public transport</u> mean that people can live <u>further</u> from the city and <u>commute</u> to work.
- Improved <u>communication services</u> (e.g. high-speed internet connections) make it easier for people to live in rural areas and <u>work from home</u>. This also means that some companies <u>no longer</u> need to be in a city centre and can move to <u>rural areas</u> where land is <u>cheaper</u>.

Regeneration

Since the <u>1990s</u> some <u>city centres</u> in <u>developed countries</u> have undergone <u>regeneration</u> to <u>reverse</u> the <u>decline</u> of urban areas because of suburbanisation, de-industrialisation and counter-urbanisation.

- To <u>attract</u> people and businesses <u>back</u> to the <u>city centre</u>, governments and private companies <u>invest</u> in <u>new developments</u>, e.g. <u>high quality flats</u> and <u>office blocks</u>, and <u>upgrade infrastructure</u>.
- Once re-urbanisation has <u>started</u> it tends to <u>continue</u> — as soon as a few businesses invest and people start to return, it encourages <u>other businesses</u> to invest.
- <u>Young</u>, <u>single people</u> often want to live <u>close to their work</u> in areas with <u>good entertainment services</u> (e.g. bars and nightclubs).

The movement of people back into urban areas is known as re-urbanisation.

Superbanisation — when the buildings start wearing capes and pants...

Some classic geography here and stuff that will come up time and time again in this topic and in Topic 5. Learning it inside out and sideways now will almost certainly reduce the pain later. Well, what are you waiting for... Get to it.

Urban Land Use

Every city is different, but they all have the same <u>dodgy run-down parts</u> and <u>posh housing areas</u>. Obviously you should use more <u>formal terms</u> to describe them in the exam — amazingly enough, they're all here...

Land Use in Cities can be Commercial, Industrial or Residential

<u>Land</u> in cities can be used for <u>different purposes</u>:

- <u>Commercial</u> — e.g. office buildings, shopping centres and hotels
- <u>Industrial</u> — e.g. factories, warehouses
- <u>Residential</u> — e.g. houses, flats and apartments (anything that people live in)

<u>Different types</u> of land use are found in <u>particular areas</u> of the city because they have <u>similar</u> requirements. This creates distinct <u>zones</u> within a city, which can be identified on maps and satellite <u>images</u>:

- The <u>central business district</u> (<u>CBD</u>) has <u>commercial</u> and <u>public buildings</u>. Look for <u>high density</u> buildings and the <u>meeting</u> of <u>major roads</u>.

- The <u>inner city</u> is mainly <u>residential</u> (low-class housing) and older <u>industry</u>. Look for <u>short</u>, <u>parallel roads</u> of <u>terraced housing</u> and <u>larger factory</u> buildings.

- The <u>suburbs</u> are mainly <u>residential</u> (medium-class housing). Look for lots of <u>short</u>, <u>curved streets</u> and <u>cul-de sacs</u>.

- The <u>rural-urban fringe</u> has a mix of <u>commercial</u> business parks and <u>residential</u> (high-class housing). Look for <u>more green space</u> between built-up areas and clusters of <u>larger office buildings</u> or <u>shopping centres</u> with <u>car parks</u>.

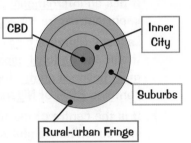

The zones of a 'model' city form concentric rings:

CBD · Inner City · Suburbs · Rural-urban Fringe

Land Use is Influenced by Accessibility, Availability, Cost and Regulations

Accessibility

1) City centres are usually <u>very accessible</u> — they are the location of the main <u>train</u> and <u>bus</u> <u>stations</u> and the <u>centre</u> of the <u>road network</u>.

2) <u>Shops</u> and <u>offices</u> locate in city centres because they need to be <u>accessible</u> to lots of people.

3) Some <u>businesses</u> now locate on the <u>edges</u> of cities — these are near <u>major motorway</u> <u>junctions</u> and <u>out-of-town airports</u>, so <u>avoid</u> <u>traffic congestion</u> in the <u>city centre</u>.

Planning Regulations

1) <u>City planners</u> try to <u>control</u> how cities develop by deciding what <u>types</u> of buildings can be built in <u>different parts</u> of the city.

2) There are often <u>strict</u> planning regulations in city centres — <u>polluting</u> industries may be <u>banned</u>.

3) Some cities have <u>strict limits</u> on development in the <u>rural-urban fringe</u>, e.g. designated greenbelt land that can't be built on. This stops the city <u>sprawling</u> into the <u>countryside</u>.

Availability

1) In the city centre almost all land is <u>in use</u> and <u>demand</u> is <u>high</u>. Businesses may <u>extend upwards</u> as ground space is limited — the <u>tallest</u> buildings are often in the <u>centre</u>.

2) <u>Brownfield</u> land in city centres, such as <u>old industrial sites</u>, may be <u>redeveloped</u> as <u>shops</u> or <u>offices</u>. Some of the <u>old</u> <u>terraced housing</u> and <u>apartment blocks</u> in inner cities are <u>redeveloped</u> as <u>luxury homes</u> for young professionals.

3) There is <u>lots of space</u> on the <u>edges</u> of cities where <u>larger buildings</u>, e.g. shopping centres, science parks, industrial estates and houses, can be built (if allowed).

Cost

1) The <u>city centre</u> has the <u>highest</u> <u>land prices</u> — the cost of land <u>falls</u> towards the <u>edge</u> of the city.

2) Some <u>businesses</u> and <u>shops</u> can <u>afford</u> to locate offices and shops in the <u>city centre</u> but there are <u>few houses</u>.

3) <u>Houses</u> tend to <u>increase</u> in <u>size</u> from the <u>inner city</u> to the <u>suburbs</u> as the <u>price</u> of land <u>decreases</u>.

A rural-urban fringe playlist — house, garage, some commercial stuff...

It's a good idea to learn the four main parts of a city and the land use in each bit, but remember that the land use is affected by many things — I'm sure city planners do this on purpose, just to make your revision awkward. Some people...

Urban Change — Case Study

Strap in, buckle up and generally prepare yourself mentally and physically for a tour of Lagos...

Lagos is the Biggest City in Africa

Lagos is a megacity in Nigeria — an emerging country and the richest country in Africa. The city's population is over 21 million, and it's one of the fastest-growing urban areas in the world.

1) Lagos is located at the outlet of the massive Lagos Lagoon (see map below) on the Atlantic western coast of Nigeria.

2) This location is ideal for its port, which is one of the biggest in Africa. The city has spread outwards from its origin on Lagos Island around the lagoon and along the coast.

3) Lagos is well connected by road to the other major towns in Nigeria, e.g. Abuja (the national capital). It has an international port and airport, making it an important centre for regional and global trade.

4) Lagos is Nigeria's biggest city for population and business. It was the national capital until 1991 and remains the main financial centre for the whole of West Africa. The city contains 80% of Nigeria's industry and lots of global companies are located there.

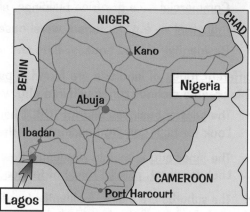

5) It is the centre of the Nigerian film industry 'Nollywood' and has a thriving music scene, which has introduced music styles such as Afrobeat and Afro hip-hop — this gives it cultural importance in Nigeria.

Different Areas of Lagos have Different Functions

1) The development of Lagos means that land use and building age varies across the city.

2) The oldest parts of the city are on Lagos Island, which is now the CBD. Many of the old buildings have been redeveloped as high rise office blocks and luxury shops. Land is very expensive.

3) By 1960 the city had spread north and east along the main road and rail links, e.g. creating Mushin. Industries developed near major transport links, e.g. Ikeja industrial estate near the airport.

4) Rapid expansion meant that by 1990 Lagos had merged with the smaller surrounding towns to form a continuous urban area. The city has continued to sprawl into the surrounding countryside.

5) It has mainly spread north as it is hemmed in by the lagoon to the east and major rivers to the west. It has also expanded west along the Lagos-Badagry express-way, e.g. in Ojo.

6) Slums have developed on less desirable land on the outskirts of Lagos throughout its history. However, over time, the city has sprawled outwards, beyond many of the slums and they now form part of the main urban area of Lagos.

	Area	Age and function
CBD	Lagos Island	Modern high-rise office buildings, local government headquarters and banks.
Inner city	Mushin	Older, high-density, low-quality houses.
	Ikeja	Large industrial estate built in the 1960s, with factories making e.g. plastics and textiles.
Suburbs	Victoria Island	Modern, high-class residential and commercial — lots of businesses and shops.
Rural-urban fringe	Ojo	Sprawling, low-density new housing on the outskirts of the city.
	Lekki	New industrial zone and port being built.

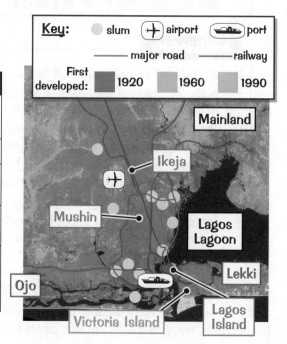

Urban Change — Case Study

Lagos's Population is Growing Rapidly

Lagos's population has <u>grown</u> for <u>different reasons</u> at different <u>times</u>:

Historic

1) The city was under <u>British rule</u> during <u>colonial</u> times and was a centre of <u>trade</u>. This attracted <u>traders</u> and <u>merchants</u> to the city.

2) Many <u>ex-slaves</u> also came to Lagos, e.g. from <u>Sierra Leone</u>, <u>Brazil</u> and the <u>West Indies</u>.

1960s-1990s

1) After Lagos gained <u>independence</u> there was <u>rapid economic development</u> — the <u>export</u> of <u>oil</u> made some people very <u>wealthy</u>.

2) The government financed lots of <u>construction projects</u>, e.g. building <u>sea ports</u>, <u>oil refineries</u> and <u>factories</u>. The <u>jobs</u> created led to <u>rapid urbanisation</u> — lots of people moved <u>to</u> Lagos from <u>rural Nigeria</u>.

3) <u>Birth rates</u> were <u>high</u> and <u>death rates</u> were <u>lower</u> leading to <u>high rates</u> of <u>natural increase</u> — a rapidly <u>growing</u> population.

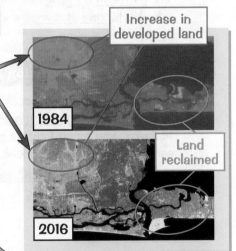

Recent

1) <u>Most</u> of the population growth in Lagos is due to <u>rural-urban migration</u>.

2) The countries <u>bordering</u> Nigeria, e.g. Chad and Niger, are <u>poor</u> and <u>involved</u> in conflict — many people leave these countries for a <u>better life</u> in Lagos.

3) There are also lots of <u>national migrants</u> from the <u>northern states</u> of Nigeria where there is lots of <u>ethnic</u> and <u>religious conflict</u> and high levels of <u>poverty</u>.

4) There is some international migration from the <u>USA</u>, the <u>UK</u> and <u>China</u>. This is mainly people who are employed by <u>foreign businesses</u> operating in <u>Lagos</u>.

5) The rate of <u>natural increase</u> is still <u>high</u> — <u>birth</u> rates are still higher than <u>death</u> rates though <u>both</u> are slowly falling.

Lagos's Growth has Caused Changes in Land Use

1) The city has expanded <u>outwards</u> — a <u>larger area</u> is now <u>built on</u>. Lots of people are forced to move to the <u>rural-urban fringe</u> as they can't afford the <u>rising house prices</u> in the <u>inner city</u>.

2) Land has been <u>reclaimed</u> from the <u>lagoon</u>. Land around the <u>CBD</u> is in <u>high demand</u> and very <u>valuable</u>, so artificial islands have been built, e.g. <u>Banana Island</u> and <u>Eko Atlantic</u> are built on <u>reclaimed land</u> and contain <u>huge</u> houses in <u>gated communities</u>.

3) Previously empty areas are now <u>built on</u>, e.g. slums are built on areas of <u>wasteland</u>. In other <u>undesirable locations</u> (like <u>Makoko</u>), people have built <u>wooden huts</u> on <u>stilts</u> in the <u>lagoon</u>.

4) The <u>land use</u> in some areas has also <u>changed</u>, for example:

- some <u>slums</u> have been <u>upgraded</u> and made more <u>permanent</u>. The huts have been <u>removed</u> and new <u>3-4 storey apartments</u> have been built in their place, e.g. in Badia East.

- some parts of the Makoko slum have been <u>cleared</u> by the government to allow <u>development</u> of desirable areas of the waterfront.

- some of the old middle-class residential areas have become <u>high-class luxury housing</u>, e.g. the old middle-class area of <u>Ikoyi</u> is now one of the <u>richest</u> neighbourhoods in Lagos with lots of <u>luxury shops</u> and hotels alongside the <u>redeveloped apartments</u>.

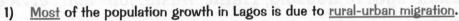

Increase in developed land

1984

Land reclaimed

2016

Lagos — growing brick by brick...

Plenty to learn on these two pages about the growth of Lagos. Make sure you've got it sorted before you move on. Because there's a lot more to come on Lagos. Turn over to see why "Everything is Awesome" isn't quite true there...

Urban Change — Case Study

People in Lagos have More Opportunities...

There is better access to employment in Lagos than in rural Nigeria and the surrounding countries:

1) Incomes are about 4 times higher in Lagos than those in rural areas and informal sector jobs mean most people can find a way of making money — the huge population means there is a large market for services.

2) Lagos is home to many of the country's banks, government departments and manufacturing industries (e.g. making food and drink). There are two major ports and a fishing industry, all of which provide employment. Rapid growth of the city means there are lots of construction jobs.

3) There are more health care centres and hospitals and a better range of medicines in Lagos and there is better access to higher education — Lagos has six universities.

4) It is possible to access electricity and water networks as well as TV and the internet.

> Even though there are major problems with the provision of services in Lagos (see below), people still have better access to resources than in rural Nigeria.

... but Lagos faces Challenges in Housing, Traffic, Waste, Jobs and Services

1 Squatter Settlements

Over 60% of the city's population live in slums.

1) Houses are often flimsy, wooden huts. These are illegally built — people face eviction if slums are demolished to clean up the city.

2) The only electricity comes from illegal connections that often cut out.

3) There are high levels of crime — many slums are patrolled by gangs called 'area boys' who both commit crimes and act as informal 'police' in the slum.

2 Traffic Congestion

Lagos has some of the worst traffic congestion in the world because:

1) There has been very little investment in transport infrastructure, despite the city growing enormously.

2) Public transport is limited, although there are plans to improve it, e.g. a light rail train.

3) The CBD is on an island, with only three bridges linking it to the rest of the city.

3 Limited Service Provision

1) There aren't enough schools for the population (e.g. there is only one primary school in Makoko) and many families can't afford to send their children to school.

2) There aren't enough health care facilities and many people can't afford to pay for treatment.

4 Poor Employment Conditions

1) There aren't enough formal jobs for the growing population — people have to make money any way they can, e.g. by scavenging in the Olusosun rubbish dump for items to sell.

2) About 60% of the population work in informal jobs (see p. 35), e.g. street sellers, barbers.

3) There's no protection for informal workers. Street-sellers' stalls are bulldozed to make way for new developments and road widening.

4) Lots of people live on less than $1.25 per day.

5 Waste Disposal

1) Most of the city doesn't have access to proper sewers, e.g. in Makoko communal toilets are shared by 15 households and most of the waste goes straight into the lagoon below — it's always full of rubbish and raw sewage. This causes health problems, e.g. cholera.

2) The huge population produces lots of waste — approximately 9000 tonnes per day.

3) Only about 40% of rubbish is officially collected and there are large rubbish dumps, e.g. Olusosun, which contain toxic waste. Waste disposal and emissions from factories are not controlled, leading to air and water pollution.

6 Water Supply

1) Only about 40% of the city is connected to the state water supply. The pipes are old and rusty — the water often gets contaminated with sewage.

2) The state water company supplies less than half of what is needed. Water is in such short supply that people pay hugely inflated prices to get water from informal sellers.

Urban Change — Case Study

There are Big Inequalities in Lagos

There are <u>big differences</u> between the <u>rich</u> and the <u>poor</u> in Lagos, which leads to differences in <u>quality of life</u>.

Rich

1) Wealthy people can afford <u>better housing</u> — the very rich live in luxurious and very expensive <u>gated communities</u>, e.g. on <u>Banana Island</u>.

2) They can also <u>afford</u> to <u>live closer</u> to <u>work</u>, so don't have to <u>face</u> traffic jams every day.

3) Lagos does not have enough electricity-generating <u>capacity</u> to satisfy the <u>whole</u> city, so neighbourhoods have to <u>take it in turns</u> to have electricity. The very wealthy improve their quality of life by running their own <u>powerful generators</u>.

Poor

The poor can't afford <u>high quality housing</u> — they end up living in <u>slums</u> on land that regularly <u>floods</u> or is close to <u>polluting factories</u>. Electricity is not available to the <u>poorest</u> people in slums, meaning they are reliant on <u>polluting cooking stoves</u> or small petrol <u>generators</u>, which cause <u>pollution</u> and <u>reduce quality of life</u>. Lack of <u>waste disposal</u> leads to <u>high health risks</u>.

The <u>inequalities</u> above make <u>political</u> and <u>economic management</u> of Lagos <u>challenging</u>:

1) There are <u>different development priorities</u>, e.g. the <u>wealthy</u> want <u>investment</u> in more high-class, modern <u>office space</u> (e.g. <u>Eko Atlantic</u>) to relieve pressure on the existing CBD, but the poor who live in slums need investment in <u>housing improvement</u> and in <u>more services</u>.

2) <u>Corruption</u> is very common in Nigeria. The government can introduce laws, e.g. to regulate traffic, but the wealthy know they can <u>ignore them</u> and <u>bribe</u> the police if they get caught.

3) The wealthy elite are <u>very powerful</u> — e.g. proposals to improve railways in and around Lagos for people and freight have been <u>stopped</u> by people who have a business interest in the lorries that currently supply the city.

The Government is Trying to make Lagos More Sustainable

1) <u>Sustainability</u> means <u>improving</u> things for people <u>today</u> without <u>negatively affecting</u> future generations. Basically, it means behaving in a way that doesn't <u>irreversibly damage the environment</u> or <u>use up resources</u> faster than they can be <u>replaced</u>.

2) Some strategies to improve sustainability are <u>top-down</u> (<u>large-scale</u>, <u>expensive</u> infrastructure projects run by <u>governments</u> and IGOs — see p. 28). In Lagos, <u>top-down</u> strategies include:

> Sustainability should consider the economy and people as well as the environment.

Improving Water Supply

The government has begun work on a <u>US $2.5 billion plan</u> which includes <u>new water treatment plants</u> and <u>distribution networks</u>. In the meantime <u>water kiosks</u> are being introduced, where people can <u>buy water</u> at a <u>lower price</u> than from informal water sellers, until they are connected.

Improving Waste Disposal

The <u>Lagos Waste Management Authority</u> (LAWMA) is working to improve <u>rubbish collection</u> by making sure collection <u>vans</u> can get to each area of the city, e.g. by doing collections at <u>night</u> when there's <u>less traffic</u>. <u>Recycling banks</u> are being put in <u>every estate</u> and people are <u>encouraged</u> to <u>sort</u> and <u>recycle</u> their <u>waste</u>.

Reducing Traffic Congestion

Two <u>light rail lines</u> are under construction to relieve <u>road congestion</u>. The lines will connect the <u>CBD</u> on <u>Lagos Island</u> with the <u>north</u> and <u>west</u> of the city (including the <u>airport</u>) along major <u>commuter routes</u>. The trains will be <u>emission free</u> to <u>limit air pollution</u> and the route will take <u>35 minutes</u> instead of up to <u>4 hours</u> by car.

Improving Air Quality

<u>Small electricity generators</u> (used by households when the power goes out) are a big source of <u>air pollution</u>. To <u>improve air quality</u> the government <u>banned</u> the <u>import</u> of small generators — instead communities are encouraged get <u>together</u> to run <u>one larger generator</u>, which will produce <u>less emissions</u> overall.

Topic 3 — Challenges of an Urbanising World

Urban Change — Case Study

Communities and NGOs are Also Trying to Improve Lagos's Sustainability

Other strategies to improve sustainability in Lagos are bottom-up (smaller-scale projects run by communities and non-governmental organisations — see p. 28). In Lagos, bottom-up strategies include:

Improving Health

CHIEF is an NGO that aims to develop sustainable health care in deprived areas of Lagos by opening community health centres, particularly for disadvantaged women and children. They also run education projects in local communities, to make people more aware of health issues.

Improving City Housing

SEAP is a Nigerian NGO that promotes sustainable livelihoods for the poorest people in society. For example, it offers small loans (microfinance) to poor communities at affordable rates, so that people can afford to get a mortgage on a house. This means that people can move out of slum housing into small affordable apartments with better access to services.

Improving Education

The Oando Foundation is a charity that is aiming to create a sustainable education system in Nigeria by improving school attendance and the quality of education on offer. The foundation involves local communities in each project so they support the school. It has 'adopted' and renovated schools in Lagos — this is reducing the number of primary children out of school. It is also working to improve teachers' skills through training programmes.

There are Pros and Cons to Top-Down and Bottom-Up Strategies

	Advantages	Disadvantages
Top-down	• Can achieve large improvements that affect the whole city, e.g. the improved water supply should provide enough water for everyone at a low cost by 2020. • Can carry out higher-cost projects that communities or NGOs would struggle to fund. • Can address economic, social and environmental sustainability.	• Often very expensive, e.g. Nigeria had to borrow almost US $1 billion from the World Bank to fund construction of its light rail line. • Top-down approaches don't always have the support of communities, who may decide to ignore or undermine the strategy. For example the bus rapid transit is often delayed due to cars and stalls blocking the bus lane. • May not help those most in need, e.g. the ban on small generators affects the poor more than the rich as they are less able to afford cleaner alternatives.
Bottom-up	• Planned with the local community, so it has their support and can target issues that most concern local people. • Often funded by donations from more developed countries or wealthy people, so there's low cost to the people they help or the Nigerian government.	• Smaller scale so projects reach fewer people. • Funds may be limited — especially during economic recessions (periods of economic decline) when the need may be greatest. Schemes often rely on donations from people in more developed countries but people can't afford to give as much during a recession. • Can lack coordination — there may be several NGOs with the same aims working separately.

La-gosh, that's a lot of case study to learn...

You might have studied a different megacity in a developing or emerging country — there are a lot to choose from. That's fine, just make sure you have enough information to cover the key points on these pages.

1) Explain two problems with waste disposal caused by rapid population growth in megacities. [4]

Revision Summary

Well, that was a whole load of fun. I bet you're dying to go and tell someone about push and pull factors or rural-urban migration now — but if you can hold it in just a little bit longer, have a go at these questions to check you really know your suburbanisation from your regeneration. Once you can answer them all in your sleep, feel free to go and share the joy with as many people you like. Although you should probably crack on with the next section instead.

Urban Growth (p.33-34) ☐

1) What is urbanisation?
2) Where is urbanisation taking place most rapidly?
3) Describe the trend in urbanisation in developed countries.
4) What is a megacity?
5) Describe the change in the global distribution of megacities since 1950.
6) Give two influences of a primate city on the country that it is in.
7) Give three push factors that lead to rural-urban migration.
8) Outline why many cities in developing countries are growing.
9) Give an example of an economic change that is leading to migration in developed countries.

Urban Characteristics and Trends (p.35-37) ☐

10) What is formal employment?
11) In which type of country does most informal employment take place?
12) What are the working conditions like in cities in developing countries?
13) Describe the urban economic structure of emerging countries.
14) What is suburbanisation?
15) Give two reasons why de-industrialisation occurs.
16) Define counter-urbanisation.
17) Give two pull factors that lead to counter-urbanisation.
18) a) What is urban regeneration?
    b) Why might it lead to re-urbanisation?
19) Describe where you might find commercial land use in a city.
20) How does accessibility affect urban land use?
21) How do planning regulations affect urban land use?

Urban Change — Case Study (p.38-42) ☑

For a megacity in a developing or emerging country that you have studied:

22) Where are the oldest buildings found?
23) Describe where most new growth is taking place in the city.
24) Give one reason why the population has grown rapidly in recent years.
25) Outline one way that population growth has led to a change in land use in the city.
26) Give three opportunities that the megacity offers to the people who live there.
27) Outline three challenges that the people in the city face.
28) Give two reasons for the differences in the quality of life within the megacity.
29) Outline one top-down initiative that is trying to make the city more sustainable.
30) Outline one bottom-up initiative that is trying to make the city more sustainable.
31) Give two advantages of top-down sustainability strategies.
32) Give two disadvantages of community-led sustainability strategies.

The UK Physical Landscape

Ah, the UK landscape. Majestic <u>mountains</u>, cracking <u>coasts</u> and raging <u>rivers</u> — I could go on all day...

The UK has large Upland and Lowland Areas, and Important Rivers

The UK's main <u>upland</u> areas (orange and red on the map below) tend to be in the <u>north</u> and <u>west</u> of the country, and <u>lowland</u> areas (green on the map) to the <u>south</u> and <u>east</u>. You need to be able to <u>identify</u> them on a map.

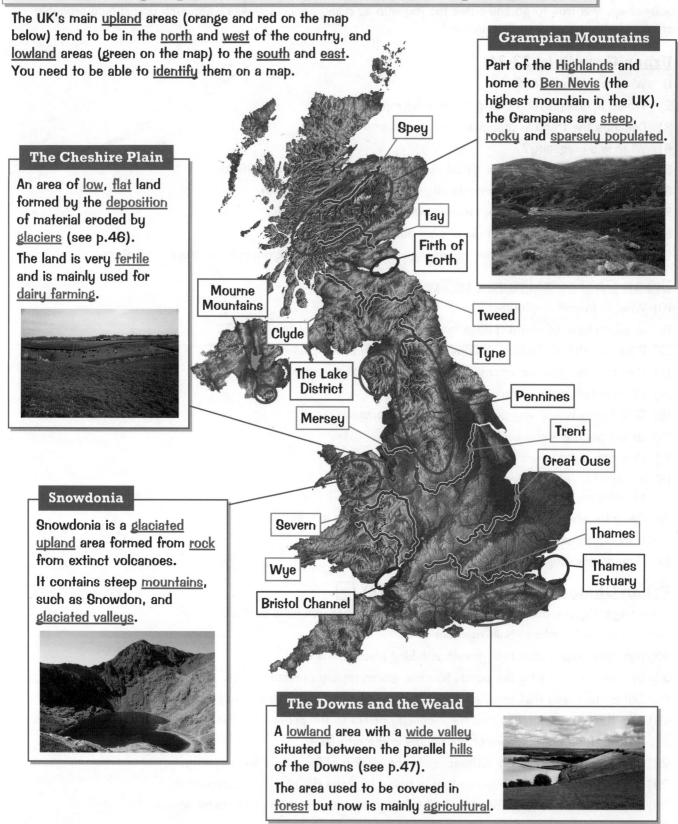

The Cheshire Plain

An area of <u>low</u>, <u>flat</u> land formed by the <u>deposition</u> of material eroded by <u>glaciers</u> (see p.46).

The land is very <u>fertile</u> and is mainly used for <u>dairy farming</u>.

Grampian Mountains

Part of the <u>Highlands</u> and home to <u>Ben Nevis</u> (the highest mountain in the UK), the Grampians are <u>steep</u>, <u>rocky</u> and <u>sparsely populated</u>.

Map labels: Spey, Tay, Firth of Forth, Tweed, Tyne, Pennines, Trent, Great Ouse, Thames, Thames Estuary, Mourne Mountains, Clyde, The Lake District, Mersey, Severn, Wye, Bristol Channel

Snowdonia

Snowdonia is a <u>glaciated</u> <u>upland</u> area formed from <u>rock</u> from extinct volcanoes.

It contains steep <u>mountains</u>, such as Snowdon, and <u>glaciated valleys</u>.

The Downs and the Weald

A <u>lowland</u> area with a <u>wide valley</u> situated between the parallel <u>hills</u> of the Downs (see p.47).

The area used to be covered in <u>forest</u> but now is mainly <u>agricultural</u>.

I think you'll find the UK physical portrait is much easier to fit on a page...

This is a lovely little introduction to the rest of the UK physical landscapes section. You can actually revise it by looking through your holiday snaps or out the window on a long journey. Or by gazing at a lovely map...

Rocks and the UK Physical Landscape

There are three types of <u>rock</u> — hard, glam and punk... erm, I mean <u>igneous</u>, <u>sedimentary</u> and <u>metamorphic</u>. There's a bit about <u>tectonic activity</u> on this page, so hit pages 14 and 15 if you need to <u>brush up</u>...

There are *Three Types* of Rocks

Rock type depends on <u>how</u> the rock was <u>formed</u>:

1) <u>Igneous</u> — igneous rocks are formed when <u>molten rock</u> (magma) from the mantle <u>cools down</u> and <u>hardens</u>. The rock forms <u>crystals</u> as it cools. Igneous rocks are usually <u>hard</u>, e.g. <u>granite</u>.

2) <u>Sedimentary</u> — sedimentary rocks are formed when layers of <u>sediment</u> are <u>compacted together</u> until they become <u>solid rock</u>. There are <u>two</u> main types in the UK:

- <u>Carboniferous limestone</u> and <u>chalk</u> are formed from <u>tiny shells</u> and <u>skeletons</u> of dead sea creatures. <u>Limestone</u> is quite <u>hard</u>, but <u>chalk</u> is a much <u>softer</u> rock.

- <u>Clays</u> and <u>shales</u> are made from <u>mud</u> and <u>clay minerals</u>. They are very <u>soft</u>.

3) <u>Metamorphic</u> — <u>metamorphic</u> rocks are formed when other rocks (igneous, sedimentary or older metamorphic rocks) are <u>changed</u> by <u>heat</u> and <u>pressure</u>. The new rocks become <u>harder</u> and more <u>compact</u>, e.g. <u>shale</u> becomes <u>slate</u> and, with further pressure and heat, slate becomes <u>schist</u>.

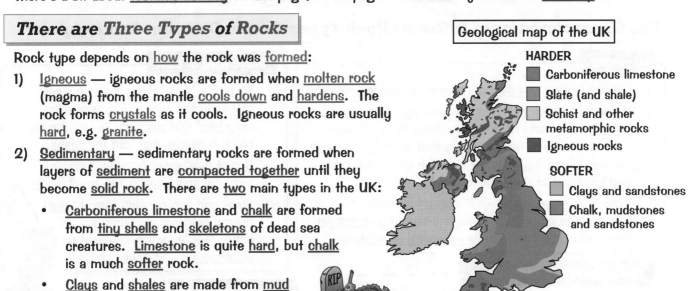

Geological map of the UK

HARDER
- Carboniferous limestone
- Slate (and shale)
- Schist and other metamorphic rocks
- Igneous rocks

SOFTER
- Clays and sandstones
- Chalk, mudstones and sandstones

There *Used to be More Tectonic Activity* in the UK

There are <u>three</u> main ways that <u>past tectonic process</u> have shaped the UK <u>landscape</u>:

1 Active Volcanoes

520 million years ago the <u>land</u> that now makes up the UK used to be much <u>closer</u> to a <u>plate boundary</u> than it is now. <u>Active volcanoes</u> forced <u>magma</u> through the <u>Earth's crust</u> which cooled to form <u>igneous rocks</u>, e.g. granite.

2 Plate Collisions

1) <u>Plate collisions</u> caused the rocks to be <u>folded</u> and <u>uplifted</u>, forming <u>mountain ranges</u>. Many of these areas remain as <u>uplands</u>, e.g. the Scottish Highlands, the Lake District and north Wales — the igneous granite is <u>hard</u> and <u>more resistant</u> to <u>erosion</u>.

2) The <u>intense heat</u> and <u>pressure</u> caused by <u>plate collisions</u> formed <u>hard metamorphic rocks</u> in northern Scotland and northern Ireland.

3 Plate Movements — UK Position

1) <u>Plate movements</u> meant that 345-280 million years ago Britain was in the <u>tropics</u> and higher sea levels meant it was partly underwater — <u>carboniferous limestone</u> formed in the <u>warm shallow seas</u>. This can be seen in the <u>uplands</u> of Peak District (northern England), south Wales and south west England.

2) The <u>youngest</u> rocks in the UK are the <u>chalks</u> and <u>clays</u> found in <u>southern England</u>. They formed in <u>shallow seas</u> and <u>swamps</u>. Chalks and clays are <u>softer</u> rocks that are more <u>easily eroded</u> — they form <u>lowland</u> landscapes.

The UK landscape rocks...

...and so will you if you can nail this page in the exam. Have a go at this question to check you've got it.

1) Give two characteristics of igneous rocks. [2]

EXAM QUESTION

Rocks and the UK Physical Landscape

Each rock type has different characteristics — and it's a good thing too, otherwise they'd be pretty boring to learn about. Oh, and I'd go grab a jumper if I were you — things get a little chilly at the bottom of the page...

The Characteristics of Different Rock Types Create Different Landscapes

Granite

1) Granite is very resistant and forms upland landscapes.

2) It has lots of joints (cracks) which aren't evenly spread. The parts of the rock where there are more joints wear down faster. Areas that have fewer joints are weathered more slowly than the surrounding rock and stick out at the surface forming tors.

3) Granite is impermeable — it doesn't let water through. This creates moorlands — large areas of waterlogged land and acidic soil, with low-growing vegetation.

Carboniferous Limestone

1) Rainwater slowly eats away at limestone through carbonation weathering (see p.49). Most weathering happens along joints in the rock, creating some spectacular features, e.g. limestone pavements (flat areas with deep weathered cracks), caverns and gorges.

2) Limestone is permeable, so limestone areas also have dry valleys and resurgent rivers (rivers that pop out at the surface when limestone is on top of impermeable rock).

Slate and Schist

1) Slate forms in layers creating weak planes in the rock. It is generally very hard and resistant to weathering but it is easily split into thin slabs.

2) Schist has bigger crystals than slate and also splits easily into small flakes.

3) Slate and schist often form rugged, upland landscapes. They are impermeable, which can lead to waterlogged and acidic soils.

Chalk and Clay

1) Chalk is harder than clay. It forms escarpments (hills) in UK lowlands and cliffs at the coast. One side of the hill is usually steep and the other side is more gentle.

2) Chalk is permeable — water flows through it and emerges as a spring where it meets impermeable rock.

3) Clay is very soft and easily eroded. It forms wide flat valleys in UK lowlands. It is impermeable so water flows over the surface — there are lots of streams, rivers and lakes.

Much of the UK Used to be Covered in Ice

1) There have been lots of glacial (cold) periods during the last 2.6 million years see p.4).

2) During some glacial periods, parts of the UK were covered in a massive ice sheet.

3) At its maximum, ice covered most of Scotland, Ireland and Wales and came as far south as the Bristol Channel in England.

4) Ice is very powerful, so it was able to erode the landscape, carving out large U-shaped valleys in upland areas such as the Lake District.

5) Glaciers also deposited lots of material as they melted. Landscapes formed by glacial meltwater and deposits extend south of the ice sheets. E.g. large parts of eastern England are covered in till (an unsorted mixture of clay, sand and rocks) deposited by melting glaciers.

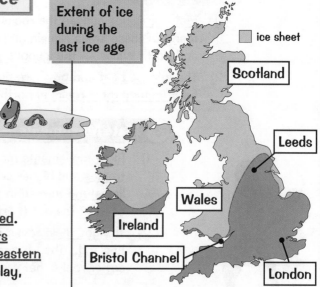

Extent of ice during the last ice age

ice sheet

Scotland

Leeds

Wales

Ireland

London

Bristol Channel

Chalk and granite — so different, they're like chalk and cheese...

Note: granite and cheese are not the same*. Anyhow, freezin' fiddlesticks — imagine half the UK covered in ice. Brrrrr. Learning how rock type and glacial processes have shaped the UK landscape will help warm you up nicely.

*This is the sort of critical revision advice you only get from CGP.

Landscape Processes — Physical

It might look like nothing's changing, but <u>rocks</u> are constantly being <u>broken down</u>, <u>moved around</u> and <u>dumped</u>...

Physical Processes *Alter the Landscape*

1) <u>Physical processes</u> are constantly <u>changing</u> the <u>landscape</u> of the UK. They include:

   • <u>Weathering</u> — weathering is the <u>breakdown</u> of rock into smaller pieces.
   It can be <u>mechanical</u>, <u>chemical</u> or <u>biological</u> (see pages 49 and 61).

   • <u>Erosion</u> — erosion <u>wears away</u> rock. During the last glacial period, <u>ice</u> eroded the landscape.
   <u>Rivers</u> and the <u>sea</u> now <u>constantly</u> erode the landscape.

   • <u>Post-glacial river processes</u> — <u>melting ice</u> at the <u>end</u> of <u>glacial periods</u> made rivers <u>much bigger</u>
   than normal with more <u>power</u> to <u>erode</u> the <u>landscape</u>. The ice also left <u>distinctive landforms</u> when
   it <u>melted</u>, e.g. hanging valleys (little valleys that are left at a higher level than the main valley).

   • <u>Slope processes</u> — including <u>mass movements</u>, e.g. rockfalls, slides, slumps and <u>soil creep</u>
   (see pages 49 and 66).

2) Physical process are affected by <u>climate</u>. For example, a <u>cold</u> climate increases the likelihood of
   <u>freeze-thaw weathering</u> (see p.61) and a <u>wet climate</u> increases the <u>number</u> of <u>streams</u> and <u>rivers</u>.

Physical Processes *Interact to Create Distinctive Upland* Landscapes...

<u>Snowdonia</u> is an <u>upland</u> landscape —
the map shows <u>tightly packed contours</u>
and there are lots of <u>rocky crags</u>.

<u>Llyn Idwal</u> is a <u>tarn</u>.
It sits in a corrie
(basin) that was
<u>hollowed out</u> by ice
during glacial times.

This <u>large U-shaped valley</u> was
eroded by ice — it has a <u>flat
floor</u> and <u>steep sides</u>. The valley
contains a <u>misfit river</u> that looks
<u>too small</u> to have created it.

There is lots of <u>rain</u> in
<u>Snowdonia</u> and the rocks
are mostly <u>impermeable</u>.
This means there are lots
of <u>streams</u> that are eroding
the steep sides of the
corrie and forming <u>gullies</u>.

<u>Freeze-thaw weathering</u> occurs on
the <u>steep back wall</u> of the corrie.
As the rocks are <u>broken up</u> there are
<u>rock falls</u>, which form <u>scree slopes</u>.

...and *Distinctive Lowland* Landscapes

<u>The Downs and the Weald</u> are
a <u>lowland</u> landscape — <u>chalk
escarpments</u> (the Downs)
lie either side of a <u>large flat
area</u> of <u>clay</u> (the Weald).
The valley is <u>flat</u> (the contour
lines on the map are
<u>widely spaced</u>).

<u>Dry valleys</u> are found in UK lowland
landscapes. These are valleys with <u>no
streams</u> visible (they flow <u>underground</u> in
the <u>permeable chalk</u>). They formed during
<u>glacial periods</u> when the <u>colder</u> climate led
to more <u>freeze-thaw weathering</u> and <u>glacial
snow melt</u> meant that <u>streams</u> had much
<u>more water</u> in them than they do today.

Large rivers, e.g. the
River Arun, <u>meander</u> on the
<u>impermeable</u> clay, <u>widening</u>
the valley floor (see p. 63).

The UK has a <u>wet climate</u> — heavy
rain can lead to <u>flooding</u>. The
overflowing river <u>deposits silt</u> on the
valley floor forming a <u>flood plain</u>.

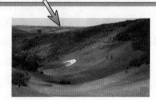

My Roman nose gives me a distinctive facial landscape...

Everything's interlinked — loads of different processes combine to create the different landscapes of the UK.
Make sure you can explain a few ways that physical processes interact to shape upland and lowland landscapes.

Landscape Processes — Human

The UK is pretty <u>small</u> and there are quite <u>a lot</u> of <u>people</u> — wherever you go, the <u>actions</u> of people have <u>changed</u> the <u>landscape</u>. I know, those hedges don't naturally grow in straight lines at the edges of fields...

Humans *have* Changed *the Landscape* Through Agriculture...

1) People have <u>cleared</u> the land of <u>forest</u> to make space for <u>farming</u>.

2) Over time <u>hedgerows</u> and <u>walls</u> have been put in to mark out <u>fields</u>.

3) Different landscapes are best for <u>different types</u> of farming:

- <u>Arable</u> — <u>flat land</u> with good <u>soil</u>, e.g. east England, is used for arable farming (growing <u>crops</u>).

- <u>Dairy</u> — warm and wet areas, e.g. south west England, are good for <u>dairy farming</u>. There are lots of <u>large</u>, <u>grassy fields</u>.

- <u>Sheep</u> — sheep farming takes place in the <u>harsher</u> conditions in the <u>uplands</u>. Sheep farming has led to a <u>lack of trees</u> on the hills (<u>young trees</u> are <u>eaten</u> or <u>trampled</u> before they get a chance to mature).

4) OS® maps show the influence of agriculture, including <u>field boundaries</u> and <u>drainage ditches</u> (dug to make the land dry enough for farming).

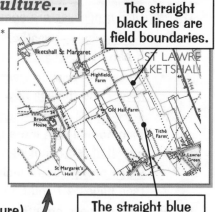

The straight black lines are field boundaries.

The straight blue lines are man-made drainage ditches.

...Forestry...

1) <u>Forestry</u> is the management of areas of <u>woodland</u> — they can be used for <u>timber</u>, <u>recreation</u> or <u>conservation</u>.

2) The UK used to be covered in <u>deciduous woodland</u>, but there is very <u>little</u> natural woodland <u>left</u>.

3) <u>Coniferous</u> (evergreen) forests have been planted for <u>timber</u>. The trees are often planted in <u>straight lines</u> — the forests don't look natural. When areas are <u>felled</u>, the landscape is left <u>bare</u>.

4) In some places, <u>deciduous</u> woodland is being <u>replanted</u> to try to <u>return</u> the area to a more <u>natural state</u>.

5) OS® maps show <u>forestry plantations</u> and areas that are being <u>managed</u>.

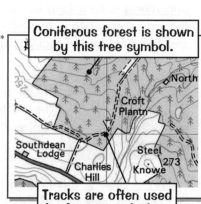

Coniferous forest is shown by this tree symbol.

Tracks are often used by forestry vehicles.

... and Settlement

1) Lots of factors influence <u>where settlements</u> have developed. For example, early settlers needed a <u>water supply</u>, somewhere that could easily be <u>defended</u> or that was <u>sheltered</u> from wind and rain.

2) Other factors such as <u>bridging points</u> over rivers and the <u>availability</u> of <u>resources</u>, e.g. wood for building, also played a part.

3) As settlements grew they further influenced the landscape. For example:

- land was <u>concreted</u> over for <u>roads</u> and <u>buildings</u>, which affected <u>drainage patterns</u>.

- some <u>rivers</u> were diverted through <u>underground channels</u>.

- some river channels were <u>straightened</u> or had <u>embankments</u> built to prevent flooding.

4) Most of the biggest cities are <u>ports</u> and <u>industrial areas</u>, e.g. London, West Midlands, Manchester and Portsmouth. These landscapes are <u>more urban</u> than natural.

5) Look for <u>buildings</u>, <u>railways</u>, <u>canals</u> and <u>embankments</u> to identify settlements on OS® maps.

The land has been raised so the railway line is level — the dashed lines show embankments.

Built-up areas

Streets   Canal

We're off to see the wizard, the wonderful wizard of OS®...

... because, because of the human-affected landscape features they show us. Coming soon to the West End.

1) Explain two ways in which humans have influenced the landscape of the UK. [4]

EXAM QUESTION

Coastal Weathering and Erosion

Weathering is the breakdown of rocks where they are and erosion is when the rocks are broken down and carried away by something, e.g. by seawater. Poor coastal zone, I bet it's worn down.

Rock is Broken Down by Mechanical, Chemical and Biological Weathering

1) Mechanical weathering is the breakdown of rock without changing its chemical composition. There's one main type of mechanical weathering that affects coasts — salt weathering:

> 1) The seawater gets into cracks in the rock.
> 2) When the water evaporates, salt crystals form. As the salt crystals form they expand, which puts pressure on the rock.
> 3) Repeated evaporation of saltwater and the forming of salt crystals widens the cracks and causes the rock to break up.

2) Chemical weathering is the breakdown of rock by changing its chemical composition. Carbonation weathering is a type of chemical weathering that happens in warm and wet conditions:

> 1) Seawater and rainwater have carbon dioxide dissolved in them, which makes them weak carbonic acids.
> 2) Carbonic acid reacts with rock that contains calcium carbonate, e.g. carboniferous limestone, so the rocks are dissolved by the rainwater.

3) Biological weathering is the breakdown of rock by living things, e.g. plant roots break down rocks by growing into cracks on their surface and pushing them apart.

Mass Movement is when Material Falls Down a Slope

Weathering and mass movement are called 'sub-aerial processes'.

1) Mass movement is the shifting of rocks and loose material down a slope, e.g. a cliff. It happens when the force of gravity acting on a slope is greater than the force supporting it.

2) Mass movements cause coasts to retreat rapidly.

3) They're more likely to happen when the material is full of water — it acts as a lubricant, and makes the material heavier.

4) The are THREE types of mass movement.

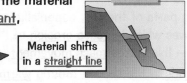
Slides: Material shifts in a straight line

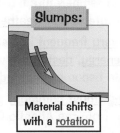
Slumps: Material shifts with a rotation

Rockfalls: Material breaks up and falls down slope

Waves Wear Away the Coast Using Three Processes of Erosion

1) Hydraulic power — waves crash against rock and compress the air in the cracks. This puts pressure on the rock. Repeated compression widens the cracks and makes bits of rock break off.

2) Abrasion — eroded particles in the water scrape and rub against rock, removing small pieces.

3) Attrition — eroded particles in the water smash into each other and break into smaller fragments. Their edges also get rounded off as they rub together.

If you find yourself slumping — have a little break from revision...

This page is packed full of information, but it's really only about how the coast is worn away and rocks are broken down into smaller pieces. Break revision into smaller pieces by learning these processes one at a time.

Coastal Landforms Caused by Erosion

Erosion by waves forms many coastal landforms over long periods of time. But don't worry, you don't have to sit around for thousands of years to see what happens, it can all be explained with a few simple diagrams.

Coastlines can be Concordant or Discordant

1) The geological structure of a coastline influences the formation of erosional landforms.

2) Hard rocks like limestone and chalk are more resistant, so it takes longer for them to be eroded and weathered by physical processes.

3) Softer rocks like clay and sandstone are less resistant, which means they are eroded more quickly.

4) Joints and faults are cracks and weaknesses in the rock. Rocks with lots of joints and faults erode faster.

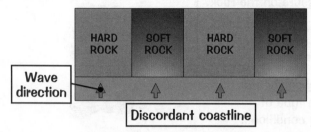

Wave direction

HARD ROCK | SOFT ROCK | HARD ROCK | SOFT ROCK

Discordant coastline

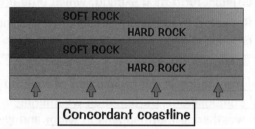

SOFT ROCK
HARD ROCK
SOFT ROCK
HARD ROCK

Concordant coastline

5) Some coastlines are made up of alternating bands of hard and soft rock that are at right angles to the coast — these are called discordant coastlines.

6) On a concordant coastline, the alternating bands of hard and soft rock are parallel to the coast.

7) Erosional landforms like bays and headlands are more common on discordant coastlines because the bands of rock are being eroded at different rates.

8) Concordant coastlines are eroded at the same rate along the coast. This means there are fewer erosional landforms.

CGP rock

The UK's Climate has an Impact on Coastal Erosion and Retreat

1) Temperature in the UK varies with the seasons. Temperatures are coldest in winter, warm through spring, hottest in summer, then cool through autumn.

2) Differences in temperature have an impact on processes along the coast, e.g. mild temperatures increase the rate of salt weathering (see previous page) because water evaporates more quickly.

3) Storms are very frequent in many parts of the UK, especially in winter. The strong winds create high energy, destructive waves which increase erosion of the cliffs. Intense rainfall can cause cliffs to become saturated — this makes mass movement (see previous page) more likely.

4) The prevailing (most common) winds in the UK are mostly warm south westerlies which bring storms from the Atlantic Ocean. The UK's south coast is exposed to these winds.

5) Cold northerly winds are also common, especially on the east coast of the UK.

Destructive Waves Wear Away the Coast

1) The waves that carry out erosional processes are called destructive waves.

2) Destructive waves are high, steep, and have a high frequency (10-14 waves per minute).

3) Their backwash (the movement of the water back down the beach) is more powerful than their swash (the movement of the water up the beach). This means material is removed from the coast.

4) Storms increase the erosional power of destructive waves, which can lead to increased rates of coastal retreat.

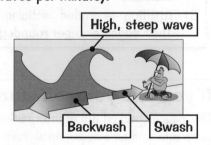

High, steep wave

Backwash | Swash

Coastal Landforms Caused by Erosion

Waves Erode Cliffs to Form Wave-cut Platforms

1) Waves cause <u>most erosion</u> at the <u>foot</u> of a cliff (see diagrams below).

2) This forms a <u>wave-cut notch</u>, which is enlarged as <u>erosion</u> continues.

3) The rock above the notch becomes <u>unstable</u> and eventually <u>collapses</u>.

4) The <u>collapsed material</u> is washed away and a <u>new</u> wave-cut notch starts to form.

5) <u>Repeated collapsing</u> results in the <u>cliff retreating</u>.

6) A <u>wave-cut platform</u> is the platform that's <u>left behind</u> as the <u>cliff retreats</u>.

Hard rock cliffs tend to be more vertical, and soft rock cliffs tend to be more sloping.

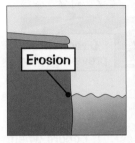
Erosion
Wave-cut notch

Unstable rock
Wave-cut notch

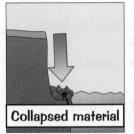
Collapsed material

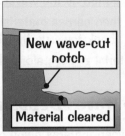
New wave-cut notch
Material cleared

Cliff retreats
Wave-cut platform

Headlands and Bays Form Along Discordant Coastlines

1) <u>Soft</u> rocks or rocks with <u>lots of joints</u> have <u>low resistance</u> to erosion. <u>Hard</u> rocks with a <u>solid structure</u> have a <u>high resistance</u> to erosion.

2) <u>Headlands</u> and <u>bays</u> form where there are <u>alternating bands</u> of <u>resistant</u> and <u>less resistant</u> rock along a coast.

3) The <u>less resistant</u> rock (e.g. clay) is eroded <u>quickly</u> and this forms a <u>bay</u> — bays have a <u>gentle slope</u>.

4) The <u>resistant</u> rock (e.g. chalk) is eroded more <u>slowly</u> and it's left <u>jutting out</u>, forming a <u>headland</u> — headlands have <u>steep sides</u>.

☐ = Less resistant rock
■ = Resistant rock
⟶ = Erosion
Headland
Bay

Headlands are Eroded to form Caves, Arches and Stacks

1) Headlands are usually made of <u>resistant rocks</u> that have <u>weaknesses</u> like <u>cracks</u>.

2) <u>Waves</u> crash into the headlands and <u>enlarge</u> the cracks — mainly by <u>hydraulic power</u> and <u>abrasion</u>.

3) <u>Repeated erosion</u> and <u>enlargement</u> of the cracks causes a <u>cave</u> to form.

4) Continued erosion <u>deepens</u> the cave until it <u>breaks through</u> the headland — forming an <u>arch</u>, e.g. Durdle Door in Dorset.

5) Erosion continues to wear away the rock <u>supporting</u> the arch, until it eventually <u>collapses</u>.

6) This forms a <u>stack</u> — an <u>isolated rock</u> that's <u>separate</u> from the headland, e.g. Old Harry in Dorset.

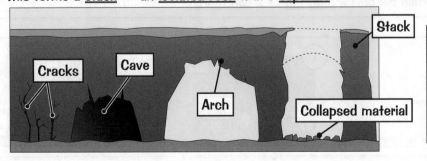
Cracks
Cave
Arch
Stack
Collapsed material

Arch
Durdle Door, Dorset

Erosion and gravity — they've always been arch enemies...

Just a few landforms to learn here, and as ever, learning the diagrams will help in the exam.

1) Explain how an arch, such as that shown above at Durdle Door, forms from a headland. [2]

EXAM QUESTION

Coastal Landforms Caused by Deposition

The <u>material</u> that's been <u>eroded</u> is <u>moved around</u> the coast and <u>deposited</u> by waves.

Transportation *is the Movement of Material*

Material is transported <u>along coasts</u> by a process called <u>longshore drift</u>:

1) <u>Waves</u> follow the <u>direction</u> of the <u>prevailing wind</u>.

2) They usually hit the coast at an <u>oblique angle</u> (any angle that <u>isn't a right angle</u>).

3) The <u>swash</u> carries material <u>up the beach</u>, in the <u>same direction as the waves</u>.

4) The <u>backwash</u> then carries material <u>down the beach</u> at <u>right angles</u>, back towards the sea.

5) Over time, material <u>zigzags</u> along the coast.

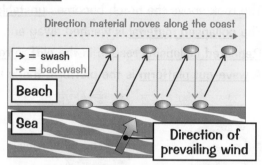

Constructive *Waves Deposit Material*

1) Deposition is when <u>material</u> being <u>carried</u> by the seawater is <u>dropped on the coast</u>. It occurs when water carrying sediment <u>slows down</u> so that it isn't moving <u>fast enough</u> to carry so much sediment.

2) Waves that <u>deposit more material</u> than they <u>erode</u> are called <u>constructive waves</u>.

3) Constructive waves are <u>low</u>, <u>long</u>, and have a <u>low frequency</u> (6-8 waves per minute).

4) The <u>swash</u> is <u>powerful</u> and it <u>carries material up the coast</u>.

5) The backwash is <u>weaker</u> and it <u>doesn't</u> take a lot of material <u>back down the coast</u>.

6) Constructive waves <u>deposit</u> material such as <u>sand</u> and <u>shingle</u> (<u>gravel</u>) along the coast to form <u>beaches</u>.

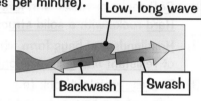

Deposited Sediment *forms Spits and Bars*

Spits

1) Spits form at <u>sharp bends</u> in the coastline, e.g. at a <u>river mouth</u>.

2) <u>Longshore drift</u> transports sand and shingle <u>past</u> the bend and <u>deposits</u> it in the sea.

3) Strong winds and waves can <u>curve</u> the end of the spit (forming a <u>recurved end</u>).

4) The <u>sheltered area</u> behind the spit is <u>protected from waves</u> — lots of material <u>accumulates</u> in this area, which means <u>plants</u> can grow there.

5) <u>Over time</u>, the sheltered area can become a <u>mud flat</u> or a <u>salt marsh</u>.

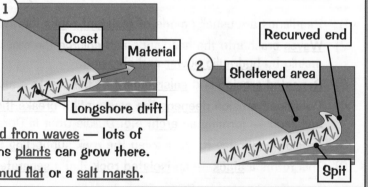

Bars

1) A bar is formed when a spit <u>joins two headlands together</u>.

2) The bar <u>cuts off</u> the bay between the headlands <u>from the sea</u>.

3) This means a <u>lagoon</u> can form <u>behind</u> the bar.

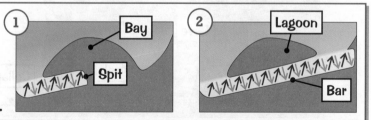

Depositing material on a beach? Sounds like littering to me.

Spits in geography have a very specific meaning. Don't get the wrong one and make a mess of your book. In the exam, you might have to identify landforms caused by deposition on a map. You'll find some help with that on the next page.

Identifying Coastal Landforms

I love <u>maps</u>, all geographers love maps. I can't get to sleep unless I've got one under my pillow. So I'm going to do you a favour and share my passion with you — check out these <u>coastal landforms</u>...

Identifying Landforms Caused by Erosion

You might be asked to <u>identify coastal landforms</u> on a <u>map</u> in the exam. The simplest thing they could ask is whether the map is showing <u>erosional</u> or <u>depositional landforms</u>, so here's how to <u>identify</u> a few <u>erosional landforms</u> to get you started:

Have a gander at pages 121-122 for more on reading maps.

Caves, Arches and Stacks

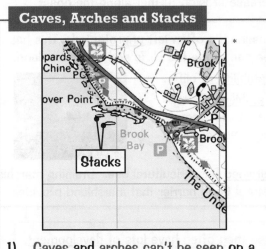

1) <u>Caves</u> and <u>arches can't be seen</u> on a map because of the rock <u>above them</u>.
2) <u>Stacks</u> look like <u>little blobs</u> in the sea.

Cliffs and Wave-cut Platforms

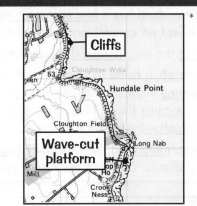

1) <u>Cliffs</u> (and other steep slopes) are shown on maps as <u>little black lines</u>.
2) <u>Wave-cut platforms</u> are shown as <u>bumpy edges</u> along the coast.

I don't need no map...

Identifying Landforms Caused by Deposition

<u>Identifying depositional landforms</u> is easy once you know that <u>beaches</u> are shown in <u>yellow</u> on maps. Here's how to <u>identify</u> a couple of <u>depositional landforms</u>:

Beaches

Shingle beach
Sand beach

1) <u>Sand beaches</u> are shown on maps as <u>pale yellow</u>.
2) <u>Shingle beaches</u> are shown as <u>white</u> or <u>yellow</u> with <u>speckles</u>.

Spits

Sharp bend
Spit

1) <u>Spits</u> are shown by a <u>beach</u> that carries on <u>out to sea</u>, but is still <u>attached</u> to the land at <u>one end</u>.
2) There might also be a <u>sharp bend</u> in the coast that caused it to form (see p. 52).

Find the spit on the map — and then wipe it off...

There are some seriously easy marks up for grabs with map questions so make sure you learn this page. You could practise looking for landforms on any maps you can find, though you might struggle with the Tube map.

Human Activity at the Coast

Ah, the <u>seaside</u>. Fish and chips, ice cream, being <u>mugged</u> by <u>seagulls</u>... you just can't beat it. The way <u>humans use</u> the coast can have an <u>effect</u> on the <u>landscape</u> and, you've guessed it, it's not always a <u>positive</u> thing...

Human Activities **have Direct** and Indirect Effects **on the Coast**

1) <u>Direct effects</u> on the coastline are the <u>immediate result</u> of <u>human activities</u>. For example, building <u>coastal defences</u> will <u>prevent erosion</u>.

2) <u>Indirect effects</u> happen as a result of the <u>direct effects</u>. For example, building coastal defences will prevent erosion in <u>one place</u>, but it can increase erosion <u>further along the coast</u>.

Agriculture

1) Agricultural land has a <u>low economic value</u> which means it's often left <u>unprotected</u>. This has a direct effect on coastal landscapes because the sea can <u>erode</u> the cliffs and shape the land.

2) <u>Changing</u> the way <u>farmland</u> is used can affect the <u>stability</u> of cliffs.

- <u>Vegetation</u> helps to bind the soil together and <u>stabilise</u> clifftops. <u>Clearing</u> vegetation from grazing land to make room for crops can <u>expose</u> the <u>soil</u> and underlying rock, leaving it vulnerable to <u>weathering</u> by wind and rain.

3) Land, e.g. <u>marshland</u>, is sometimes <u>reclaimed</u> and <u>drained</u> for agricultural use. Draining marshland directly affects the coast because it <u>reduces</u> the natural <u>flood barrier</u> that marshland provides.

Development

1) Coastal areas are popular places to <u>live</u> and <u>work</u>, so they often have lots of <u>development</u>, e.g. hotels and <u>infrastructure</u> (roads, rail, power lines etc.).

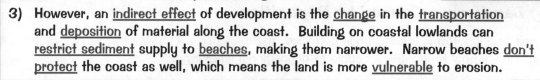

2) Coasts with lots of <u>settlement</u> may have more <u>coastal defences</u> than other areas because people want to <u>protect</u> their <u>homes</u> and <u>businesses</u>. This has a <u>positive</u> direct effect on the coastline because the land is <u>better protected</u> against erosion.

3) However, an <u>indirect effect</u> of development is the <u>change</u> in the <u>transportation</u> and <u>deposition</u> of material along the coast. Building on coastal lowlands can <u>restrict sediment</u> supply to <u>beaches</u>, making them narrower. Narrow beaches <u>don't protect</u> the coast as well, which means the land is more <u>vulnerable</u> to erosion.

Industry

1) Coastal <u>quarries</u> expose large areas of rock, making them more <u>vulnerable</u> to chemical <u>weathering</u> and <u>erosion</u>.

2) <u>Gravel</u> has been extracted from some <u>beaches</u> for use in the <u>construction industry</u>, e.g. for making concrete. This has <u>removed</u> material from the coast and <u>increased</u> the <u>risk</u> of <u>erosion</u> because there's <u>less</u> material to protect cliffs.

3) <u>Industrial growth</u> at <u>ports</u> has led to increased pressure to build on <u>salt marshes</u>. These areas provide <u>flat land</u> and <u>sheltered water</u>, which are ideal for <u>ports</u> and <u>industry</u>, but are also <u>natural flood barriers</u>. Building on them leaves the land <u>more vulnerable</u> to <u>erosion</u>.

Coastal Management

1) <u>Coastal management</u> is about <u>protecting coastal landscapes</u> from the <u>impacts</u> of <u>erosion</u>.

2) Some <u>management strategies</u> (see p. 57) alter <u>sediment movement</u>, which <u>reduces</u> the amount of <u>protective</u> beach material further along the coast — this <u>increases erosion</u>.

3) Coastal defences can also <u>reduce erosion</u>. This has a direct effect on the coast because it <u>prevents</u> the landscape from <u>changing</u>, i.e. <u>retreating</u>.

Building sandcastles — the most important coastal activity...

1) Explain one way in which industry has an effect on coastal landscapes. [2]

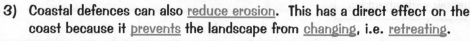

EXAM QUESTION

Coastal Landscape — Example

Holderness in East Yorkshire has one of the <u>highest rates of coastal erosion</u> in Europe. What a claim to fame...

The Holderness Coast is on the East Coast of England

1) The Holderness coastline is <u>61 km long</u> — it stretches from <u>Flamborough Head</u> (a headland) to <u>Spurn Head</u> (a spit).

2) <u>Erosion</u> is causing the cliffs to <u>collapse</u>. About <u>1.8 m of land</u> is <u>lost</u> to the sea <u>every year</u> — in some places, e.g. <u>Great Cowden</u>, the rate of erosion has been <u>over 10 m per year</u> in recent years.

3) The cliffs are mostly made of <u>boulder clay</u> which is <u>easily eroded</u>. It's likely to <u>slump</u> when it's <u>wet</u>, causing the cliffs to collapse.

4) <u>Beaches</u> along the Holderness coast are <u>narrow</u>, which means they <u>don't</u> provide enough <u>protection</u> for the cliffs from the sea's <u>erosional power</u>.

5) Holderness faces the <u>prevailing wind direction</u>, which brings waves from the <u>north east</u> all the way from the <u>Norwegian Sea</u>. Waves <u>increase in power</u> over this <u>long distance</u>, so the coast is battered by <u>highly erosive waves</u>.

6) Eroded material is moved <u>south along</u> the coast by <u>longshore drift</u> instead of staying in the place it came from, <u>exposing</u> a <u>new</u> area of cliff to erosion and causing the <u>coastline</u> to <u>retreat</u>.

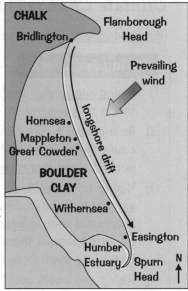

Parts of Holderness are Protected by Coastal Defences

1) <u>Over 11 km</u> of the Holderness coastline is protected by <u>hard engineering strategies</u> (see p. 57) because:

- There are <u>towns</u> and <u>villages</u> like Hornsea (population: over 8000), Withernsea (population: over 6000) and Mappleton where <u>people live</u>.
- There is important <u>infrastructure</u> like the <u>B1242 road</u> which links many of the towns and businesses along the coast.
- The <u>gas terminal</u> at <u>Easington</u> supplies <u>25%</u> of the UK's gas and is <u>right on the edge</u> of the <u>cliff</u>.

2) <u>Coastal defences</u> called <u>groynes</u> have been built at Mappleton.

3) There are also groynes and a sea wall at <u>Hornsea</u> and at <u>Withernsea</u>.

The Defences have Caused Problems Further Along the Coast

1) <u>Groynes</u> protect <u>local areas</u> but cause <u>narrow beaches</u> to form <u>further down</u> the Holderness coast. This increases erosion down the coast, e.g. <u>Great Cowden</u> (south of <u>Mappleton</u>) has lots of <u>farms</u> and <u>caravan parks</u> that are now <u>at risk</u> of <u>falling into the sea</u>.

2) The material produced from the erosion of Holderness is <u>normally transported south</u> into the <u>Humber Estuary</u> and <u>down</u> the <u>Lincolnshire coast</u>. Reducing the amount of material that's eroded and transported south <u>increases</u> the <u>risk</u> of <u>flooding</u> in the Humber Estuary, because there's <u>less material</u> to slow the floodwater down.

3) The rate of <u>coastal retreat</u> along the <u>Lincolnshire coast</u> has increased because <u>less new material</u> is being added.

4) <u>Spurn Head</u> is <u>at risk</u> of <u>being eroded away</u> because <u>less material</u> is being <u>added to it</u>.

5) <u>Bays</u> are forming <u>between</u> the <u>protected areas</u>, and the protected areas are becoming <u>headlands</u> which are being eroded <u>more heavily</u>. This means <u>maintaining the defences</u> in the protected areas is becoming <u>more expensive</u>.

Extreme caravanning — the latest craze in Great Cowden...

You don't have to learn this example if you've studied a different one in class — just make sure you know you it inside out. Located examples are always a speedy route to impressing the examiner and securing some extra marks.

Coastal Flooding

Coastal areas are <u>increasingly at risk</u> from <u>flooding</u> by the sea. The <u>bad news</u> is, this can cause a lot of <u>problems</u> for the <u>environment</u> and the <u>people</u> living there. The good news — what? There isn't any? Oh...

Climate Change is Increasing the Risk of Coastal Flooding

<u>Rising sea levels</u> and an increased <u>frequency of storms</u> are making coastal flooding more likely.

Rising Sea Levels

1) <u>Rising sea levels</u> (see p.7) pose a threat to <u>low-lying</u> and <u>coastal areas</u>.

2) An increase in sea levels could cause <u>higher tides</u> that would <u>flood</u> coastal areas <u>more frequently</u>.

3) Higher tides could also remove <u>larger amounts</u> of material from <u>beaches</u>. This could lead to <u>increased erosion</u> of cliffs because there's <u>less material</u> to <u>protect</u> them from the sea.

4) Rising sea levels could <u>expose</u> more of the coastline to <u>erosion</u> — <u>beaches</u> could become <u>narrower</u> as the sea will be able to <u>move further inland</u>.

Storm Frequency

1) <u>Climate change</u> is causing <u>storms</u> to become <u>more frequent</u>.

2) Storms give the sea more <u>erosional power</u> — areas of <u>hard rock</u> will be <u>more vulnerable</u> to erosion and areas of <u>soft rock</u> will erode <u>more quickly</u>.

3) The sea will also have more <u>energy</u> to <u>transport</u> material. <u>High-energy waves</u> can move more material for <u>greater distances</u>, which could lead to some areas being <u>starved</u> of material. This leaves these areas <u>vulnerable</u> to <u>erosion</u> and to <u>flooding</u>.

4) <u>Storm surges</u> (see p.10) could become <u>more frequent</u> and <u>sea level rise</u> could cause surges to <u>reach</u> areas <u>further inland</u>.

There are Threats to People and the Environment

Threats to People

1) <u>Low-lying coastal areas</u> could be <u>permanently flooded</u> or <u>flood</u> so often that they become <u>impossible</u> to inhabit.

2) Coastal <u>industries</u> may be shut down because of <u>damage</u> to <u>equipment</u> and <u>buildings</u>, e.g. <u>fishing boats</u> can be destroyed.

3) There's a risk of damage to <u>infrastructure</u> like <u>roads</u> and <u>rail networks</u>. For example, railway lines in <u>Dawlish</u>, <u>Devon</u> run <u>parallel</u> to the sea and are <u>badly affected</u> by flooding. Storms in 2014 damaged <u>flood defences</u> and parts of the <u>track</u>.

4) There's a <u>booming tourist industry</u> in coastal areas. Flooding and erosion can <u>put people off visiting</u>. Fewer tourists means <u>businesses</u> that <u>rely on tourism</u> may <u>close</u>, leading to a loss of <u>livelihoods</u>.

Threats to the Environment

1) <u>Ecosystems</u> will be affected because <u>seawater</u> has a <u>high salt content</u>. Increased salt levels due to coastal flooding can <u>damage</u> or <u>kill</u> organisms in an ecosystem. It can also affect <u>agricultural land</u> by reducing <u>soil fertility</u>.

2) The <u>force</u> of floodwater can <u>uproot</u> trees and plants, and <u>standing</u> floodwater drowns some trees and plants.

3) Some <u>conservation areas</u> are threatened by coastal erosion. For example, there are <u>lagoons</u> on the <u>Holderness coast</u> that are protected. The lagoons are separated from the sea by a <u>bar</u>. If this is <u>eroded</u> it will connect the lagoons to the <u>sea</u> and they would be <u>destroyed</u>.

Forget the bucket and spade — where's my rubber dinghy...

Let's face it, it's no fun living near the sea if you're going to be flooded. No amount of donkey rides can comfort you if you lose your home and job to flooding. Let's lighten the mood with a little exam practice:

1) Outline how coastal flooding poses a threat to people. [3]

Coastal Management

The aim of coastal management is to protect people and the environment from the impacts of erosion and flooding. Not all coastal areas can be managed though — the amount of money available is limited.

Coastal Defences Include Hard and Soft Engineering

Hard Engineering

Man-made structures built to control the flow of the sea and reduce flooding and erosion.

Soft Engineering

Schemes set up using knowledge of the sea and its processes to reduce the effects of flooding and erosion.

	Defence	What it is	Benefits	Costs
Hard Engineering	**Sea Wall**	A wall made out of a hard material like concrete that reflects waves back to sea.	It prevents erosion of the coast. It also acts as a barrier to prevent flooding.	It creates a strong backwash, which erodes under the wall. Sea walls are very expensive to build and to maintain.
Hard Engineering	**Groynes** ← longshore drift	Wooden or stone fences that are built at right angles to the coast. They trap material transported by longshore drift.	They create wider beaches which slow the waves. This gives greater protection from flooding and erosion. They're a fairly cheap defence.	They starve beaches further down the coast of sand, making them narrower. Narrower beaches don't protect the coast as well, leading to greater erosion and floods.
Soft Engineering	**Beach Replenishment**	Sand and shingle from elsewhere (e.g. from the seabed) or from lower down the beach are added to the upper part of beaches.	It creates wider beaches which slow the waves. This gives greater protection from flooding and erosion.	Taking material from the seabed can kill organisms like sponges and corals. It's a very expensive defence. It has to be repeated.
Soft Engineering	**Slope Stabilisation**	Slopes are reinforced by inserting concrete nails into the ground and covering the slope with metal netting.	It prevents mass movement by increasing the strength of the slope.	Slope stabilisation is very expensive and sometimes very difficult to install.
Soft Engineering	**Strategic Realignment**	Removing an existing defence and allowing the land behind it to flood.	Over time the land will become marshland — creating new habitats. Flooding and erosion are reduced behind the marshland.	People may disagree over what land is allowed to flood, e.g. flooding farmland would affect the livelihood of farmers.

1) Another option is to do nothing — no new coastal defences are built and erosion and flooding are dealt with as they happen.

2) It doesn't cost anything to let the coast retreat naturally, but infrastructure (e.g. for tourism) may be lost.

3) People might also be forced to move away from the area because of the risk of erosion and flooding.

Management Strategies need to be Sustainable

1) In order to protect the coast and avoid conflict, management strategies need to be sustainable. This means making sure erosion and flooding are controlled without causing more problems elsewhere (e.g. erosion further down the coast) or affecting the people who live and work at the coast (e.g. farmers and business owners). Strategies also need to be cheap to avoid conflicts about the spending of public money.

2) Integrated Coastal Zone Management (ICZM) is an approach that aims to protect the coast while taking everyone's interests into account — this makes it easier to find solutions that people can all agree on.

3) It's also a long-term approach so it can be adapted to any future needs and changes along the coastline. This makes it a sustainable approach to managing the coast.

Good management strategies have warm-ups to reduce groyne strains...

Wow, that sure is a mighty fine table. It seems like a lot to remember but I promise you, it's really not that tough. Make sure you know at a least a couple of benefits and costs for each strategy so you'll be a winner in the exam.

Revision Summary

Well this is most irregular. A revision summary halfway through a section? Absolute madness. I'm just glad the great old editor Cornelius Gerald Parsnipish never lived to see this — he'd be literally furious with rage.

Anyway, you've coasted through half the section — that means it's time to find out just how much of this information has been deposited in your noggin. Have a go at the questions below. If you're finding it tough, just look back at the pages in the section and then have another go. You'll be ready to move on to the next half when you can answer all of these questions without breaking sweat.

Rocks and the UK Physical Landscape (p. 44-46) ☑

1) a) How are igneous rocks formed?
   b) What are sedimentary rocks formed from?
   c) Describe how metamorphic rocks are formed.
2) Give two ways in which tectonic activity has shaped the UK landscape.
3) Outline the characteristics of slate and schist.
4) Explain how the UK landscape has been shaped by glacial periods.

Landscape Processes (p. 47-48) ☑

5) Give three physical processes that alter the landscape.
6) a) Give an example of a lowland landscape.
   b) Outline how physical processes have created this landscape.
7) How does forestry change the landscape?
8) How does settlement alter the landscape?

Coastal Processes and Landforms (p. 49-53) ☐

9) How does salt weathering break up rock?
10) What are the three types of erosion caused by waves? Explain how they work.
11) What is the difference between a discordant and a concordant coastline?
12) What are the characteristics of destructive waves?
13) Describe how erosion can turn a crack in a cliff into a cave.
14) How does longshore drift transport sediment along a coast?
15) What are the characteristics of constructive waves?
16) Where do spits form?
17) What do stacks look like on a map?
18) How are cliffs shown on a map?
19) On maps, what do speckles on top of yellow shading tell you?

Human Activity and Coastal Management (p. 54-57) ☑

20) Explain how agriculture can have a direct effect on the coast.
21) How does development affect the coast?
22) Give one effect of coastal management on the coastline.
23) Describe one human process that is causing change on a named coastal landscape.
24) Why does sea level rise increase the risk of coastal flooding?
25) a) Give two threats of coastal flooding to people.
    b) Give two threats of coastal flooding to the environment.
26) What is the difference between hard and soft engineering? Give an example of each.
27) What are the disadvantages of using groynes for coastal management?
28) What is strategic realignment?
29) How are coastal management strategies being made more sustainable?

River Landscapes

You're probably best off going to the loo <u>before</u> you start this. It's all about <u>flowing water</u>...

A River's Long Profile and Cross Profile Vary Over its Course

1) The <u>path</u> of a river as it <u>flows downhill</u> is called its <u>course</u>.

2) Rivers have an <u>upper course</u> (closest to the <u>source</u> of the river), a <u>middle course</u> and a <u>lower course</u> (closest to the <u>mouth</u> of the river).

3) Rivers form <u>channels</u> and <u>valleys</u> as they <u>flow downhill</u>.

4) They <u>erode</u> the landscape — <u>wear it down</u>, then <u>transport</u> the material to somewhere else where it's <u>deposited</u>.

5) The <u>shape</u> of the <u>valley</u> and <u>channel changes</u> along the river depending on whether <u>erosion</u> or <u>deposition</u> is having the <u>most impact</u> (is the <u>dominant process</u>).

6) The <u>long profile</u> of a river shows you how the <u>gradient</u> (steepness) <u>changes</u> over the different courses.

7) The <u>cross profile</u> shows you what a <u>cross-section</u> of the river looks like.

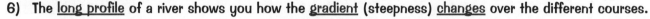

Course	Gradient	Valley and channel shape	Cross profile
Upper	<u>Steep</u>	<u>V-shaped</u> valley, steep sides <u>Narrow</u>, <u>shallow</u> channel	
Middle	<u>Medium</u>	<u>Gently sloping</u> valley sides <u>Wider</u>, <u>deeper</u> channel	
Lower	<u>Gentle</u>	<u>Very wide</u>, <u>almost flat</u> valley <u>Very wide</u>, <u>deep</u> channel	

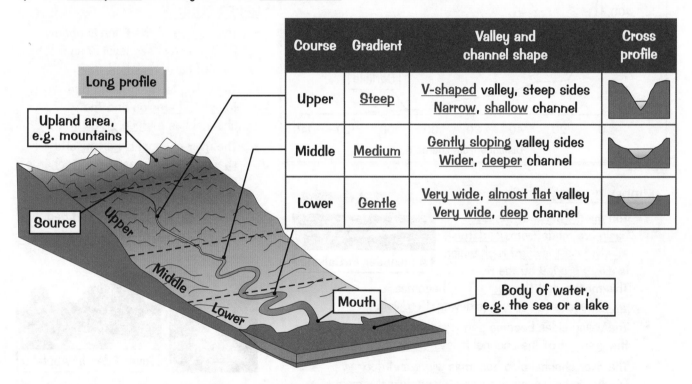

Long profile

Upland area, e.g. mountains

Source

Upper

Middle

Lower

Mouth

Body of water, e.g. the sea or a lake

Vertical and Lateral Erosion Change the Cross Profile of a River

Erosion can be <u>vertical</u> or <u>lateral</u> — both types happen at the <u>same time</u>, but one is usually <u>dominant</u> over the other at <u>different points</u> along the river:

There's more on the processes of erosion on the next page.

Vertical erosion

This <u>deepens</u> the river valley (and channel), making it <u>V-shaped</u>. It's dominant in the <u>upper course</u> of the river. High <u>turbulence</u> causes the <u>rough, angular particles</u> to be scraped along the river bed, causing intense <u>downwards</u> erosion.

Lateral erosion

This <u>widens</u> the river valley (and channel) during the formation of <u>meanders</u> (see page 63). It's dominant in the <u>middle</u> and <u>lower courses</u>.

Don't show me that cross profile — just go with the flow...

Sit back, close your eyes and imagine gently babbling brooks. Then you'd best get on with learning this page. Make sure you can describe a river's long profile and its cross profile at different points along its course.

River Landscapes

Grab a paddle and hold on to your <u>hat</u> — it's time for a <u>voyage</u> along a <u>northern river</u>.

The River Eden's Landscape Changes *Along its* Course

1) The River Eden is in <u>north-west England</u>, between the mountains of the <u>Lake District</u> and the <u>Pennines</u>. It's <u>145 km long</u> from source to mouth.

2) The River Eden's <u>source</u> is in the Pennine hills in south Cumbria. It flows north-west through <u>Appleby-in-Westmorland</u> and <u>Carlisle</u>. Its mouth is in the <u>Solway Firth</u> at the Scottish border.

Eden basin

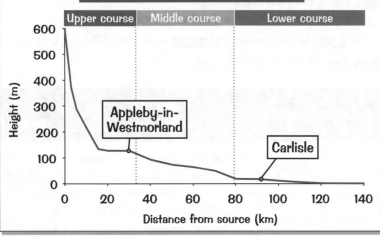

LONG PROFILE OF THE RIVER EDEN

Upper course | Middle course | Lower course

Height (m) — Appleby-in-Westmorland — Carlisle

Distance from source (km)

UPPER COURSE

- The <u>source</u> of the Eden is about <u>600 m</u> above sea level in an area of <u>hard</u>, <u>resistant rock</u>.
- The valley is <u>steep-sided</u> due to <u>vertical erosion</u> and the channel has a <u>steep gradient</u>.
- The <u>river channel</u> is <u>narrow</u> and <u>shallow</u> — this means the <u>discharge</u> (see p. 67) is <u>low</u>. The <u>velocity</u> (speed) is <u>low</u> due to <u>friction</u> from the <u>rough channel sides</u> and <u>bed</u>.
- The river carries <u>large</u>, <u>angular stones</u>.

River Eden at Appleby

MIDDLE COURSE

- The <u>middle parts</u> of the <u>Eden basin</u> are made from <u>sandstone</u>, a <u>soft</u>, <u>less-resistant rock</u> which is <u>easily eroded</u> by the river. This means that the <u>river valley</u> becomes <u>wider</u> because of <u>lateral</u> (sideways) <u>erosion</u>.
- The valley sides become <u>gentle slopes</u> and the <u>gradient</u> of the channel is <u>less steep</u>.
- The river channel also becomes <u>wider</u> and <u>deeper</u>. Discharge <u>increases</u> as more <u>streams</u> join the main river.
- The river's <u>sediment load</u> is made up of <u>smaller</u> and <u>more rounded</u> rocks than it was in the <u>upper course</u> as erosion continues (see next page).

A meander at Salkeld

LOWER COURSE

- In the lower course, the <u>valley</u> is <u>very wide</u> and <u>flat</u>.

- By the time the Eden reaches <u>Carlisle</u>, it's only <u>a few metres</u> above sea level.
- The river has a <u>high velocity</u> (it's <u>flowing fast</u>) because there's <u>very little friction</u> from the channel's <u>smooth sides</u>. It also has a <u>very large discharge</u> because two other rivers (the Caldew and the Petteril) join the Eden in Carlisle.
- The <u>river channel</u> is <u>very wide</u> and <u>deep</u> — in the centre of Carlisle, the Eden is more than <u>50 m</u> wide. <u>Material</u> carried by the river is <u>fine</u> and <u>well-rounded</u> — most of it is carried by <u>suspension</u> or <u>solution</u> (see next page).

River Eden at Carlisle

The Eden basin — a physical geographer's paradise...

You don't have to use this named river if you've studied another in class, just make sure you know how the river's landscape changes over its course. Splitting it up into the upper, middle and lower courses will make it much easier to learn.

River Processes

Rivers <u>scrape</u> and <u>smash rocks up</u>, <u>push</u> them about, then <u>dump them</u> when they've had enough...

Weathering Helps Shape River Valleys

Weathering <u>breaks down rocks</u> on the valley sides.
<u>Freeze-thaw weathering</u> is a type of <u>mechanical weathering</u> (see p. 49):

1) <u>Freeze-thaw weathering</u> happens when the temperature alternates <u>above</u> and <u>below</u> 0 °C (the <u>freezing point</u> of water).

2) Water <u>gets into</u> rock that has <u>cracks</u>, e.g. granite. When the water <u>freezes</u> it <u>expands</u>, which puts <u>pressure</u> on the rock. When the water <u>thaws</u> it <u>contracts</u>, which <u>releases</u> the pressure on the rock.

3) <u>Repeated freezing</u> and <u>thawing</u> widens the cracks and causes the rock to <u>break up</u>.

Chemical and biological weathering also affect river valleys.

There are Four Processes of Erosion

The <u>processes of erosion</u> that occur along <u>coasts</u> also occur in <u>river channels</u>:

1) <u>Hydraulic action</u> — the <u>force</u> of the water <u>breaks rock particles away</u> from the <u>river channel</u>.

2) <u>Abrasion</u> — eroded <u>rocks</u> picked up by the river <u>scrape</u> and <u>rub</u> against the <u>channel</u>, wearing it away. <u>Most erosion</u> happens by <u>abrasion</u>.

3) <u>Attrition</u> — eroded <u>rocks</u> picked up by the river <u>smash into each other</u> and break into <u>smaller fragments</u>. Their <u>edges</u> also get <u>rounded off</u> as they rub together. The <u>further</u> material travels, the more <u>eroded</u> it gets — attrition causes <u>particle size</u> to <u>decrease</u> between a river's <u>source</u> and its <u>mouth</u>.

4) <u>Solution</u> — river water <u>dissolves</u> some types of rock, e.g. <u>chalk</u> and <u>limestone</u>.

The faster a river's flowing, the more erosion happens.

Transportation is the Movement of Eroded Material

The <u>material</u> a river has <u>eroded</u> is <u>transported downstream</u>.
There are <u>four processes</u> of transportation:

Traction

<u>Large</u> particles like boulders are <u>pushed</u> along the <u>river bed</u> by the <u>force of the water</u>.

Saltation

<u>Pebble-sized</u> particles are <u>bounced along</u> the <u>river bed</u> by the <u>force of the water</u>.

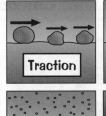

Traction Saltation

Suspension Solution

Suspension

<u>Small</u> particles like silt and clay are <u>carried along</u> by the water.

Solution

<u>Soluble materials dissolve</u> in the water and are <u>carried along</u>.

Deposition is When a River Drops Eroded Material

Deposition is when a river <u>drops</u> the <u>eroded material</u> it's <u>transporting</u>.

It happens when a river <u>slows down</u> (loses velocity).

There are a <u>few reasons</u> why rivers slow down and deposit material:

1) The <u>volume</u> of <u>water</u> in the river <u>falls</u>.

2) The <u>amount</u> of <u>eroded material</u> in the water <u>increases</u>.

3) The water is <u>shallower</u>, e.g. on the <u>inside of a bend</u>.

4) The river <u>reaches</u> its <u>mouth</u>.

I can't bear the suspension — just go ahead and dump me...

There are lots of very similar names to remember here — try not to confuse saltation, solution and suspension. And yes, confusingly, solution is both a process of erosion and transportation. Now saltate on over to the next page...

River Landforms — Erosion

If you don't know anything about <u>waterfalls</u> then you haven't been watching enough <u>shampoo adverts</u>. Now's your chance to find out all about them and other landforms made by <u>erosion</u>.

Waterfalls and Gorges are Found in the Upper Course of a River

1) <u>Waterfalls</u> form where a river flows over an area of <u>hard rock</u> followed by an area of <u>softer rock</u>.

2) The <u>softer rock</u> is <u>eroded</u> (by <u>hydraulic action</u> and <u>abrasion</u> — see previous page) <u>more</u> than the <u>hard rock</u>, creating a '<u>step</u>' in the river.

3) As water goes over the step it <u>erodes more and more</u> of the softer rock.

4) A <u>steep drop</u> is eventually created, which is called a <u>waterfall</u>.

5) The <u>hard rock</u> is eventually <u>undercut</u> by erosion. It becomes <u>unsupported</u> and <u>collapses</u>.

6) The collapsed rocks are <u>swirled around</u> at the foot of the waterfall where they <u>erode</u> the softer rock by <u>abrasion</u>. This creates a deep <u>plunge pool</u>.

7) Over time, <u>more undercutting</u> causes <u>more collapses</u>. The waterfall will <u>retreat</u> (move back up the channel), leaving behind a steep-sided <u>gorge</u>.

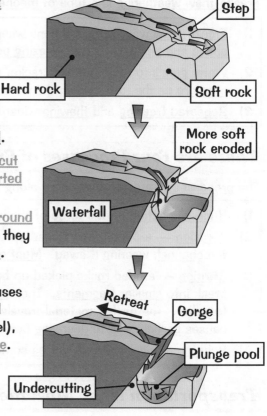

Interlocking Spurs are Nothing to do with Cowboys

1) In the <u>upper course</u> of a river most of the <u>erosion</u> is <u>vertically downwards</u>. This creates <u>steep-sided</u>, <u>V-shaped valleys</u>.

2) The rivers <u>aren't powerful enough</u> to <u>erode laterally</u> (sideways) — they have to <u>wind around</u> the <u>high hillsides</u> that stick out into their paths on either side.

3) The <u>hillsides that interlock</u> with each other (like a zip if you were looking from above) as the river winds around them are called <u>interlocking spurs</u>.

Interlocking spurs along a river in Shropshire

Some river landforms are beautiful — others are gorge-ous...

Step over the hard rock and plunge into the pool — that's how I remember how waterfalls are formed. Geography examiners love river landforms (they're a bit weird like that) so make sure you learn how they form.

Topic 4 — The UK's Evolving Physical Landscape

River Landforms — Erosion and Deposition

When a river's <u>eroding</u> and <u>depositing</u> material, <u>meanders</u> and <u>ox-bow lakes</u> can form.
Australians have a different name for <u>ox-bow lakes</u> — billabongs. Stay tuned for more incredible facts.

Meanders *are Formed by* Erosion *and* Deposition

Rivers develop <u>large bends</u> called <u>meanders</u> in their <u>middle</u> and <u>lower courses</u>, in areas where there are both <u>shallow</u> and <u>deep</u> sections in the channel:

1) The <u>current</u> (the flow of the water) is <u>faster</u> on the <u>outside</u> of the bend because the river channel is <u>deeper</u> (there's <u>less friction</u> to <u>slow</u> the water down).

2) So more <u>erosion</u> (<u>abrasion</u> and <u>hydraulic action</u> — see p. 61) takes place on the <u>outside</u> of the bend, forming <u>river cliffs</u>.

3) The <u>current</u> is <u>slower</u> on the <u>inside</u> of the bend because the river channel is <u>shallower</u> (there's <u>more friction</u> to <u>slow</u> the water down).

4) So eroded material is <u>deposited</u> on the <u>inside</u> of the bend, forming <u>slip-off slopes</u>.

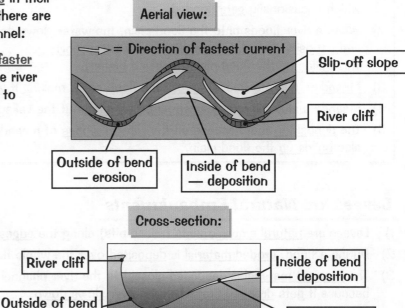

Ox-Bow Lakes *are Formed from* Meanders

Meanders get <u>larger</u> over time — they can eventually turn into an <u>ox-bow lake</u>:

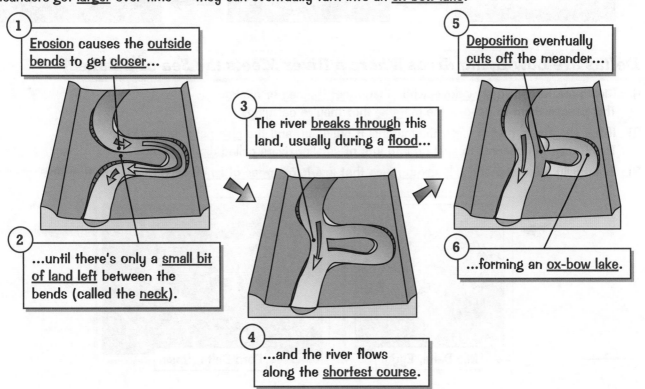

1 <u>Erosion</u> causes the <u>outside bends</u> to get <u>closer</u>...

2 ...until there's only a <u>small bit of land left</u> between the bends (called the <u>neck</u>).

3 The river <u>breaks through</u> this land, usually during a <u>flood</u>...

4 ...and the river flows along the <u>shortest course</u>.

5 <u>Deposition</u> eventually <u>cuts off</u> the meander...

6 ...forming an <u>ox-bow lake</u>.

Fun fact — 'meanders' is a rubbish anagram of 'dreamers'...

In the exam, don't be afraid to draw diagrams of river landforms — examiners love a good diagram and they can help make your answer clear. Oh, and bonus CGP grammar tip: say "Her and me" or "She and I", not "Me and 'er"...

River Landforms — Deposition

When <u>rivers dump material</u> they don't do it by text message — they make attractive <u>landforms</u> instead.

Flood Plains are Flat Areas of Land that Flood

1) The <u>flood plain</u> is the <u>wide valley floor</u> on either side of a river which occasionally <u>gets flooded</u>.

2) When a river <u>floods</u> onto the flood plain, the water <u>slows down</u> and <u>deposits</u> the <u>eroded material</u> that it's <u>transporting</u>. This <u>builds up</u> the flood plain (makes it <u>higher</u>).

3) <u>Meanders migrate</u> (move) <u>across</u> the flood plain, making it <u>wider</u>.

4) Meanders also migrate <u>downstream</u>, <u>flattening</u> out the valley floor.

5) The <u>deposition</u> that happens on the <u>slip-off slopes</u> of meanders also <u>builds up</u> the flood plain.

Flood plain

All these landforms are found in the lower course of a river.

Levees are Natural Embankments

1) Levees are <u>natural embankments</u> (raised bits) along the <u>edges</u> of a <u>river channel</u>.

2) During a flood, <u>eroded material</u> is <u>deposited</u> over the whole flood plain.

3) The <u>heaviest material</u> is <u>deposited closest</u> to the river channel, because it gets <u>dropped first</u> when the river <u>slows down</u>.

4) <u>Over time</u>, the <u>deposited material builds up</u>, creating <u>levees</u> along the edges of the channel.

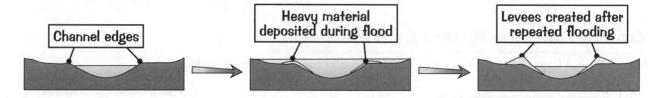

Channel edges

Heavy material deposited during flood

Levees created after repeated flooding

Deltas are Low-Lying Areas Where a River Meets the Sea or a Lake

1) Rivers are forced to <u>slow down</u> when they <u>meet the sea</u> or a <u>lake</u>. This causes them to <u>deposit</u> the <u>material</u> that they're carrying.

2) If the <u>sea doesn't wash away</u> the material it <u>builds up</u> and the <u>channel gets blocked</u>. This forces the channel to <u>split up</u> into lots of <u>smaller rivers</u> called <u>distributaries</u>.

3) Eventually the material <u>builds up so much</u> that <u>low-lying areas of land</u> called <u>deltas</u> are <u>formed</u>.

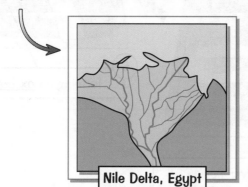
Nile Delta, Egypt

Ebro Delta, Spain

Sediment blockages — some rivers get dealt a bad hand...

These depositional landforms might not be as exciting as waterfalls, but you still need to know about them.

1) Explain how a delta is formed.   [3]

EXAM QUESTION

Identifying River Landforms

You can know all the facts about <u>rivers</u>, but if you don't know what their <u>features</u> look like on <u>maps</u> then some of the exam questions will be a wee bit tricky. Here's something I prepared earlier...

*Contour Lines **Tell you the Direction** a River Flows*

<u>Contour lines</u> are the <u>orange lines</u> drawn all over maps. They tell you about the <u>height</u> of the land (in metres) by the numbers marked on them, and the <u>steepness</u> of the land by how <u>close together</u> they are (the <u>closer</u> they are, the <u>steeper</u> the slope).

It sounds obvious, but rivers <u>can't</u> flow uphill. Unless gravity's gone screwy, a river flows <u>from higher</u> contour lines <u>to lower</u> ones. Have a look at this map of Cawfell Beck:

Take a peek at pages 121-122 for more on reading maps.

1 The <u>height values</u> get <u>smaller</u> towards the <u>west</u> (left), so west is <u>downhill</u>.

2 Cawfell Beck is flowing from <u>east</u> to <u>west</u> (right to left).

3 A <u>V-shape</u> is formed where the contour lines <u>cross</u> the river. The V-shape is <u>pointing uphill</u> to where the river came from.

*Maps contain **Evidence for River Landforms***

Exam questions might ask you to look at a <u>map</u> and give the <u>evidence</u> for a <u>landform</u>. Remember, different landforms are found in the <u>upper</u> and <u>lower course</u> — you can use this evidence to help you <u>identify</u> them.

Evidence for the Upper Course

<u>Waterfalls</u> are often marked on maps. The <u>symbol for a cliff</u> (black, blocky lines) and <u>close contour lines</u> can also be evidence of waterfalls.

The nearby land is <u>high</u> (712 m).

The river <u>crosses lots</u> of <u>contour lines</u> in a <u>short distance</u>, which means it's <u>steep</u>.

The river's <u>narrow</u> (a <u>thin</u> blue line).

The <u>contour lines</u> are very <u>close together</u> and the valley floor is narrow. This means the river is in a <u>steep-sided V-shaped</u> valley.

Evidence for the Lower Course

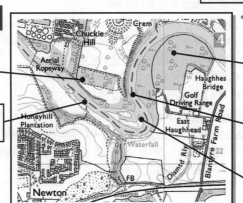

The nearby land is <u>low</u> (less than 15 m).

The river doesn't <u>cross any contour lines</u> so it's <u>very gently sloping</u>.

The river meanders across a large flat area (<u>no contours</u>), which is the <u>flood plain</u>.

The river's <u>wide</u> (a <u>thick</u> blue line).

The river has <u>large meanders</u> and an <u>ox-bow lake</u> may be formed here.

My contours are largely a result of too much chocolate...

Its important to understand what maps are showing, so read this page like there's no tomorrow, then find a map and explain to anyone who'll listen the evidence it provides for the many beautiful and varied features of rivers.

River Landscapes and Sediment Load

What do you get if you cross <u>rivers</u>, <u>climate</u>, <u>geology</u> and <u>slope processes</u>? A <u>river landscape</u>, of course...

River Landscapes and Sediment Load are Influenced by Physical Factors

<u>Climate</u>, <u>geology</u> and <u>slope processes</u> all help to <u>shape river landscapes</u> and affect the <u>sediment load</u> (the <u>material</u> carried by a river):

Climate

1) Rivers in <u>wetter climates</u> have a <u>higher discharge</u> (see next page) because there's <u>more water</u> entering the <u>river channel</u>.

2) Higher discharge increases the <u>rate of erosion</u> — if a river has a <u>higher volume of water</u>, it has <u>more power</u> to <u>erode</u> the river banks and bed. This <u>adds</u> material to the river's <u>load</u>.

3) It also shapes the landscape, forming <u>V-shaped valleys</u> in the river's upper course (through <u>vertical erosion</u>) and a <u>wide</u>, <u>flat</u> <u>flood plain</u> in the lower course (through <u>lateral erosion</u>).

4) <u>Transportation</u> also <u>increases</u> when there's a higher discharge because the river has more <u>energy</u> to <u>carry</u> material.

5) Weathering increases the river's sediment load and can affect the shape of the landscape, e.g. <u>freeze-thaw weathering</u> makes rockfalls more likely (see p. 61).

Geology

1) Rivers flowing through areas of <u>hard rock</u> have a <u>slower</u> rate of erosion because hard rocks are <u>more resistant</u>. This means the river will have a <u>lower sediment load</u>.

2) Areas with <u>softer rocks</u> will experience <u>more erosion</u> — this adds <u>more material</u> to the river's <u>sediment load</u>.

3) Landscapes with <u>more resistant rocks</u> tend to have <u>steeper valley sides</u>. Landscapes with <u>less resistant rocks</u> have <u>gentle sloping valley sides</u>.

4) <u>Waterfalls</u> form where there is a layer of <u>hard rock</u> on top of <u>softer</u> rock.

5) <u>Interlocking spurs</u> (see p. 62) form where <u>softer rock</u> is eroded <u>first</u>, leaving areas of <u>harder rock sticking out</u>.

Slope Processes

1) <u>Vertical erosion</u> by rivers makes valley sides <u>steeper</u>, <u>increasing</u> the movement of material <u>down</u> the slopes.

2) <u>Mass movement</u>, e.g. <u>slumping</u> (see p. 49), can add large amounts of material to the river's load. Mass movements are more likely during colder weather (<u>freeze-thaw weathering</u> loosens material) and during periods of intense rainfall (the saturated ground becomes <u>heavier</u> and <u>less stable</u>).

Soil creep creates mini terraces on gentle slopes called 'terracettes'.

3) <u>Soil creep</u> is when <u>soil particles</u> move down a slope because of <u>gravity</u>. It's caused by the <u>expansion</u> and <u>contraction</u> of the soil. <u>Water</u> adds <u>weight</u> to the soil and makes it <u>expand</u> — this causes it to <u>move down the slope</u>. When the soil <u>dries out</u>, it <u>contracts</u>. Soil creep can add lots of <u>fine</u> material to the river's load.

Soil creep — likes to hang around in dark valleys...

More often than not, it's a combination of climate, geology and slope processes that shape river landscapes and influence sediment load. I'm sure you've reached peak excitement about rivers by now, but keep it together for just a bit longer...

Topic 4 — The UK's Evolving Physical Landscape

River Discharge

We've not really talked much about the actual <u>water</u> in a river. Well, all that's about to change — hooray.

Hydrographs *Show the Change* in *River Discharge*

1) River discharge is simply the <u>volume of water</u> that flows in a river per second. It's measured in <u>cumecs</u> — cubic metres per second (m^3/s).

2) <u>Storm hydrographs</u> show the changes in river discharge around the time of a <u>storm</u>:

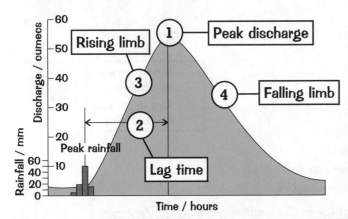

① <u>Peak discharge</u>: The <u>highest discharge</u> in the period of time you're looking at.

② <u>Lag time</u>: The <u>delay</u> between <u>peak rainfall</u> and <u>peak discharge</u>.

③ <u>Rising limb</u>: The <u>increase</u> in river discharge as <u>rainwater</u> flows into the river.

④ <u>Falling limb</u>: The <u>decrease</u> in river discharge as the river returns to its <u>normal level</u>.

3) Lag time happens because most rainwater <u>doesn't land directly</u> in the river channel — there's a <u>delay</u> as rainwater <u>gets to the channel</u>. It gets there by <u>flowing quickly overland</u> (called <u>surface runoff</u>, or just <u>runoff</u>), or by <u>soaking into the ground</u> (called <u>infiltration</u>) and flowing <u>slowly underground</u>.

Storm Hydrographs *are Affected* by *Different Factors*

1) If <u>more water</u> flows as <u>runoff</u> the <u>lag time</u> will be <u>reduced</u>. This means <u>discharge</u> will <u>increase</u> and the <u>hydrograph</u> will be <u>steeper</u> because <u>more water</u> gets to the river in a <u>shorter space of time</u>.

2) There are <u>physical</u> and <u>human</u> factors that affect <u>lag time</u>, <u>discharge</u> and the <u>shape</u> of the <u>hydrograph</u>:

GEOLOGY — water <u>can't infiltrate</u> into <u>impermeable</u> rocks, so there's <u>more runoff</u>.

SOIL TYPE — more <u>impermeable</u> soils (e.g. clays) <u>can't absorb</u> as much water as <u>sandy soils</u>, which <u>increases runoff</u>. <u>Shallower soils</u> also become saturated <u>more quickly</u> than <u>deeper soils</u>.

SLOPE — the <u>steeper</u> the slope, the <u>less infiltration</u> and the <u>higher</u> the <u>runoff</u>.

DRAINAGE BASIN TYPE — <u>circular</u> drainage basins have a <u>shorter lag time</u> and <u>higher discharge</u> than <u>narrow basins</u> because water reaches the <u>main river channel</u> <u>at the same time</u>. In a narrower basin, water from the <u>far end</u> of the basin <u>takes a long time</u> to reach the main channel.

ANTECEDENT CONDITIONS — previously <u>wet</u> or <u>very cold weather</u> can <u>increase runoff</u> because water can't infiltrate <u>saturated</u> or <u>frozen soil</u>.

'Antecedent' is just a fancy word for 'previous'.

URBANISATION — water <u>can't infiltrate</u> into <u>impermeable</u> surfaces (e.g. tarmac or concrete), so there's <u>more runoff</u>. <u>Gutters</u> and <u>drains</u> quickly take runoff to rivers, which <u>rapidly increases discharge</u>.

DEFORESTATION — trees <u>take up water</u> from the ground and <u>store it</u>, which <u>reduces</u> runoff. <u>Cutting down</u> trees <u>increases runoff</u> and causes <u>more</u> <u>water</u> to enter the river channel, which <u>increases discharge</u>.

Revision lag time — the time between starting and getting bored...

Hydrographs look scary, but they're not too bad — just keep going until the knowledge infiltrates your brain.

1) Explain how changing land use can change the shape of a storm hydrograph. [4]

River Flooding

Flooding happens when the <u>level</u> of a river gets <u>so high</u> that it <u>spills over its banks</u> onto the <u>flood plain</u>.

The River Eden is Prone to Flooding

1) The <u>River Eden</u> (see p. 60) runs through <u>North Cumbria</u>.

2) <u>Flooding</u> in the Eden basin is <u>common</u> and some areas, e.g. <u>Carlisle</u>, are <u>very prone</u> to flooding.

3) A <u>combination</u> of <u>physical factors</u> and <u>human activities</u> increase the risk of flooding in this area:

Carlisle is built where the rivers Eden, Caldew and Petteril meet.

North Pennines · **Carlisle** · **Lake District**

~ River Eden and its tributaries
⌐ ⌐ Area drained by the River Eden

Physical Factors

- Cumbria is on the <u>west coast</u> of the UK, facing the prevailing <u>south-westerly</u> winds — the <u>climate</u> is <u>mild and wet</u>.

- It's one of the <u>wettest</u> parts of the UK, often experiencing periods of <u>intense rainfall</u>. Many of the UK's <u>highest rainfall records</u> have been recorded in Cumbria.

- The Eden basin is bordered by the <u>Lake District</u> to the west and the <u>North Pennines</u> to the east. Both these areas are made up of <u>hard</u>, <u>impermeable rocks</u>. This means water <u>can't soak</u> into the ground and <u>runs off</u> into the <u>river channel</u>.

- <u>Snowfall</u> is <u>common</u> on higher ground during the <u>winter months</u>. Snow melt can add <u>lots of water</u> to the river channel in a <u>short space of time</u>.

Human Activities

- Carlisle is a <u>large built-up area</u> and there has been lots of <u>development</u> on the Eden's <u>flood plain</u>. This has affected the flood plain's ability to <u>absorb</u> and <u>store floodwater</u>. The lack of <u>soil</u> or <u>vegetation</u> means there's <u>little infiltration</u> of rainfall, which leads to <u>high surface runoff</u>.

- <u>Natural woodland</u> and <u>heathland</u> have been <u>cleared</u> from many upland areas in the Eden basin. This <u>increases</u> surface <u>runoff</u> when it rains, and means that <u>more water</u> ends up in the river channel <u>more quickly</u>.

- Parts of the Eden valley have been <u>drained</u> to make them <u>more suitable</u> for <u>farming</u>. <u>Drainage ditches</u> mean water flows rapidly to the <u>river channel</u>.

4) The <u>interaction</u> of <u>physical</u> and <u>human factors</u> led to flooding in the Eden basin (including <u>severe flooding</u> in <u>Carlisle</u>) on <u>5th and 6th December 2015</u>.

- <u>Antecedent conditions</u> — November 2015 was the <u>second wettest</u> November ever <u>recorded</u> in Cumbria — this had an impact on <u>antecedent conditions</u> because <u>soils</u> were already <u>saturated</u> and <u>river discharge</u> was <u>high</u>.

- <u>Heavy rainfall</u> — during Storm Desmond more than <u>300 mm</u> fell across the Cumbrian hills in <u>24 hours</u>. This was the <u>highest rainfall</u> ever recorded in the UK.

- <u>Short lag time</u> — the rainwater across the drainage basin <u>quickly</u> reached the <u>main channel</u> at Carlisle.

- <u>Blockages</u> — <u>debris</u> carried by the floodwater <u>blocked bridges</u> and smaller channels, <u>forcing water</u> out of the river channel.

- <u>Insufficient drainage</u> — runoff from <u>impermeable surfaces</u> in Carlisle ran quickly into <u>drainage systems</u>. These <u>couldn't cope</u> with the volume of water and <u>overflowed</u>, making the flooding <u>worse</u>.

Flooding — sometimes brought on by the stress of exams...

...so take it easy and go over the page again. Make sure you know understand how physical and human processes are interacting to cause flooding on a named river and you'll be home and dry.

River Flooding

Aahh, déjà vu. River flooding is becoming more and more frequent in the UK. Luckily for you, I've got just the page to tell you all about the reasons why. So find yourself a spot of high ground and get reading...

The Risk of Flooding is Increasing in the UK

Flood risk is increasing in the UK because of two main factors:

Increased Frequency of Storms

1) The frequency of storms in the UK is increasing — this could be a consequence of global climate change (see page 7).

2) It is also thought that storms are becoming more extreme — more intense rainfall is increasing the scale of flood events.

3) More periods of wet weather mean that the ground is saturated, making flooding more likely.

Land Use Change

1) As the UK's population grows, there's more pressure to expand urban areas. This leads to an increase in impermeable surfaces (e.g. concrete), which cause rapid surface runoff.

2) Removing vegetation and permeable surfaces means that water that would have been stored in the soil or plants and trees now flows quickly downstream.

3) Lots of development, e.g. house building, is taking place on flood plains. These areas are naturally prone to flooding and this increases the risk to developed areas.

4) More people living on flood plains mean that there are more people at risk of flooding if flood defences fail.

Flooding Threatens People and the Environment

Threats to People

1) People can be killed or injured by floodwater.
2) Roads, bridges and rail lines can be damaged or destroyed.
3) Floodwater is often contaminated with sewage, which can lead to a lack of clean drinking water.
4) Possessions can be damaged or washed away.
5) People can be made homeless as their properties are inundated or damaged.
6) Businesses may be forced to shut down because of flood damage and disrupted power supplies. This leads to a loss of livelihoods.

2015 floods in Carlisle

Threats to the Environment

1) Floodwater contaminated with sewage and rubbish can pollute rivers, damaging wildlife habitats.
2) Farmland can be ruined by silt and sediment deposited after a flood.
3) River banks are eroded, causing huge changes to the river landscape, e.g. widening of the river channel and increased deposition downstream.
4) The force of floodwater can uproot trees and plants, and standing floodwater may cause those that survive the initial wave of water to die.

Farmland ruined by flooding

Buy a canoe now, we're all doomed. DOOOOMED I tell ye...

Ahem. Sorry. The impacts of river flooding and coastal flooding are very similar — make sure you don't get them muddled up. Have a go at this exam question before the floodwaters wash away your pen and paper:

1) Explain two reasons why the risk of river flooding is increasing in the UK. [4]

River Management

Floods can be <u>devastating</u>, but there are a number of different <u>strategies</u> to stop them or lessen the blow.

Engineering can Reduce the Risk of Flooding or its Effects

There are <u>two</u> types of strategy to <u>deal with flooding</u>:

1) <u>Hard engineering</u> — <u>man-made structures</u> built to <u>control the flow</u> of rivers and <u>reduce flooding</u>.
2) <u>Soft engineering</u> — schemes set up using <u>knowledge</u> of a <u>river</u> and its <u>processes</u> to <u>reduce the effects of flooding</u>.

Different <u>hard engineering</u> strategies have different <u>costs</u> and <u>benefits</u>:

FLOOD WALLS — flood walls are <u>artificial barriers</u> built along river banks. They're designed to increase the <u>height</u> of the <u>river banks</u>, allowing the river channel to <u>hold more water</u>. However, flood walls are <u>very expensive</u> and they can be <u>unsightly</u> and <u>block the view</u> of the river.

EMBANKMENTS — embankments are <u>high banks</u> that are built <u>along</u> or near the <u>river banks</u>. They stop the river <u>flowing</u> into built-up areas during a <u>flood</u>, protecting <u>buildings</u> and <u>infrastructure</u> on the flood plain. They can be made from <u>earth</u> or other <u>natural materials</u>, making them <u>less unsightly</u> than flood walls. They're quite <u>expensive</u> to build and there's a risk of <u>severe flooding</u> if the water rises <u>above</u> the level of the embankments or if they <u>break</u>.

FLOOD BARRIERS (FLOODGATES) — floodgates, e.g. the <u>Thames Barrier</u>, are built on <u>river estuaries</u> to stop flooding from <u>storm surges</u> (see p. 10) or <u>very high tides</u>. They can be <u>shut</u> when there's a <u>surge forecast</u> to prevent flooding and they protect a <u>large area</u> of land, e.g. central London. Floodgates are <u>very expensive</u> to build and need to be <u>maintained regularly</u>.

FLOOD BARRIERS (DEMOUNTABLE) — demountable flood barriers provide <u>temporary</u> protection against flooding. The barriers are <u>only put up</u> when there's a <u>flood forecast</u> so there's always a risk they might not be put up <u>in time</u>. Demountable flood barriers are quite <u>expensive</u> to build, but they <u>don't spoil</u> the look of attractive locations.

<u>Soft engineering</u> strategies also have <u>costs</u> and <u>benefits</u>:

FLOOD PLAIN RETENTION — this strategy involves <u>maintaining</u> the river's <u>flood plain</u>, i.e. by <u>not building</u> on it. It helps <u>slow</u> floodwaters down and maintain the flood plain's <u>ability</u> to <u>store water</u>. <u>No money</u> has to be spent on building flood defences, but it <u>restricts development</u> and <u>can't</u> be used in <u>urban areas</u>.

RIVER RESTORATION — this involves making the river <u>more natural</u>, e.g. by removing man-made levees, so that the flood plain can <u>flood naturally</u>. There's <u>less risk</u> of flooding <u>downstream</u> because <u>discharge</u> is <u>reduced</u>. The river is left in its <u>natural state</u>, so there's very <u>little maintenance</u> required. However, river restoration can increase <u>local flood risk</u>, especially if <u>nothing</u> is done to prevent <u>major flooding</u>.

Flood your mind — with knowledge of flood defence schemes...

Would you look at that — it's the end of rivers. It looks like there's a lot of stuff to learn here, but it's not difficult at all. Make sure you have at least a couple of costs and benefits for each strategy stashed away in your brain.

Revision Summary

Wat-er load of fun that was. Have a go at the questions below and then go back over the topic to check your answers. If something's not quite right, pore over the page again. Once you can answer everything correctly you're ready to sail away, sail away, sail away... to the next topic.

River Landscapes and Processes (p.59-61) ☑

1) What does a river's long profile show?
2) Describe the cross profile of a river's lower course.
3) What is the difference between vertical and lateral erosion?
4) Compare the sediment size and shape in a river's upper and lower courses.
5) How does a river's discharge change along its course?
6) Describe the process of freeze-thaw weathering.
7) What's the difference between abrasion and attrition?
8) Name two processes of transportation.
9) When does deposition occur?

River Landforms (p.62-65) ☐

10) Where do waterfalls form?
11) What are interlocking spurs?
12) a) Where is the current fastest on a meander?
    b) What feature of a meander is formed where the flow is fastest?
13) Name the landform created when a meander is cut off by deposition.
14) What is a flood plain?
15) Outline the main features of a delta.
16) What do the contour lines on a map show?
17) Give two pieces of map evidence for a waterfall.
18) Give two pieces of map evidence for a river's lower course.

River Landscapes, Sediment Load and Discharge (p.66-67) ☐

19) Explain how climate influences sediment load.
20) Give two ways geology influences river landscapes.
21) What is soil creep?
22) What is river discharge?
23) What is lag time?
24) Describe one physical factor and one human factor that alter storm hydrographs.

River Flooding and Management (p.68-70) ☐

25) Outline two physical factors that increase the risk of flooding on a named river.
26) What human activities are causing flooding on a river you have studied?
27) Outline two ways in which land use change is increasing the risk of flooding.
28) a) Give two threats of flooding to people.
    b) Give two threats of flooding to the environment.
29) Define hard engineering.
30) Define soft engineering.
31) Describe the costs of using flood walls to reduce the risk of flooding.
32) Describe the benefits of river restoration.

UK Human Landscape

Warning. This topic is all about why <u>places</u> and <u>people</u> in the UK are <u>changing</u>. Once you've read it there's no going back — there'll be <u>geography</u> everywhere you look. I'm sorry. I'm really so so sorry.

Population Density *is Highest* **in Urban Cores**

The <u>population distribution</u> in the UK is very <u>uneven</u>.

- Population density is <u>highest</u> in <u>cities</u>, e.g. London, Glasgow, Birmingham.
- It's also high in areas <u>around</u> major cities, or where <u>major cities</u> have developed into <u>conurbations</u> — towns that have merged to form <u>continuous urban areas</u>, e.g. Merseyside includes Liverpool, Knowsley and St Helens.

- <u>Upland areas</u> such as northern Scotland and central Wales are mostly <u>rural</u>. Rural areas are <u>sparsely</u> populated.
- Other <u>rural areas</u> include the south west and north of England and Northern Ireland.

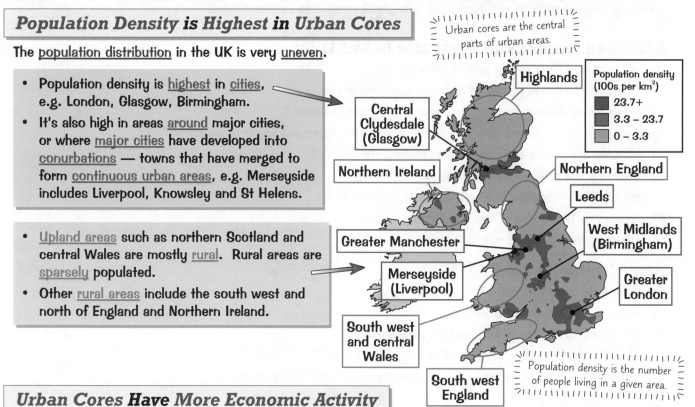

Urban cores are the central parts of urban areas.

Population density (100s per km²)
- 23.7+
- 3.3 – 23.7
- 0 – 3.3

Highlands
Central Clydesdale (Glasgow)
Northern Ireland
Northern England
Leeds
West Midlands (Birmingham)
Greater Manchester
Merseyside (Liverpool)
Greater London
South west and central Wales
South west England

Population density is the number of people living in a given area.

Urban Cores **Have** *More Economic Activity*

The <u>amount</u> and <u>type</u> of <u>economic activity</u> is different in <u>urban</u> and <u>rural</u> areas:

Urban Cores

1) Urban core areas have a higher concentration of <u>economic activity</u> — <u>60%</u> of jobs in cities are found there.
2) The main <u>employment opportunities</u> are in the <u>tertiary</u> sector (e.g. retail and finance) and in <u>manufacturing</u> (e.g. electronics and food and drink).
3) Lots of people live in <u>cities</u> because there are <u>more jobs available</u> there, which are often <u>better paid</u>.

Rural Areas

1) Rural areas usually have <u>fewer job opportunities</u>.
2) There is more <u>primary industry</u> — e.g. <u>farming</u>, <u>forestry</u>, <u>fishing</u> and <u>quarrying</u>.
3) Some areas also have a <u>seasonal tourism industry</u>, e.g. cafés and hotels in the <u>Lake District National Park</u> in northern England.
4) Some rural settlements that are near <u>urban areas</u> have become <u>commuter settlements</u> — people <u>live</u> there and <u>travel</u> into <u>urban</u> areas for <u>work</u>.

See page 35 for more on the types of economic sector.

Urban Cores **Have** *A Younger Population*

1) The <u>age structure</u> of <u>urban</u> and <u>rural</u> areas is different.
2) There is a <u>higher proportion</u> of <u>younger</u> people in <u>big cities</u>, such as London, Bristol and Manchester — people often live in cities to be closer to their <u>jobs</u>, so a higher proportion of the population is of <u>working age</u>.
3) There is a higher proportion of <u>older</u> people in <u>rural</u> areas, e.g. <u>Northern Ireland</u> and <u>Scotland</u>. <u>Older</u> people <u>move out</u> of <u>cities</u> to retire to a more peaceful environment and <u>younger</u> people <u>leave rural areas</u> to work in cities.

Proportion of people over 65
- Low
- Medium
- High
- Very high

Cor, blimey! What a page...

There, that wasn't so bad. It may seem pretty obvious stuff but the ideas on this page form the basis of everything that's coming up. So, head down and stick at it 'til you know the key differences between urban and rural areas.

UK Human Landscape

Things are never as rosy as they look... Some areas have <u>problems</u>. And where there are problems, we need <u>solutions</u>. (The solution to the problem of your exam is to read this page and learn it, by the way.)

Some Rural Areas of the UK Have High Levels of Poverty

Some rural areas of the UK are <u>struggling</u> to <u>grow economically</u>. These include:

1) <u>Isolated</u> rural areas on the <u>periphery</u> (edge) of the UK (e.g. north Wales, north west Scotland), which are relatively <u>inaccessible</u>. There are <u>few employment opportunities</u> because they are difficult to farm and have few natural resources. <u>Young people</u> have to <u>leave</u> to find jobs elsewhere — <u>depopulation</u> leads to <u>loss of services</u> (e.g. shops, doctors surgeries) because they can no longer be supported.

2) Rural areas around the <u>former industrial areas</u>, e.g. north east England and parts of the Midlands, where the loss of <u>manufacturing industry</u> has caused <u>high unemployment</u> and new jobs haven't been created.

UK and EU Government Policies Aim to Reduce Differences in Wealth

There are lots of <u>strategies</u> to <u>reduce</u> the differences in <u>wealth</u> between <u>thriving urban cores</u> (see previous page) and rural areas with <u>high levels of poverty</u>. These happen at a range of <u>scales</u> and may involve <u>county councils</u>, the <u>national government</u> and the <u>European Union</u> (<u>EU</u>).

1 Creating Enterprise Zones

1) The UK government has created <u>55 Enterprise Zones</u> across England, Scotland and Wales.

2) These offer companies a range of benefits for locating in enterprise zones, including: <u>reduced taxes</u>, <u>simpler planning rules</u>, and <u>improved infrastructure</u> (e.g. superfast broadband).

3) These measures can be used to <u>encourage</u> companies to <u>locate</u> in areas of <u>high unemployment</u>, bringing <u>jobs</u> and <u>income</u> which could help <u>poorer rural</u> areas to develop.

4) For example, the new <u>Dorset Green</u> Enterprise Zone already has two <u>high tech engineering companies</u> and hopes to attract <u>55</u> more <u>businesses</u>, creating <u>2000 new jobs</u> in the region.

2 Transport Infrastructure

1) The <u>UK government</u> plans to link London, Birmingham, Leeds and Manchester with a new <u>high speed rail line</u>, HS2. This will increase <u>capacity</u> and allow <u>faster journeys</u> into major cities — promoting <u>industry</u> and <u>jobs</u> in poorer rural areas in the north of England.

2) On a local scale, Lancashire county council has built a <u>new road</u> to link the <u>port</u> of Heysham in Lancashire to the <u>M6</u>. This will encourage <u>businesses</u> to <u>invest</u> by <u>reducing travel times</u> and <u>easing congestion</u>, creating more <u>job opportunities</u> for people in the <u>surrounding rural areas</u>.

3 Regional Development

1) The EU has used the <u>European Regional Development Fund</u> (<u>ERDF</u>) to promote <u>growth</u> in poorer rural areas by investing in <u>small high-tech businesses</u>, providing <u>training</u> to improve local people's <u>skills</u> and funding infrastructure, e.g. high speed broadband to attract businesses. For example, the EU funded <u>superfast broadband</u> in Cornwall. This attracts <u>digital businesses</u>, such as Gravitas, and links regeneration projects and new research and development centres in the region. This is <u>creating</u> skilled <u>jobs</u> in the area, attracting young <u>graduates</u> and <u>boosting</u> the local <u>economy</u>.

2) The <u>Common Agricultural Policy</u> (<u>CAP</u>) is an EU initiative to make sure <u>EU farmers</u> can earn a <u>living</u> from farming. It includes <u>training</u> for farmers and <u>assistance</u> for young farmers starting up as well as <u>subsidies</u> for <u>rural diversification</u> projects (see p. 82).

3) In <u>2016</u> the UK voted to <u>leave</u> the EU, which means <u>future</u> regional development plans are <u>uncertain</u>.

All aboard the Enterprise — due to embark to zone development...

Make sure you know how the government and the EU have tried to reduce differences in wealth in the UK.

1) Explain two ways in which government policies can help rural areas to develop. [4]

Migration

The UK's population is changing because people are constantly moving about — they do have their reasons though. If you grab a pen and a notebook and don't go wandering off I'll tell you all the latest trends.

Migration *Influences the* Age Structure *and* Distribution *of People in the UK*

1) Roughly half the UK's population growth is driven by natural increase (more births than deaths), and about half by migration.

2) Between 1970 and 1982 more people left the UK than moved to the UK. There has been a constant flow of British people leaving the UK since 1970 — mostly to Australia, the USA, France and Spain.

3) Overall, since 1983 more people have moved to the UK than have left and net migration has generally been increasing — net migration has more than doubled in the last 10 years.

4) National and international migration affect the distribution and age structure of the population:

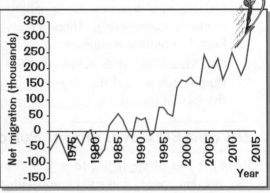

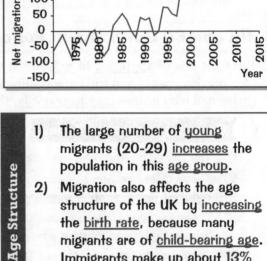

Distribution

1) Young national migrants and most international migrants move to major cities — this is where most jobs are and where universities are located. The most popular destinations for international migrants are London and the West Midlands.

2) There has been lots of counter-urbanisation (see p.36) as wealthy people move out of cities to seek a better quality of life in rural areas — the London region has the highest number of people leaving.

3) Many older people move to coastal areas in the east and south west of England when they retire.

Age Structure

1) The large number of young migrants (20-29) increases the population in this age group.

2) Migration also affects the age structure of the UK by increasing the birth rate, because many migrants are of child-bearing age. Immigrants make up about 13% of the UK population, but account for about 27% of babies born.

UK Immigration Policy *has Increased Diversity*

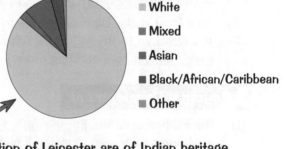

1) After the second world war, the UK encouraged immigration from Commonwealth countries, e.g. the Caribbean, India and Pakistan, to fill skills shortages in the UK workforce.

2) Later, entry was restricted but work permits for migrants with desirable skills, e.g. IT, were made available — many highly skilled Indians and Pakistanis still come to the UK.

3) This has meant that the UK has a high proportion of people of Caribbean and Asian ethnicity — nearly 10%. This is much higher in some regions, e.g. 29% of the population of Leicester are of Indian heritage.

4) Since 1995 the EU has allowed free movement of people within member countries to find work — this increased the number of people migrating to the UK from Europe, e.g. from Germany.

5) In 2004 eight new countries joined the EU. Lots of people moved from these countries, e.g. Poland and Hungary, to find jobs in the UK. This was mainly in low-skilled jobs, e.g. catering and agriculture.

6) Between 2001 and 2011, the proportion of non-British white people increased more than any ethnic group — Polish people are now one of the largest non-UK born groups.

7) International immigration has increased cultural diversity — immigrants introduce languages, food, arts, festivals and fashion from their own culture giving the UK a rich mix.

My new juggling class is increasing mi-grate diversity of skills...

...though a gag-writing class would probably be more useful. Once you're clear on how migration and immigration policies are affecting the UK population, proceed to the next page in an orderly fashion. No pushing at the back.

Topic 5 — The UK's Evolving Human Landscape

The UK Economy

You might have worked out that while it's all tickety boo in some cities, other places are having a tougher time. Well, it's largely down to how the UK economy has changed over time, so if you're sitting comfortably...

Primary and Secondary Industries have Declined

1) Since 1960 jobs in primary industries have decreased. Farming has become more mechanised so fewer people are needed. The mining industry also declined due to competition from abroad and cheaper alternative fuels.

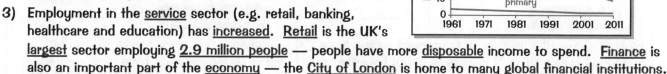

2) Jobs in secondary industries have also decreased — people employed in manufacturing fell from 36% of the workforce in 1961 to just 9% in 2011. This was partly a result of global shift (see p.36).

3) Employment in the service sector (e.g. retail, banking, healthcare and education) has increased. Retail is the UK's largest sector employing 2.9 million people — people have more disposable income to spend. Finance is also an important part of the economy — the City of London is home to many global financial institutions.

4) Quaternary industries, e.g. IT and research and development (R&D) are increasing, making use of the UK's skilled university graduates. In 2013, nearly £30 billion was spent on R&D in the UK.

Secondary Industry has Declined in Burnley

1) Burnley is a town in Lancashire, about 20 miles north of Manchester.

2) In the early 20th Century Burnley had a thriving economy based on textiles — it was one of the world's leading cotton weaving towns.

3) From 1914, the textiles industry in the UK began to collapse — partly due to cheap imports. The last cotton mill closed in the 1980s.

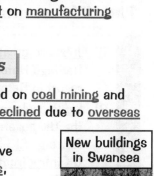
Derelict street due to poverty and depopulation

4) Other primary and secondary industries also struggled. Several major factories closed in the 1990s and early 2000s with the loss of hundreds of jobs.

5) Burnley has struggled to recover economically. The employment rate is only about 65% and wages are well below the UK average — low-skilled service sector jobs don't pay well. There is very little population growth — with few jobs on offer, people are more likely to leave than to move there.

6) The manufacturing skills existing in the area and the low costs of operating there have begun to attract aerospace engineering firms — meaning the area is still largely dependent on manufacturing industries for employment.

Tertiary and Quaternary Sectors are Growing in South Wales

1) For much of the 18th and 19th centuries, the economy of South Wales was based on coal mining and ironmaking. In the 20th century, coal mining and iron working in South Wales declined due to overseas competition. Unemployment levels were high, and many people lived in poverty.

2) In 1992, the different parts of the region started to work together more to achieve economic growth. They aimed to improve transport networks, attract businesses, increase skills and draw visitors to the area.

New buildings in Swansea
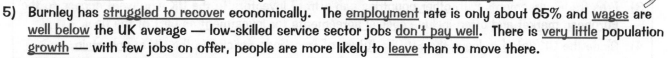

3) Costs are lower than London and the south east, making it easier to start up new businesses. Universities (in Swansea and Cardiff) supply a skilled labour force.

4) This has helped to attract private investors in high tech industries — South Wales is now home to lots of new digital and media companies and is a thriving economic region.

5) As wealth increases, people have more money to spend on services, creating more jobs in these industries.

There's been a decline in the manufacturing of cake in my office...

The decline of secondary industry had a massive impact on the UK economy and has a whole host of knock-on effects. Go over this page til you've well and truly nailed it — it'll really help with the massive case study coming up on p. 77.

UK Links with the Wider World

It's not just people that move to the UK — businesses do too. And more and more of them are coming.

FDI is Increasing in the UK...

1) A company based in one country can invest money in a different country
— this is foreign direct investment (FDI). FDI can take two forms:
   - companies can buy land or buildings and locate their factory or office there.
   - companies can buy all or part of an already existing business.

2) FDI has been increasing in the UK — it rose from £726 billion in 2010 to £1 065 billion in 2014.

3) Most of this investment comes from transnational corporations (TNCs — see p.26).

... Due to Globalisation, Free Trade Policies and Privatisation

Globalisation

Globalisation is the process of countries become more integrated (see p.26). It is increasing FDI because:

1) Transport and communications links have improved making it easier for companies to operate in the UK.

2) London has developed as a global financial centre — many foreign banks, e.g. the German Deutsche Bank, have located here because of the business culture and networking opportunities.

Privatisation

Services that were previously run by the UK government have been offered to private firms. This has increased FDI because foreign firms can buy them or merge them with their existing businesses.

For example, many UK electricity boards are now owned by foreign companies — Scottish Power is owned by the Spanish energy company, Iberdrola.

Free Trade Policies

1) Free trade policies reduce import and export restrictions, making it easier for countries to trade.

2) Free trade is promoted between member countries of the EU. This increases FDI from the EU because companies can move goods and services freely between the UK and their home country.

3) Free trade agreements with other countries can attract investors to the UK who want access to the European market and often include special agreements for investment as part of the deal.

4) Since the UK voted to leave the EU, the future of free trade policies in the UK is uncertain.

The UK Economy is Increasingly Affected by TNCs

On the plus side...

1) Jobs are created, e.g. the US firm Grand Heritage Hotel Group is investing in a new resort in Derbyshire creating 1000 jobs.

2) Large scale projects can be built that the UK government can't afford to pay for, e.g. £15 billion has been invested in UK infrastructure, such as offshore wind turbines, sub-sea power cables etc.

3) TNCs often lead the way in developing new products, technology and business practices which can be used by other firms to increase productivity.

But there are also downsides...

1) It can lead to over-reliance on TNCs — if there's a problem elsewhere in the world, the UK's economy is affected, e.g. the world economic recession led to redundancies at the Nissan factory in Sunderland in 2009.

2) There are big effects if TNCs choose to relocate or change suppliers, e.g. many UK farmers are dependent on just one or two large TNCs who buy their produce.

3) Local businesses struggle to compete against TNCs, e.g. in some towns the arrival of the coffee chain Starbucks has forced independent coffee shops to close down.

I'm privatising my revision in hope some bright spark will invest...

Phew, economics is complicated stuff. You need to know why FDI is increasing and the effect of TNCs.

1) Explain two reasons why foreign direct investment is increasing in the UK.   [4]

Dynamic UK Cities — Case Study

London — where the streets are <u>paved with gold</u> and everyone has <u>tea</u> with the <u>Queen</u> on a Friday afternoon.

London is a Global City in South East England

1) London is sited on the <u>flat floodplain</u> of the <u>River Thames</u> where it meets the sea.

2) It is the UK's <u>capital city</u> and is an essential part of the UK's economy. <u>Over 20%</u> of the UK's <u>income</u> comes from London.

3) It is the centre of the UK's <u>transport</u> system. It was a major <u>port</u> until 1981 and still has <u>shipping links</u>. There are two major <u>international airports</u> (Heathrow and Gatwick) plus three <u>smaller</u> ones, e.g. London City Airport. There is easy <u>access</u> to <u>mainland Europe</u> via the Channel Tunnel.

4) It has a major <u>influence</u> on its <u>surrounding area</u>. Companies are attracted to the region by the <u>proximity</u> to London, which <u>increases jobs</u> and <u>wealth</u>. The <u>South East</u> and <u>East of England</u> are the two biggest <u>regional economies</u> in the UK outside London.

5) London's important <u>globally</u> too — it's a <u>world city</u> and, along with New York, one of the two most important <u>financial centres</u> in the world. There are more <u>foreign banks</u> in London than <u>anywhere else</u>.

You Need to Know the City's Structure

Land use and <u>building age varies</u> across the city (see p. 37).

	Area (example)	Main Land Use	Description
CBD (Central Business District)	<u>City of London</u>	Commercial	Mix of <u>new high-rise office blocks</u> and <u>historical</u> buildings. Land is <u>expensive</u> so building <u>density</u> is <u>high</u>. There are a <u>few small parks</u>.
Inner city	<u>Newham</u>	Low-class residential	<u>High-density</u>, <u>old</u> terraced housing, <u>1960s-70s high-rise flats</u> and <u>modern apartment</u> buildings. <u>Poor</u> environmental quality, some <u>green space</u>.
	<u>Chelsea</u>	High-class residential	<u>80%</u> houses built <u>before 1919</u>. Land is <u>expensive</u> so building <u>density</u> is <u>high</u>. Lots of <u>large terraced houses</u>, some converted into <u>flats</u>. High quality <u>green space</u> — most houses have <u>gardens</u>.
Suburbs	<u>Surbiton, Kingston upon Thames</u>	Middle-class residential	Good quality <u>20th century semi-detached</u> housing, along with <u>shops</u> and <u>restaurants</u>. Most houses have <u>gardens</u> and there are <u>large</u> areas of good quality <u>green space</u>.
Rural-urban fringe	<u>Crockenhill, Sevenoaks</u>	High-class residential	<u>Large</u>, <u>detached</u> and <u>semi-detached</u> houses with <u>gardens</u> — the area is surrounded by <u>countryside</u>.
	<u>Thurrock</u>	Industrial, commercial	Industry includes <u>oil refineries</u>, <u>manufacturing</u> and a <u>container port</u>. Lakeside <u>retail</u> park opened in <u>1990</u>.

Migration is Causing Parts of London to Grow

1) The <u>population</u> of London is now over <u>8.5 million people</u> and it's <u>growing</u> due to:

   • <u>International migration</u> — <u>net</u> migration to London in 2014 was <u>100 thousand people</u>.

   • <u>National migration</u> — within the UK, <u>young</u> adults move <u>to</u> the city for <u>work</u> or to <u>study</u>.

   • <u>Internal population growth</u> — the <u>young population</u> means there are <u>more births</u> than <u>deaths</u> in the city.

2) <u>Inner city</u> London has the <u>highest rate</u> of people moving <u>in</u> and <u>out</u> including both the <u>wealthiest</u> and <u>poorest</u> people. <u>Highly skilled</u> people move to the <u>inner city</u> to work in <u>high-paid jobs</u> (e.g. in banking) along with <u>low-paid migrants</u> looking for jobs in the <u>service sector</u> (e.g. cleaning and catering).

3) Migrants who have been in London for <u>longer</u> tend to move out to the <u>suburbs</u> as they become more <u>settled</u>. About 50% of the population of the Outer London boroughs of <u>Harrow</u> and <u>Hounslow</u> are <u>foreign-born</u>.

Topic 5 — The UK's Evolving Human Landscape

Dynamic UK Cities — Case Study

Migration Influences the Character of Different Parts of the City

Age Structure — there is now a high percentage of people aged 25-34 in inner city London and a lower proportion of people over 65. Most immigrants are of working age.

Ethnicity — ethnic diversity is higher in inner city areas, e.g. 52% of people are foreign born in Newham compared to 29% in Kingston upon Thames, but it's increasing rapidly in some suburbs, e.g. Bexley.

Population — population growth rates are increasing in inner city areas because of high immigration rates and because many migrants are of child-bearing age (so birth rates are higher).

Housing — the high rate of immigration is leading to overcrowding. Poorer immigrants often live in older terraces and 1960s-70s council tower blocks in the inner city, which are more affordable.

Services — in inner city areas where immigration rates are high, there is an increasing demand for services such as education and health care (e.g. for school places and maternity care). However, these areas are often amongst the poorest parts of the city, so it's difficult to provide what's needed.

Culture — London is very culturally diverse, with more than 200 languages spoken. Many immigrants choose to settle near people with the same ethnic background, giving the area a distinct ethnic character, e.g. Chinatown. Lots of food, music and goods from that culture can be found there.

There is Lots of Inequality in London

1) The Index of Multiple Deprivation (IMD) combines data on employment, health, education, crime, housing, services and the environment to give an overall figure for the quality of life in an area. Deprived areas have a low quality of life.

2) This map shows how the IMD varies across London. Deprivation is highest in the inner city and in parts of north London. East London is generally more deprived than west London.

Most deprived

Least deprived

3) Poorer people are limited in where they can live:
   - they can only afford poor quality housing, often in the inner city.
   - they may need to live close to work if they don't have a car or can't afford public transport.

   This can make it difficult for them to leave deprived areas — they become trapped in a cycle of poverty.

4) Deprivation affects people's access to jobs and services, widening the gap between the rich and poor:

Services — Rapid population growth and high turnover of people puts pressure on services, e.g. health and education. Funding services is also harder in deprived areas, where councils get less money from taxes and businesses.

Employment — There are fewer manufacturing jobs in the inner city — new industries locate on the outskirts, so it's harder for people to find suitable work. Average income in Kensington and Chelsea is more than £130 000 but less than £35 000 in Newham. More than 25% of London's population are living in poverty, due to unemployment or low wages.

Education — The best state schools, e.g. Holland Park, are very over-subscribed and difficult to get into. Wealthy parents are able to send their children to fee-paying schools, but many children from poorer families end up in under-performing state schools. This can lead to a cycle of poverty, e.g. where a lack of education leads a limited range of job opportunities, and lower incomes.

Health — Unhealthy lifestyles, e.g. drinking, smoking and poor diets, are more common in deprived areas — life expectancy is about 5 years lower in poorer areas of the city than in wealthier areas. Health care is free on the NHS but services are often overwhelmed and poorer people can't afford private health care.

Learning about inequality — quality, innit...

You're not done with this case study yet, not by a long way. But our gag team threatened mutiny if I didn't put one here.

Dynamic UK Cities — Case Study

London has seen both <u>decline</u> and <u>growth</u>. It's a bit like a seesaw really — some areas are <u>going down</u> while others are on the <u>way up</u>. Decline may be <u>depressing</u>, but (spoiler alert) things have been done to <u>help</u>...

Parts of the *Inner City* and *CBD Have Declined*

<u>De-industrialisation</u> (see p.36) and <u>depopulation</u> led to <u>decline</u> in the <u>central</u> areas of London.

1) The <u>decline</u> of the <u>docks</u> and <u>manufacturing</u> industries in London's <u>East End</u> led to mass <u>unemployment</u> — 20% of jobs were lost between 1966 and 1976 in the dockland areas.

2) <u>De-industrialisation</u> and <u>unemployment</u> in the second half of the 20th century led to many families <u>moving away</u> from the area. Further <u>depopulation</u> of the inner city was caused by <u>suburbanisation</u>, the building of <u>satellite towns</u>, e.g. Milton Keynes, and <u>slum clearance</u> (old terraces were demolished and replaced with high-rise flats, e.g. the Aylesbury estate, Southwark).

3) As people moved away, many buildings were left <u>derelict</u>. There was also a <u>decrease</u> in local <u>services</u>, e.g. shops, schools and health care facilities, as there weren't enough <u>people</u> or <u>money</u> to continue them.

4) <u>De-centralisation</u> (when shops and businesses <u>move out</u> of the CBD) caused further <u>decline</u>. Many shops struggled to pay the <u>high rents</u> in the city centre and moved to <u>less central</u> locations, e.g. Lewisham. New <u>high-tech</u> industries located in <u>business parks</u>, e.g. North London Business Park, on the <u>edge</u> of London where land is <u>cheaper</u> and there are better <u>transport links</u> and easier <u>access</u>.

5) The growth of <u>e-commerce</u> (online shopping) has recently put further <u>pressure</u> on <u>high street shops</u>. Some firms have <u>moved</u> to distribution centres on the <u>edge</u> of the city where they can distribute goods to online shoppers more easily. Others have been forced to <u>close down</u>.

Parts of the *Rural-Urban Fringe* and *Inner City have seen Economic Growth*

Financial and business services and TNC investment

- The <u>growth</u> of <u>finance</u> and <u>business</u> services is <u>revitalising</u> the <u>CBD</u>. The City of London has emerged as a global centre for <u>banking</u>, <u>insurance</u> and <u>law</u> companies, which benefit from being <u>close</u> to each other.

- Many <u>TNCs</u> locate their <u>sales</u> and <u>marketing</u> departments and <u>headquarters</u> in London because of its <u>importance</u> as a <u>financial centre</u>. TNCs based in London include HSBC, Shell, GlaxoSmithKline and Virgin Atlantic Airways. These in turn attract <u>further investment</u> as they help to cement London's <u>identity</u> as a <u>global</u> city.

Gentrification and studentification

- Some areas, e.g. Islington, have been <u>gentrified</u> — <u>wealthier</u> people move in to <u>run down areas</u> and <u>regenerate</u> them by <u>improving</u> their houses. New <u>businesses</u> are springing up in gentrified areas to cater for the wealthier newcomers.

- Other areas, e.g. Camden, have been <u>studentified</u> — a high student population has led to <u>thriving services</u> and <u>entertainment venues</u>, generating <u>new jobs</u> and <u>wealth</u> for the area.

Urban sprawl

- Most <u>growth</u> has taken place in the <u>rural-urban fringe</u>. Large <u>shopping centres</u>, e.g. Bluewater, have been built on the <u>edge</u> of the city where land is <u>cheaper</u> and there is <u>less congestion</u> and <u>more parking space</u>.

- <u>Industrial</u> areas, e.g. Crossways Business Park by the QEII bridge, have also been developed on the <u>outskirts</u> of London.

- The availability of <u>jobs</u> has <u>attracted</u> many people to <u>live</u> there.

Leisure and culture

- London hosted the <u>Olympic games</u> in 2012, with most <u>investment</u> taking place in London's <u>East End</u>. This was one of London's <u>most deprived</u> areas but the area now has <u>new transport links</u> and the <u>athletes' village</u> has been developed into a modern <u>housing estate</u>. The sports stadiums are <u>open</u> for <u>community use</u> as well as <u>world sporting events</u>. New <u>jobs</u> have been <u>created</u> and lots of people are <u>moving to</u> the area.

Topic 5 — The UK's Evolving Human Landscape

Dynamic UK Cities — Case Study

London Docklands *was Regenerated and Rebranded*

1) Rebranding is about improving a place's image so that people will want to go there. It usually involves regeneration — making actual improvements to an area, e.g. new buildings and services. It also involves using marketing to improve the reputation of a place.

2) The London Docklands area was regenerated and rebranded in 1980s-90s as a centre for finance and business, with new office space in Canary Wharf as well as shopping centres and housing developments.

Positive Impacts	Negative Impacts
• Transport links were improved — the new Docklands Light Railway and Jubilee Line extension carry thousands of passengers every day. • The environment has been improved and quality green space created, e.g. the Thames Barrier Park. • Businesses have been attracted back, creating jobs — Canary Wharf is now home to many media organisations and global banks, e.g. Barclays. • The population has increased and people have more money to spend in local shops and cafés, so many businesses have thrived.	• Many local people were forced out. 36% of the local population were unskilled workers and most lived in council housing, so couldn't afford the new houses and weren't suited to the new jobs. • Some traditional businesses, e.g. pubs, and old community centres closed, and were replaced with services for the wealthier newcomers, e.g. expensive restaurants and artisan bakeries. • Existing communities were destroyed — local people were moved to new towns and estates on the edge of London, e.g. Chigwell in Essex.

Strategies are Needed to Make Urban Living More Sustainable

Sustainable strategies are about improving things for people today without negatively affecting future generations. They need to consider the environment, the economy and people's social well-being.

Big cities need so many resources that it's unlikely they'd ever be truly sustainable. But things can be done to make a city (and the way people live there) more sustainable.

Employment — increasing employment opportunities reduces poverty and improves economic sustainability. The London Living Wage encourages businesses to pay a fair wage that takes into account the high cost of living in London. Skills programmes, e.g. En-route to Sustainable Employment, mean that people can progress to higher paid jobs.

Recycling — more recycling means fewer resources are used, e.g. metal cans can be melted down and used to make more cans. Waste recycling schemes include the collection of household recycling boxes and recycling facilities for larger items, e.g. fridges. However, only 33% of rubbish in London is recycled — the lowest level in the whole of England.

Green spaces — green spaces have environmental benefits and make sure cities remain places where people want to live and work. London is 40% public green space with lots of parks in the city centre, e.g. Hyde Park, and larger open areas on the outskirts, e.g. Hampstead Heath.

Transport — noise and air pollution can be reduced, for example:
• congestion charging discourages drivers from entering the city centre at peak times.
• self-service bicycles and bike lanes make it easier and safer for people to cycle instead of drive.
• electric buses and zero-emission taxis are helping to reduce emissions from public transport.

Housing — the BedZED development is a large-scale sustainable community in south London. The houses have thick insulation, solar heating systems and water-saving appliances, all of which help to reduce energy consumption and conserve resources. The houses are built from locally-sourced materials, giving them a smaller carbon footprint, and many properties on the development have subsidised rents (making them more affordable).

Rebranding — burning yourself on the iron... again...

You need to know about decline and growth in your chosen city as well as how life there can be improved. If that sounds dull, it might help to rebrand your revision as 'super fun time'. Yeah OK, that's probably not gonna work.

Dynamic UK Cities — Case Study

Like two hippos on a trampoline, London and its surrounding area are influences on each other...

London and its Surrounding Rural Areas are Interdependent

London is connected to the rural areas around it — they rely on each other for goods and services.

Labour

1) Many people commute into London from the surrounding rural areas to work, e.g. around 40% of people in Sevenoaks District (north west Kent) work in London.

2) Students and young professionals move into London — they often want to live close to their work in areas with good entertainment facilities, e.g. Camden has lots of pubs, clubs and restaurants.

Goods

1) London relies on the surrounding rural areas for food — many farmers sell their produce to supermarkets and wholesalers who transport it into the city.

2) Many rural people travel into London to do some of their shopping — there is a greater selection of high street and luxury shops, e.g. Harrods™.

Services

1) London has excellent hospitals and private schools as well as specialist services, e.g. Great Ormond Street children's hospital — people travel from the surrounding rural areas to use them.

2) Many Londoners travel into the countryside for leisure activities, e.g. to play golf, walk in country parks, go horse riding etc.

The interdependence of urban and rural areas has costs and benefits:

Benefits	Costs
• Some businesses in rural areas (e.g. pubs with restaurants) have seen an increase in business as newer residents have higher disposable incomes. • Some farmers have made money from selling land or buildings or diversifying their business (see next page). • Some existing houses have been improved, e.g. traditional Kentish oast houses have been renovated and turned into houses. • There is less pressure on housing in London.	• Some villages, e.g. Ivy Hatch, may become commuter settlements — where people live in rural areas but work in London. This leaves villages empty during the day, so some shops and services may close because of reduced demand (see next page). • New housing estates have been built on open countryside, e.g. at Dunton Green, which has affected wildlife habitats. • Lots of commuters drive to Sevenoaks to catch the train into London — the additional traffic is increasing air pollution and congestion and causing parking issues.

Interdependence is Causing Changes to Rural Areas

1) Sevenoaks District is a largely rural area to the south east of London. Lots of people are moving there from London for a better quality of life (counter-urbanisation — see page 36). This puts pressure on housing, pushing up prices — house prices have risen by over 250% since 1995 due to the high demand.

Kentish oast house

2) The population of Sevenoaks District is changing. Lots of people retire there because it is a peaceful, pleasant environment. At the same time, younger people are leaving, and many move into London for work. Sevenoaks District has a much higher than average proportion of people aged over 50, and a much lower than average proportion of people in their twenties.

3) London has a huge population of people with more leisure time and higher incomes than in the past. This creates demand for leisure and recreation services, e.g. tea rooms, golf courses and riding schools in the surrounding rural areas.

Dynamic UK Cities — Case Study

There are Lots of Challenges for Rural Areas Around London

Quality of life can be measured using the Index of Multiple Deprivation (IMD — see page 78). Rural areas usually have lower IMD scores (higher quality of life) because people are generally wealthier and more people are retired (so aren't looking for work). However, there are challenges is some areas:

Employment

1) Employment deprivation is concentrated in a few small pockets, e.g. Swanley and Merstham.

2) Increased use of technology in agriculture and increasing farm sizes has decreased the number of workers needed in rural areas, e.g. Kent now has fewer agricultural workers and manufacturing has declined by more than 30% since 1998. Finding alternative employment can be a challenge.

Housing

Sevenoaks District is among the 30% most deprived areas for housing affordability. House prices in the Sevenoaks area are much higher than the UK average. This creates a challenge in providing affordable housing for young people, whose incomes are often lower.

Health Care and Education

1) Ageing populations require more health care and special facilities, e.g. nursing homes.

2) Some GP surgeries in smaller communities are threatened by closure. West Kingsdown surgery nearly closed in 2016.

3) Schools in some villages are closing due to declining numbers of pupils, e.g. there is now no secondary school in Edenbridge.

4) This creates challenges:
   - Many elderly people in rural areas don't own a car so they can struggle to get to shops and health care facilities.
   - Young people may have to travel long distances to get to school and for leisure activities.

Rural Diversification Creates Economic Opportunities

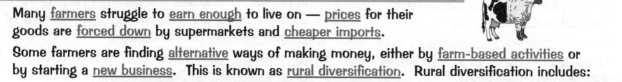

Mo-aa. Ba-oo.

1) Many farmers struggle to earn enough to live on — prices for their goods are forced down by supermarkets and cheaper imports.

2) Some farmers are finding alternative ways of making money, either by farm-based activities or by starting a new business. This is known as rural diversification. Rural diversification includes:

	Example	Environmental impacts
Farm shops	Stanhill Farm in Wilmington, Kent has opened a farm shop selling produce from the farm and the local area.	Land can continue to be farmed. More varieties of crop are grown using more environmentally-friendly methods than monoculture (growing large areas of one crop for supermarkets).
Accommodation	Tanner Farm Park in Kent has turned some land into a large touring caravan and camping park.	Large caravan parks can be unsightly. There is more pressure on the natural environment from the large numbers of visitors — through increased use of water and energy and the amount of waste generated.
Leisure activities	The Hop Farm in Kent has an animal petting area, children's rides and places to eat.	Land is built on to create car parks, visitor facilities etc. Traffic increases in the area, leading to air pollution.

3) Tourism can also create new economic opportunities in rural areas. For example, Leeds Castle (in Kent) is a historic building that has developed various attractions (e.g. a maze and golf course) and events to encourage more people to visit. However, this can mean that new tourist facilities are built on greenfield land and lead to an increase in traffic congestion.

Rural challenges — the coconut shy and welly wanging...

And there you have it, that's the last of this enormous case study. Have a go at this question to celebrate.

1) Explain two challenges faced by rural areas surrounding a major city in the UK. [4]

EXAM QUESTION

Revision Summary

Phew, who knew there was so much to know about the UK's human landscape... you'd think it'd be enough just to look out the window or wander down your local high street, but unfortunately it's all a bit more complicated than that. There's a lot to get your head round in this section, so make sure you're clear on the basics by working your way through these questions — try to do them without looking back at the pages (unless you get really stuck, in which case I'll allow you a quick peek).

UK Human Landscape (p.72-73) ☑

1) Which areas of the UK have a high population density?
2) Describe the main economic activities in rural areas.
3) Describe the difference in age structure between urban cores and rural areas.
4) What is an enterprise zone?
5) Give two ways that transport infrastructure can reduce differences in wealth in urban and rural areas.
6) Give one example of regional development in the UK.

UK Links with the Wider World (p.74-76) ☑

7) Name one of the main countries that people from the UK emigrate to.
8) 'The UK has positive net migration.' What does this mean?
9) Give two ways that national migration affects the distribution of population in the UK.
10) How does international migration affect the age structure of the UK?
11) Give two examples of UK immigration policy.
12) How has the proportion of people employed in secondary industries in the UK changed since 1960?
13) Describe two other changes to the employment structure of the UK over the last 50 years.
14) Outline the differences in economic structure in two contrasting regions of the UK.
15) What is foreign direct investment (FDI)?
16) Describe how globalisation is increasing FDI in the UK.

Dynamic UK Cities — Case Study (p.77-82) ☑

For a major city in the UK that you have studied:

17) How is the city connected to the country it is located in?
18) Describe the land use in the inner city.
19) Describe the variations in environmental quality in the city.
20) How has migration affected the ethnicity in different parts of the city?
21) Give one reason why there is inequality in health.
22) Outline two reasons for decline in the inner city and/or CBD.
23) Give two parts of the city that have experienced economic growth.
24) What is gentrification?
25) What is rebranding?
26) Give two positive and two negative effects that rebranding has had on people.
27) Outline two strategies that are improving sustainability in the city.
28) Give three examples of interdependence between the city and the surrounding rural areas.
29) Give two benefits that interdependence has.
30) Explain why a rural area has experienced pressure on housing due to its links with the city.
31) Give two examples of rural diversification.
32) Give two environmental impacts from tourism projects in rural areas.

Fieldwork

Ah, <u>fieldwork</u>. Time to venture into the <u>outside world</u> armed only with a <u>clipboard</u> and a <u>geographical hat</u>*...

*Geographical hat not always supplied.

You have to Write About Two Fieldwork Investigations in the Exam

1) Fieldwork is <u>assessed</u> in the third part (<u>Part C</u>) of <u>Paper 2</u>. There's no <u>coursework</u>, but in the exam you need to be able to <u>write about</u> fieldwork that you have done.

2) You need to have done at least one <u>physical</u> and one <u>human</u> fieldwork investigation. The <u>physical</u> one will be on <u>either</u> 'Coastal Change and Conflict' <u>or</u> 'River Processes and Pressures'. The <u>human</u> one will be on <u>either</u> 'Dynamic Urban Areas' <u>or</u> 'Changing Rural Areas'. You'll be asked about <u>both</u> your physical and human fieldwork investigation in the exam.

(annotation) Your teacher will tell you which topics you're doing.

3) The fieldwork part of the exam has <u>two</u> types of questions:

- You'll have to answer questions about <u>your investigation</u> — you might be asked about your <u>question</u> or <u>hypothesis</u>, <u>methods</u>, what <u>data</u> you <u>collected</u> and <u>why</u>, how you <u>presented</u> and <u>analysed</u> it, how you could <u>extend your research</u> and so on.

- You'll also be asked about fieldwork techniques in <u>unfamiliar</u> situations. You might have to answer questions about <u>techniques</u> for <u>collecting data</u>, how to <u>present data</u> you've been given or how <u>useful</u> the <u>different techniques</u> are.

For Each of your Investigations, You'll Need to Know...

① Why You Chose Your Question

You may need to explain <u>why</u> the question or hypothesis you chose is <u>suitable</u> for a <u>geographical investigation</u>.

If you study <u>different sites</u> in the <u>study area</u>, make sure you know <u>why</u> they were <u>suitable</u> for the study. This could include that they gave a <u>good overall representation</u> of the study area or that they could be <u>compared</u> (if your investigation was a <u>comparison</u>).

② How and Why You Collected Data

You may need to <u>describe</u> and <u>justify</u> what data <u>you collected</u>. This includes whether it was <u>primary data</u> (data that you collected <u>yourself</u>) or <u>secondary</u> data (data that <u>someone else</u> collected and you <u>used</u>), <u>why</u> you collected or used it, <u>how</u> you <u>measured</u> it and <u>how</u> you <u>recorded</u> it.

③ How You Processed and Presented Your Data

The way you <u>presented</u> your data, and <u>why</u> you <u>chose</u> that option, could come up. You may need to <u>describe what you did</u>, <u>explain</u> why it was <u>appropriate</u>, and discuss <u>how</u> you <u>adapted</u> your presentation method for <u>your data</u>. You might also be asked for a <u>different way</u> you <u>could</u> have presented your data.

(annotation) There's more on analysing, concluding and evaluating on p. 86.

④ What Your Data Showed

You'll need to know:
- A <u>description</u> of your data.
- How you <u>analysed</u> your data.
- An <u>explanation</u> of your data.

This might include <u>links</u> between your <u>data sets</u>, the <u>statistical techniques</u> you used, and any <u>anomalies</u> (odd results) in the data that you spotted.

(annotation) There's more on statistical techniques on pages 127-128.

⑤ The Conclusions You Reached

This means you may need to <u>explain how</u> your data provides <u>evidence</u> to <u>answer</u> the <u>question</u> or <u>support</u> the <u>hypothesis</u> you set at the <u>beginning</u>.

⑥ What Went Well, What Could Have Gone Better

You might be asked to <u>evaluate</u> your fieldwork:
- Were there <u>problems</u> in your <u>data collection methods</u>?
- Were there <u>limitations</u> in your <u>data</u>?
- What <u>other data</u> would it have been <u>useful</u> to have?
- How <u>reliable</u> are your <u>conclusions</u>?

No, you can't get a tractor to do your field work for you...

Don't worry if your fieldwork doesn't quite go to plan. It's more important that you can write about it and say why things went wrong. It does help if you at least attempt to make it work though — another read through won't go amiss.

Completing Fieldwork

The fun part of fieldwork is going out and doing it — but before you grab your anorak and rush out the door, there are a couple of important things you need to keep in mind...

You Need to Know How You're Going to Collect Your Data

1) There are rules set by the exam board about the type of data that you have to collect in your fieldwork.

2) You might need to use specialist techniques to collect your data. For example, you may need to measure the gradient of a beach using a clinometer or pantometer, or the velocity of a river by timing how long it takes for a float to travel between two points.

3) To get the best results, you'll need to know how to carry out these techniques accurately and consistently. In the exam, you could get asked to explain why you chose the method you used.

There are Different Types of Data that You Can Collect

1) There are two types of data that you can use in your investigations — primary and secondary (see p.84).

2) Sometimes, you'll need to use sampling techniques when you're collecting primary data:

- Random sampling is where samples are chosen at random, e.g. picking pebbles on a beach.
- Systematic sampling is where samples are chosen at regular intervals — this is useful in places where what you want to investigate changes frequently, e.g. the number of pedestrians in an area.
- Stratified sampling is where you choose samples from different groups to get a good overall representation. This type of sampling is useful if you need to collect people's perceptions, e.g. of pollution in their area, and need to ask people of different ages.

3) The data you collect can be quantitative or qualitative:

- Quantitative data is numerical data, e.g. the number of pedestrians in an urban area. It's based on things you can measure.
- Qualitative data is based on information that can't be measured, e.g. opinions. For your fieldwork investigations, it's likely that you'll need to collect data on people's views, e.g. what residents think about quality of life in their area.

4) You need to use at least two secondary data sources for each of your investigations. One of these must be a source from a list decided by the exam board. You can choose any other sources you want to use yourself. The source that you have to use depends on which investigation you're carrying out:

- **GEOLOGY MAPS** — for Coastal Changes and Conflicts
- **FLOOD RISK MAPS** — for River Processes and Pressures
- **CENSUS DATA** — for Dynamic Urban Areas and Changing Rural Areas

You Need to Think About Health and Safety

1) You'll need to think about safety when choosing the sites you're going to study.

2) You need to know how to carry out a risk assessment for the sites you choose to study:

- Identify the specific risks at the site,
- Give them a risk rating up to 10 (where 10 is the most severe risk),
- Write down how they can be managed.

E.g.

Risk Identified	Risk Rating	How can it be managed?
Risk of accidents whilst surveying traffic passing through junction.	7	Wear a fluorescent vest and choose a safe place to stand away from the traffic flow.

Pantometers — useful for measuring a dog's stick-chasing field work...

'But what do I do with all the data I've collected?', I hear you cry — just wander over to the next page and I'll explain...

Analysing, Concluding and Evaluating

Analysis, conclusions and evaluations can be pretty tricky, so here's a load of stuff to help you with them.

You need to Describe and Explain what the Data Shows

Analysing and interpreting data is about:

1) Describing what the data shows — you need to describe any patterns and correlations (see pages 123-126) and look for any anomalies. Make sure you use specific points from the data and reference what graph, table etc. you're talking about. You might also need to make comparisons between different sets of data. Statistical techniques (see pages 127-128) help make the data more manageable, so it's easier to spot patterns and make comparisons.

2) Explaining what the data shows — you need to explain why there are patterns and why different data sets are linked together. Use your geographical knowledge to help you explain the results and remember to use geographical terms.

Conclusions are a Summary of the Results

A conclusion is a summary of what you found out in relation to the original question. It should include:

1) A summary of what your results show.

2) An answer for the question you are investigating, and an explanation for why that is the answer.

3) An explanation of how your conclusion fits into the wider geographical world — think about how your conclusion and results could be used by other people or in further investigations.

> Be careful when drawing conclusions. Some results show a link or correlation, but that doesn't mean that one thing causes the other.

Evaluations Identify Problems in the Investigation

Evaluation is all about self assessment — looking back at how good or bad your study (or the data you are given in the exam) was. You need to be able to:

1) Identify any problems with the methods used and suggest how they could be improved. Think about things like the size of the data sets, if any bias (unfairness) slipped in and if other methods would have been more appropriate or more effective.

2) Describe how accurate the results are and link this to the methods used — say whether any errors in the methods affected the results.

3) Comment on the validity of your conclusion. You need to talk about how problems with the methods and the accuracy of the results affect the validity of the conclusion. Problems with methods lead to less reliable and accurate results, which affects the validity of the conclusion.

> Accurate results are as near as possible to the true answer — they have few errors.
>
> Reliable means that data can be reproduced.
>
> Valid means that the data answers the original question and is reliable.

For example:

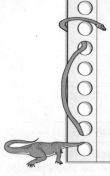

I concluded that the river flowed faster further downstream. However, one problem with my data collection method was that it was difficult to put the float in at exactly the same point each time. This reduced the accuracy of my measurements. To make my investigation more accurate, I could have placed a tape measure across the river to mark the exact point of entry. Another problem was that I only took two readings at each site and I only used one upstream site and one downstream site. To make my data more reliable I could have taken more readings at each site, and used a larger number of sites both upstream and downstream. These improvements would have produced a more valid conclusion.

Evaluation — could do with a hair cut, otherwise fine...

Bit of a weird one this — you need to remember how you analysed your data, the conclusion of your investigations and the evaluation for your studies. So make sure you have some points ready to go before you hit the exam. But you also need to be able to analyse, conclude and evaluate based on someone else's data that you might be given in the exam.

Global Ecosystems

Time for a whistle-stop tour of the <u>world's ecosystems</u>. All aboard...

You Need to Know the Global Distribution of Major Biomes

1) <u>Biomes</u> are large-scale, <u>global ecosystems</u> with distinctive vegetation.

2) An <u>ecosystem</u> includes all the <u>living</u> and <u>non-living</u> things in an area.

3) The <u>climate</u> in an area determines what <u>type of biome</u> forms. So different parts of the world have <u>different biomes</u> because they have <u>different climates</u>.

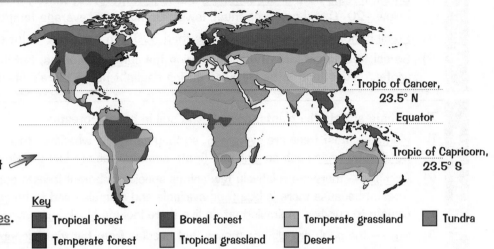

Tropic of Cancer, 23.5° N

Equator

Tropic of Capricorn, 23.5° S

Key
■ Tropical forest   ■ Boreal forest   ■ Temperate grassland   ■ Tundra
■ Temperate forest   ■ Tropical grassland   ■ Desert

Tropical Forests Have a Hot, Wet Climate

See pages 95-97 for more on tropical forests.

Climate

1) The climate is <u>the same all year</u> round — there are <u>no definite seasons</u>.

2) It's <u>hot</u> (the temperature is generally between <u>20-28 °C</u> and only varies by a few degrees over the year). This is because near the <u>equator</u> the <u>Sun</u> is <u>overhead</u> all year round.

3) Because tropical forests are found near the <u>equator</u>, <u>day length</u> is the same (about <u>12 hours</u>) <u>all year</u> round. This means the forests get plenty of <u>sunshine</u> all year.

4) <u>Rainfall</u> is very <u>high</u>, around 2000 mm per year. It <u>rains every day</u>, usually in the <u>afternoon</u>.

Characteristics

The climate affects the <u>plants</u>, <u>animals</u> and <u>soil</u> in tropical forests:

Evergreen plants don't drop their leaves in a particular season.

1) <u>Plants</u> — most trees are <u>evergreen</u> to take advantage of the <u>continual growing season</u>. Plants grow <u>quickly</u> and are <u>adapted</u> to take in <u>maximum light</u>.

2) <u>Animals</u> — the <u>dense</u> vegetation provides lots of <u>food</u> and different <u>habitats</u>, so there are lots of <u>different species</u> of animal, for example <u>gorillas</u>, <u>jaguars</u>, <u>anacondas</u>, <u>tree frogs</u> and <u>sloths</u>. There are loads of species of <u>insects</u> and <u>birds</u>.

3) <u>Soil</u> — plants <u>grow quickly</u> and shed leaves all year round. These <u>decompose</u> quickly, so there's a constant supply of <u>nutrients</u> in the <u>soil</u>, and these nutrients are <u>cycled quickly</u>.

Temperate Forests Have a Mild, Wet Climate

Climate

1) Temperate forests have <u>four</u> distinct <u>seasons</u>. The <u>summers</u> are <u>warm</u> and the <u>winters</u> are <u>cool</u>.

2) <u>Rainfall</u> is very <u>high</u> (up to 1500 mm per year) and there's <u>rain all year</u> round.

3) Days are <u>shorter</u> in winter and <u>longer</u> in summer — the <u>hours</u> of <u>sunshine vary</u> through the year.

Characteristics

The climate affects the <u>plants</u>, <u>animals</u> and <u>soil</u> in temperate forests:

1) <u>Plants</u> — the <u>mild, wet climate</u> supports <u>fewer</u> plant species than tropical forests, but <u>more</u> than boreal forests (see next page). Forests are often made up of <u>broad-leaved trees</u> that <u>drop their leaves</u> in autumn (e.g. oak), <u>shrubs</u> (e.g. brambles) and <u>undergrowth</u> (e.g. ferns).

2) <u>Animals</u> — the <u>mild</u> climate and range of <u>plants</u> provides <u>food</u> and <u>habitats</u> for <u>mammals</u> (e.g. foxes, squirrels), <u>birds</u> (e.g. woodpeckers, cuckoos) and <u>insects</u> (e.g. beetles, moths).

3) <u>Soil</u> — plants lose their leaves in <u>autumn</u>, and the leaf litter decomposes quite <u>quickly</u> in the <u>moist, mild</u> climate. This means that <u>soils</u> are relatively <u>thick</u> and <u>nutrient-rich</u>.

Global Ecosystems

Boreal Forests *Have a Cold, Dry Climate*

The boreal biome is also called the taiga.

Climate

1) <u>Boreal forests</u> have <u>short summers</u> and <u>long winters</u>. In winter, average <u>temperatures</u> are below <u>−20 °C</u> and can drop much lower. In summer, average temperatures are about <u>10 °C</u>.

2) <u>Precipitation</u> is <u>low</u> — generally <u>less than 500 mm</u> per year. A lot of this falls as <u>snow</u>.

3) Boreal forests get lots of <u>daylight</u> during the <u>summer</u> months, but little or none during the <u>winter</u>. Skies tend to be <u>clear</u>, so during daylight hours there's plenty of <u>sunshine</u>.

See pages 101-102 for more about the characteristics of the taiga.

Characteristics

The climate affects the <u>plants</u>, <u>animals</u> and <u>soil</u> in boreal forests:

1) <u>Plants</u> — most trees are <u>evergreen</u>, so they can grow whenever there's <u>enough light</u>. <u>Coniferous trees</u> such as <u>pine</u> and <u>fir</u> are common, as are low-growing <u>mosses</u> and <u>lichen</u>.

2) <u>Animals</u> — there are relatively <u>few</u> animal species in boreal forests compared to e.g. tropical forests, because there is <u>less food</u> available and animals need to be <u>adapted</u> to the cold climate to survive. Animals that do live there include <u>black bears</u>, <u>wolves</u>, <u>elk</u> and <u>eagles</u>.

3) <u>Soil</u> — the <u>cool</u>, <u>dry climate</u> means that needles from the trees <u>decompose slowly</u>, so soils are quite <u>thin</u>, <u>nutrient-poor</u> and <u>acidic</u>. In some areas the ground is <u>frozen</u> for most of the year.

There are *Two Types* of Grassland

Climate

1) <u>Tropical</u> grasslands have quite <u>low rainfall</u> (800-900 mm per year) and <u>distinct wet and dry seasons</u>. Temperatures are <u>highest</u> (around 35 °C) just <u>before</u> the wet season and <u>lowest</u> (about 15 °C) just <u>after</u> it. They are found around the <u>equator</u>, so they get <u>lots of sunshine</u> all year round.

2) <u>Temperate</u> grasslands have <u>hot summers</u> (up to 40 °C) and <u>cold winters</u> (down to −40 °C). They receive <u>250-500 mm</u> precipitation each year, mostly in the <u>late spring</u> and <u>early summer</u>. Because they're <u>further</u> from the <u>equator</u>, the amount of <u>light</u> they receive <u>varies</u> through the year.

Characteristics

Rainfall is <u>too low</u> to support many <u>trees</u> in <u>tropical</u> or <u>temperate</u> grasslands, which affects <u>animals</u> and <u>soil</u>:

1) <u>Tropical</u> grasslands consist mostly of <u>grass</u>, <u>scrub</u> and <u>small plants</u>, with a few <u>scattered trees</u>, e.g. acacia. They are home to lots of <u>insects</u>, including <u>grasshoppers</u>, <u>beetles</u> and <u>termites</u>. Larger animals include <u>lions</u>, <u>elephants</u>, <u>giraffes</u>, <u>zebras</u> and <u>antelope</u>. Grass <u>dies back</u> during the <u>dry</u> season, forming a <u>thin</u>, <u>nutrient-rich soil</u>, but nutrients are <u>washed out</u> of the soil during the wet season.

2) <u>Temperate</u> grasslands are also dominated by <u>grasses</u> and <u>small plants</u>, and have very <u>few trees</u>. They are home to <u>fewer</u> animal species than tropical grasslands — mammals include <u>bison</u> and <u>wild horses</u>, and rodents such as <u>mole rats</u>. <u>High temperatures</u> in summer mean that decomposition is <u>fast</u>, so soils are relatively <u>thick</u> and <u>nutrient-rich</u>.

Deserts *Have Low Rainfall*

Not every desert is hot — some are mild (e.g. the Atacama desert) and some are cold (e.g. the Gobi desert).

Climate

1) Rainfall is very low — <u>less than 250 mm</u> per year. It might only rain <u>once</u> every two or three years.

2) <u>Hot</u> desert <u>temperatures</u> range from very <u>hot</u> in the <u>day</u> (e.g. 45 °C) to <u>cold</u> at <u>night</u> (below 0 °C).

3) Hot deserts get more <u>daylight</u> during the <u>summer</u> than the <u>winter</u>. Because there is little <u>cloud cover</u>, they get lots of hours of <u>sunshine</u> every day.

Characteristics

The climate affects the <u>plants</u>, <u>animals</u> and <u>soil</u> in deserts:

1) <u>Plants</u> — plant growth is <u>sparse</u> due to <u>lack of rainfall</u>. A few plants do grow, e.g. <u>cacti</u>, <u>thornbushes</u>.

2) <u>Animals</u> — relatively <u>few</u> animal species live in hot deserts — those that do are <u>adapted</u> to cope with the harsh climate. Animals that live there include <u>lizards</u>, <u>snakes</u>, <u>insects</u> and <u>scorpions</u>.

3) <u>Soil</u> — the <u>sparse</u> vegetation means that there is <u>little leaf litter</u>, and the <u>dry</u> climate means that organic matter is <u>slow</u> to <u>decompose</u>. As a result, soils are mostly <u>thin</u> and <u>nutrient-poor</u>.

Global Ecosystems

Tundra *Has a Cold, Dry Climate*

Climate

1) Temperatures are low — around 5-10 °C during the summer and lower than −30 °C in the winter.
2) Precipitation is also very low — less than 250 mm per year. Most of this falls as snow.
3) Tundra is found at high latitudes, so it gets near-continuous daylight in the summer and little or no daylight in the winter. There is more cloud cover in the summer.

Characteristics

The climate affects the plants, animals and soil in tundra regions:

1) Plants — the cold climate and lack of light in winter make it hard for plants to grow, and there are hardly any trees. Vegetation includes mosses, grasses and low shrubs.
2) Animals — the cold climate and lack of vegetation means that relatively few animal species live in the tundra. Those that do include Arctic hares, Arctic foxes, mosquitoes and lots of birds. Some animals migrate south for the winter.
3) Soil — the sparse vegetation produces little leaf litter, and the cold, dry climate means that organic matter decomposes slowly, so soil is thin and nutrient-poor. There is a layer of permafrost (permanently frozen ground) below the soil surface, which can stop water from draining away.

Biome Distribution *is Affected by Local Factors*

Climate (i.e. temperature, rainfall and sunshine hours) is the main factor influencing biome distribution, but there are other factors that alter distribution at a smaller scale:

Altitude is the height above sea level.

1) Altitude — higher altitudes are colder, so fewer plants grow there, which also limits the number of animal species. This means there's not much organic matter, so soils are thin or non-existent.
2) Rock type — some rock types are easily weathered (see p.46) to form soils, and different rock types contain different minerals. This affects how nutrient-rich the soil is. Some rocks are also permeable (water can flow through them) and others are impermeable (they don't let water through).
3) Soil type — more nutrient-rich soils can support more plants. The acidity and drainage of soils also varies, affecting the plants that can grow. E.g. peat soils are very acidic, so only acid-tolerant plants such as conifers can grow, and clay soils are sticky, so water can't flow through very easily.
4) Drainage — if drainage is poor, soil gets waterlogged and only plants adapted to wet conditions can grow there. Very wet areas may be home to aquatic species of plants and animals.

The Biotic and *Abiotic Components of Biomes Interact*

The biotic components are the living parts of a biome — e.g. plants (flora) and animals (fauna).
The abiotic components are the non-living parts — e.g. soil, water, rock, atmosphere.
The different components interact with each other, for example:

1) Water availability affects the plants that can grow — e.g. if the soil is very dry, only desert plants such as cacti will be able to survive. Plants take in water from the soil and release it into the atmosphere, providing moisture for further rainfall.
2) The type and density of vegetation that grows affects the type of soil that forms, and the type of soil that forms affects the type of vegetation that can grow — e.g. dense vegetation cover and lots of leaf fall means that lots of nutrients will be added to the soil, which can then support more plant growth.
3) Some organisms cause biological weathering. This is when rocks in the ground are broken up into smaller pieces by living things, e.g. tree roots breaking rocks up as they grow.

Global echo-systems — they go round and round and round...

Don't be fooled into thinking that just because you've read the pages you know it all — you need to learn where these biomes are found, what they're like and the factors that affect their distribution. Phew, no time to waste...

Humans and the Biosphere

Resources are just all the things we use — and it turns out we use an <u>awful lot of them</u> and get pretty much everything from the <u>biosphere</u>. I know, I thought everything came from Santa too...

The Biosphere *Provides Lots of Resources*

1) The <u>biosphere</u> includes <u>all</u> parts of the <u>Earth</u> that are <u>occupied</u> by <u>living organisms</u> — it's the <u>plants</u>, <u>animals</u>, <u>bacteria</u> and <u>fungi</u> as well as the <u>soil</u> and <u>water</u> that they live in.

2) <u>Living organisms</u> provide loads of <u>goods</u> that people need to <u>survive</u>. These are used by <u>indigenous</u> people (people who are <u>native</u> to an area) and others who live <u>locally</u>. For example:

> **FOOD** — Many indigenous people get all of their <u>food directly</u> from <u>plants</u> and <u>animals</u>. Some <u>forage</u> for food, picking wild <u>fruit</u>, <u>vegetables</u> and <u>nuts</u>, hunting and trapping <u>animals</u> and catching <u>fish</u>. Others <u>grow</u> food for their <u>own use</u>, e.g. growing <u>cereals</u>, <u>fruit</u> and <u>vegetables</u> and raising <u>livestock</u>.

> **MEDICINE** — Lots of plants have <u>medicinal</u> properties and are used to <u>cure illnesses</u> and keep people <u>healthy</u>. Plant species in <u>tropical forests</u> have been used to create over <u>7000 drugs</u>, e.g. quinine from the cinchona tree is used to treat malaria.

> **BUILDING MATERIALS** — <u>Trees</u> and other <u>plants</u> are often used as <u>building materials</u>, e.g. <u>pine</u> from <u>taiga forests</u> (see p.103) is used to make <u>furniture</u> and to build <u>houses</u>. <u>Sap</u> from trees can be used as <u>glue</u> or to make buildings <u>waterproof</u>, <u>reeds</u> and <u>straw</u> can be used for <u>roofs</u> and <u>plant fibres</u> can be used to make <u>rope</u>.

> **FUEL** — Indigenous people rely on <u>plants</u> and <u>animals</u> for <u>fuel</u> for <u>cooking</u> and <u>keeping warm</u>. <u>Wood</u>, <u>moss</u>, <u>dried grass</u> and <u>dried animal dung</u> is burnt as fuel. Some indigenous people in areas with little vegetation (like the <u>tundra</u>), use <u>animal fat</u>, e.g. blubber from seals, as fuel for <u>oil lamps</u>.

Humans *Exploit the Biosphere*

The biosphere is also <u>exploited</u> by companies for <u>commercial gain</u> (to make a <u>profit</u>). <u>Increasing demand</u> and <u>improving technology</u> is increasing the <u>scale</u> of commercial exploitation. For example:

> **Energy** — Demand for energy is <u>increasing</u> as the world <u>population increases</u> and people have more <u>electronic devices</u>, e.g. laptops and phones (see p.92). Large areas of <u>forest</u> are <u>cut down</u> to <u>clear land</u> for the growing of <u>crops</u> that can be used to make <u>biofuels</u>, or to make way for <u>coal mines</u> or <u>power stations</u>. Some areas of <u>tropical forest</u> have been <u>flooded</u> by the building of <u>hydroelectric dams</u>. Drilling for <u>oil</u> and <u>gas</u> in the <u>tundra</u> is damaging the biosphere because pipelines are <u>melting</u> the <u>permafrost</u>.

> **Water** — Demand for water is also <u>increasing</u> because of increases in global <u>population</u> — people use water for <u>washing</u>, <u>irrigating farmland</u> etc. Water resources, e.g. <u>lakes</u>, <u>rivers</u> and <u>aquifers</u> (underground water stores), can be <u>over-exploited</u> — this is happening in <u>arid areas</u> like the <u>Sahara desert</u>. This can cause damage to the biosphere, as <u>plants</u> and <u>animals</u> no longer have enough water to <u>survive</u>.

> **Minerals** — Minerals such as <u>gold</u> and <u>iron</u> are used in <u>building</u>, <u>scientific instruments</u>, <u>electrical appliances</u> and lots of other things — and demand for them is <u>increasing</u>. Minerals are often extracted by <u>mining</u>. Mines in <u>tropical forests</u> are responsible for lots of <u>deforestation</u> and <u>toxic chemicals</u> are <u>washed</u> into streams and rivers, <u>killing wildlife</u>. <u>Open pit mining</u> removes <u>large areas</u> of the land <u>surface</u> (see p.103).

Fridges — vital for all your re-sauce needs...

Indigenous people use resources in a sustainable way because they aren't being used more quickly than they're replaced. Commercial exploitation is a whole different story — resources are used up much faster than they can be replaced.

Role of the Biosphere

The <u>biosphere</u> is basically the <u>world's life support</u> and has several <u>really important</u> jobs to do.

The Biosphere Helps to Regulate the Gases in the Atmosphere...

1) The biosphere helps to <u>control</u> the proportion of different <u>gases</u> in the atmosphere:

- <u>Plants</u> take in <u>carbon dioxide</u> (CO_2) and give out <u>oxygen</u> during <u>photosynthesis</u>.
- <u>Animals</u> take in <u>oxygen</u> from the air and give out <u>carbon dioxide</u> when they breathe.

2) Maintaining the <u>balance</u> of gases in the atmosphere is <u>important</u> because:

- Most <u>living organisms</u> need <u>oxygen</u> to survive.
- <u>Increased</u> levels of <u>CO_2</u> lead to <u>global warming</u> (see p.6).
- <u>Increased</u> levels of <u>CO_2</u> can also make the <u>oceans acidic</u>, <u>affecting</u> the <u>organisms</u> that live there.
- <u>Some CO_2</u> is needed to keep the Earth <u>warm enough</u> to support life.

Forests are essential in maintaining the balance of gases because they take in huge amounts of CO_2 and release huge amounts of oxygen.

... to Keep Soil Healthy...

The biosphere is important for maintaining <u>soil nutrients</u> and <u>structure</u>:

- <u>Plant roots</u> and <u>animals</u> (e.g. earthworms) spread nutrients through the soil — this helps to maintain <u>soil structure</u> and <u>fertility</u>, which allows plants to <u>grow</u>.
- The <u>roots</u> of vegetation also <u>hold</u> the soil together — without this, the soil can be <u>eroded</u> by wind and rain.
- Vegetation <u>intercepts</u> (catches) rainfall before it reaches the ground. This helps to prevent <u>leaching</u> — where <u>nutrients</u> in the soil are <u>washed downwards</u> out of reach of <u>plants</u>.

The nutrient cycle is the way that nutrients move through an ecosystem. For more on nutrient cycles, see p.96.

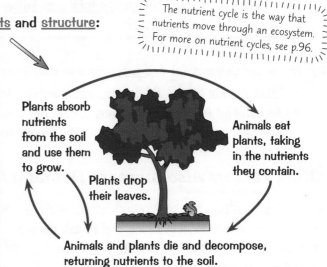

Plants absorb nutrients from the soil and use them to grow.

Animals eat plants, taking in the nutrients they contain.

Plants drop their leaves.

Animals and plants die and decompose, returning nutrients to the soil.

... and to Regulate the Water Cycle

1) The <u>water cycle</u> (or <u>hydrological cycle</u> if you're feeling fancy) is the movement of water between the <u>land</u>, bodies of <u>water</u> (e.g. lakes, rivers, the sea) and the <u>atmosphere</u>. It looks a bit like this. ⟹

2) The biosphere is an important <u>control</u> on the water cycle:

- Water is <u>taken up</u> by plants, so <u>less</u> reaches rivers. This helps to prevent <u>flooding</u> (see p.67) and <u>soil erosion</u>.
- Plants also help to <u>regulate</u> the <u>global water cycle</u> by <u>storing</u> water and releasing it into the atmosphere <u>slowly</u>. Large areas of <u>forest</u>, e.g. the Amazon rainforest, can reduce the <u>risk</u> of <u>drought</u> and <u>flooding</u> in areas a long way away.

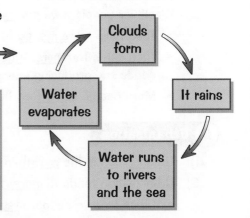

Clouds form

It rains

Water runs to rivers and the sea

Water evaporates

Bios fear — that feeling you get at family reunions...

So, the biosphere is pretty important for keeping the Earth ticking over comfortably, as it turns out. If you've got all that then head on over to the next page — I'll be with you after I've planted this tree and fed my pet earthworm Gavin.

Demand for Resources

In my day, there were a measly <u>6 billion</u> people in the world and enough <u>potato waffles</u> and <u>floppy disks</u> to keep everyone happy. Unfortunately, things are a bit more <u>complicated</u> nowadays...

Population Growth is Increasing Demand for Resources

1) The world's population is <u>increasing</u>. <u>More people</u> require <u>more resources</u> (e.g. food, water and energy), so demand <u>increases</u>.

2) The world's population is <u>predicted</u> to continue to <u>rise</u>:

Population Projections

- Population projections are <u>predictions</u> of <u>how many people</u> there will be in the world in the <u>future</u>.

- We know <u>past</u> and <u>present</u> values of population pretty <u>accurately</u>, but it's <u>more difficult</u> to predict <u>future</u> global population — it gets <u>harder</u> the <u>further forward</u> in time you go.

- The <u>UN</u> has made three <u>predictions</u> about <u>population growth</u> up to the <u>end of this century</u>. The <u>highest</u> prediction shows the <u>world's total population</u> reaching <u>14 billion people</u>.

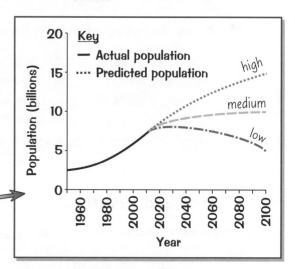

3) Increased demand for <u>one resource</u> can also increase demand for <u>another</u>, for example:

- <u>More people</u> means that <u>more food</u> needs to be grown, which increases demand for <u>water</u>.

- As demand for <u>water</u> increases, it may need to be <u>transported</u> from areas where there's plenty to areas where there's not enough — this takes lots of <u>energy</u>.

Other Factors Also Increase Demand for Resources

These factors are affecting the regional demand for resources.

Increasing <u>wealth</u>, <u>urbanisation</u> and <u>industrialisation</u> are increasing the demand for resources.

In <u>emerging</u> countries, e.g. China and Brazil, there has been <u>rapid industrialisation</u> and <u>urbanisation</u> and people are getting <u>wealthier</u> (see pages 33-34).

Over the next few decades most <u>economic</u> growth is expected to take place in <u>Africa</u>.

1 Increasing Wealth

1) <u>Economic development</u> means that people are getting <u>wealthier</u> (more <u>affluent</u>).
2) Wealthier people have <u>more disposable income</u>, which affects their <u>resource consumption</u>:

- They have <u>more money</u> to spend on <u>food</u> and they often buy <u>more</u> than they <u>need</u>.
- They can afford <u>cars</u>, <u>fridges</u>, <u>televisions</u> etc., all of which use <u>energy</u>. Manufacturing these goods and producing energy to run them also uses a lot of <u>water</u>.
- More people can <u>afford</u> flushing toilets, showers, dishwashers etc. This <u>increases water use</u>.

2 Urbanisation

1) <u>Urbanisation</u> is the <u>growth</u> in the <u>proportion</u> of a country's population living in urban areas.
2) Urbanisation tends to <u>increase resource consumption</u> because:

- Cities tend to be more <u>resource-intensive</u> than rural areas — street lights and neon signs use <u>energy</u>, and fountains and urban parks require <u>water</u>.
- Food and water have to be <u>transported</u> long distances to meet the increased demand in cities, and <u>waste</u> needs to be <u>removed</u> — this increases <u>energy use</u>.

Demand for Resources

(3) **Industrialisation**

1) Industrialisation is the shift in a country's main economic activity from primary production (e.g. farming) to secondary production (e.g. manufacturing goods).

2) Manufacturing goods such as cars, chemicals and electrical appliances uses a lot of energy — e.g. to run machines or heat components so they can be shaped. Manufacturing also uses a lot of water — e.g. for cooling and washing components. As countries become more industrialised, their demand for energy and water increases.

3) Industrialisation is increasing the production of processed goods, e.g. foods such as margarine. This increases the demand for ingredients such as palm oil, which are often grown on huge plantations.

Malthus **and** *Boserup* **Had Different** *Theories* **About Resource Supply**

Malthus and Boserup both came up with theories about how population growth and resource availability are related:

Malthus's Theory

- Thomas Malthus was an 18th-century economist. He thought that population was increasing faster than supply of resources, so eventually there would be too many people for the resources available.

- He believed that, when this happened, people would be killed by catastrophes such as famine, illness and war, and the population would return to a level that could be supported by the resources available.

- The point where the lines cross on the graph is the point of catastrophe — population starts to decrease after this, until it is low enough that there are enough resources to support it again.

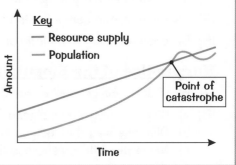

Boserup's Theory

- Ester Boserup was a 20th-century economist. Her theory was that however big the world's population grew, people would always produce sufficient resources to meet their needs.

- She thought that, if resource supplies became limited, people would come up with new ways to increase production (e.g. by making technological advances) in order to avoid hardship.

- The graph shows that, as population increases to be equal with resource supply, resource supply increases so there are always enough resources available for the population.

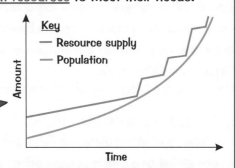

Neither theory has been proved completely right or completely wrong. There have been famines in some areas, but on a global scale, food production has so far kept up with population growth.

Famine, illness, war — Malthus sounds like a proper fun sponge...

Phew, that's it for this section. But before you go, have a crack at this exam-style question:

1) Explain two reasons why the demand for resources is increasing. [4]

Revision Summary

If the biosphere is your thing, this section's for you. On the other hand, if resource supply theories are your thing, this section's for you. Yep, it's got it all. Before you get too excited and read it all again, give these questions a bash to see how much you know. If there were any that you couldn't answer, head back for another look. Repeat this process until you ~~fall asleep~~ have all the information firmly stored in your head.

Global Ecosystems (p.87-89) ☐

1) What is a biome?
2) Why do different parts of the world have different biomes?
3) Where are temperate forests found?
4) Give one biome that is mostly found between the Tropics of Cancer and Capricorn.
5) True or false: tropical forests have a distinct summer and winter.
6) Describe the climate of tropical forests.
7) Describe the soil in the temperate forest biome.
8) Give one way that climate affects vegetation in boreal forests.
9) Describe the climate of temperate grasslands.
10) How is the vegetation in temperate grasslands different from that in tropical grasslands?
11) What kinds of plants grow in hot deserts?
12) What is the soil like in hot deserts?
13) What sorts of animals are found in the tundra biome?
14) Give two local factors that can affect biome distribution.
15) Give two abiotic components of biomes.
16) Describe one way that biotic and abiotic components interact.

Human Use of the Biosphere (p.90) ☐

17) What does 'indigenous' mean?
18) a) Give one way that indigenous people rely on the biosphere for food.
    b) Give one way that indigenous people rely on the biosphere for fuel.
    c) Name two other resources that indigenous people get from the biosphere.
19) What is meant by the phrase 'commercial exploitation of the biosphere'?
20) Give two examples of how the biosphere is exploited for water.

Role of the Biosphere (p.91) ☐

21) How does the biosphere regulate the composition of the atmosphere?
22) Give one reason why maintaining the balance of gases in the atmosphere is important.
23) Describe one way in which the biosphere helps to keep soil healthy.
24) a) Sketch the water cycle.
    b) How does the biosphere affect the water cycle?

Demand for Resources (p.92-93) ☐

25) True or false: global population is fairly steady.
26) How does global population change affect the demand for resources?
27) What impact does urbanisation have on the demand for resources?
28) Name two other factors that can affect resource demand.
29) a) What did Malthus believe would happen to resource supply as population increased?
    b) What did Boserup believe would happen to resource supply as population increased?

Tropical Rainforests

It's time to venture deep into the heart of the rainforest and find out some of its special features. First up, how all the different parts of the ecosystem are connected. Grab your bug spray and watch out for spiders...

Rainforests are *Interdependent* Ecosystems

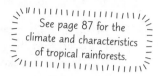
See page 87 for the climate and characteristics of tropical rainforests.

The biotic (living) components of rainforests (plants, animals and people) and the abiotic (non-living) components (climate, soils, water) are closely related — if one of them changes, the others are affected. For example:

1) The warm and wet climate means that plants grow quickly. The dense leaf cover protects the forest floor from wind and heavy rainfall, while root systems hold the soil together — this stops it being eroded.

2) The lack of wind near the forest floor means that many plants there have to rely on bees, butterflies, or other animals for pollination. Symbiotic relationships between plants and animals (where they each depend on the other for survival) are very common in tropical rainforests. For example:

> Agouti (a rodent) are one of the only animals who can crack open the hard seed pod of the Brazil nut to eat the nut inside. Sometimes, the agouti bury the nuts — these can sprout into new seedlings. If the agouti became extinct, the Brazil nut trees would decline and so could all the other animals who live in or feed on the Brazil nut trees. People who sell Brazil nuts to make a living may also be affected.

3) There are lots of epiphytes (plants that grow on other plants) in rainforests. They get access to light by growing high up on other plants, but they don't have access to the nutrients in the soil — they are dependent on rainfall to provide water and nutrients.

4) Changes to the rainforest ecosystem can have knock-on effects on the whole ecosystem. For example, deforestation reduces the amount of CO_2 being absorbed from the atmosphere, which adds to the greenhouse effect and changes the climate (see p.6).

Plants are *Adapted* to the Hot, Wet Climate

Tropical rainforests have a layered structure — they are stratified. This affects how much sunlight can reach the different levels of vegetation. Plants are adapted to the conditions found in each layer.

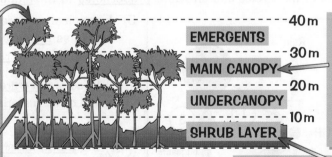

The emergents are the tallest trees, which poke out of the main canopy layer. They have straight trunks and only have branches and leaves at the top where they can get light. They also have big roots called buttress roots to support their trunks.

The undercanopy is made up of younger trees that have yet to reach their full height. They can only survive where there are breaks in the canopy to let a little bit of light through.

The main canopy is a continuous layer of trees. Like emergents, they only have leaves at the top. The dense layer of leaves shades the rest of the forest.

The shrub layer is nearest the ground where it's quite dark. Shrubs have large, broad leaves to absorb as much of the available light as they can.

EMERGENTS — 40 m
— 30 m
MAIN CANOPY — 20 m
UNDERCANOPY
— 10 m
SHRUB LAYER

Plants also have other adaptations, for example:

1) Plants have thick, waxy leaves with pointed tips. The pointed tips (called drip-tips) channel the water to a point so it runs off — that way the weight of the water doesn't damage the plant, and there's no standing water for fungi and bacteria to grow in. The waxy coating of the leaves also helps repel the rain.

2) Many trees have smooth, thin bark as there is no need to protect the trunk from cold temperatures. The smooth surface also allows water to run off easily.

3) Climbing plants, such as lianas, use the tree trunks to climb up to the sunlight.

4) Plants drop their leaves gradually throughout the year, meaning they can go on growing all year round.

Tropical Rainforests

Animals *have Also Adapted to the Physical Conditions*

Animals are adapted in different ways so that they can find food and escape predators:

1) Many animals spend their entire lives high up in the canopy. They have strong limbs so that they can spend all day climbing and leaping from tree to tree, e.g. howler monkeys.

2) Some animals have flaps of skin that enable them to glide between trees, e.g. flying squirrels. Others have suction cups for climbing, e.g. red-eyed tree frogs.

3) Some animals are camouflaged, e.g. leaf-tailed geckos look like leaves so they can hide from predators.

4) Many animals are nocturnal (active at night), e.g. sloths. They sleep through the day and feed at night when it's cooler — this helps them to save energy.

5) Some animals are adapted to the low light levels on the rainforest floor, e.g. anteaters have a sharp sense of smell and hearing, so they can detect predators without seeing them.

6) Many rainforest animals can swim, e.g. jaguars. This allows them to cross river channels.

Nutrients are Cycled Quickly in Tropical Rainforests

1) The nutrient cycle is the way that nutrients move through an ecosystem.

2) Nutrients are stored in three ways in the ecosystem.
   - living organisms (biomass),
   - dead organic material, e.g. fallen leaves (litter),
   - the soil.

3) In the cycle, nutrients are transferred between these three stores.

4) The store and transfer of nutrients in different ecosystems can be shown as flow diagrams. The size of the circles and arrows is proportional to the amount of nutrients.

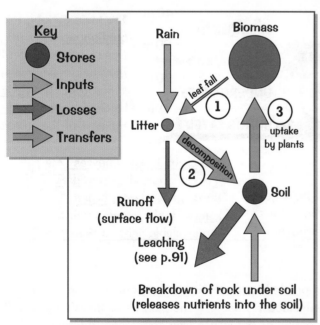

Key
- Stores
- Inputs
- Losses
- Transfers

Rain · Biomass · leaf fall · (1) · (3) · Litter · uptake by plants · decomposition · (2) · Soil · Runoff (surface flow) · Leaching (see p.91) · Breakdown of rock under soil (releases nutrients into the soil)

5) In tropical rainforests most nutrients are stored as biomass and the transfer of nutrients is very rapid. This is because:

(1) Trees are evergreen, so dead leaves and other material fall all year round.

(2) The warm, moist climate means that fungi and bacteria decompose the dead organic matter quickly. The nutrients released are soluble (they dissolve in water) and are soaked up by the soil.

(3) Dense vegetation and rapid plant growth mean that nutrients are rapidly taken up by plants' roots.

Nutrient cycles — yum, bikes you can eat...

Yikes, that was quite an introduction to rainforests. There's a lot to learn here, so get crackin'.

1) Explain two ways that animals are adapted to the conditions found in tropical rainforests. [4]

EXAM QUESTION

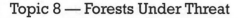

Tropical Rainforests

As the <u>sweat</u> drips down your face and the <u>leeches</u> cling to your shins, you may be wondering what <u>effect</u> <u>rapid nutrient cycling</u> has on the <u>rainforest</u>. Or then again maybe not — but I'm gonna tell you anyway...

Rainforests Have *Very High Biodiversity*...

1) <u>Biodiversity</u> is the <u>variety</u> of organisms living in a particular area — both <u>plants</u> and <u>animals</u>.

2) Rainforests have extremely <u>high biodiversity</u> — they contain around <u>50%</u> of the world's <u>plant</u>, <u>animal</u> and <u>insect species</u>, and may contain <u>around half</u> of <u>all life</u> on Earth. This is because:

- The rainforest biome has been around for a <u>very long time</u> (10s of millions of years) <u>without</u> the <u>climate changing</u> very much, so there has been lots of time for <u>plants</u> and <u>animals</u> to <u>evolve</u> to form <u>new species</u>.

- The <u>layered structure</u> of the rainforest provides lots of different <u>habitats</u> — plants and animals <u>adapt</u> to become highly <u>specialised</u> to their particular <u>environment</u> and <u>food source</u> (their '<u>ecological niche</u>') so lots of <u>different species</u> develop.

- Rainforests are <u>stable</u> environments — it's <u>hot</u> and <u>wet all year round</u>. They are also very <u>productive</u> (the plants <u>grow quickly</u> and <u>all year round</u>, producing lots of <u>biomass</u>) because of the high rate of nutrient cycling (see previous page). This means that plants and animals don't have to cope with <u>changing conditions</u> and there is always <u>plenty</u> to <u>eat</u> — so they are able to <u>specialise</u> (see above).

...and *Complex Food Webs*

1) <u>Food chains</u> show <u>what's eaten by what</u> in an ecosystem.

2) They always start with a <u>producer</u>, e.g. a plant. Producers <u>make their own food</u> using energy from the Sun.

> Consumers are organisms that eat other organisms. 'Primary' means 'first', so primary consumers are the first consumers in a food chain. Secondary consumers are second and tertiary consumers are third.

3) Producers are eaten by <u>primary consumers</u>, e.g. fruit bats and insects. Primary consumers are then eaten by <u>secondary consumers</u>, e.g. snakes, and secondary consumers are eaten by <u>tertiary consumers</u>, e.g. crocodiles and jaguars.

4) All these organisms eventually die and get broken down by <u>decomposers</u>.

5) Ecosystems usually contain many <u>different</u> species — which means <u>lots</u> of different possible <u>food chains</u>. <u>Food webs</u> show how all the food chains <u>overlap</u>.

Food webs in <u>tropical rainforests</u> are very <u>complex</u>:

- there are <u>so many different species</u> that there are <u>loads</u> and <u>loads</u> of <u>links</u> — e.g. jaguars also eat deer, sloths, tapir, monkeys and so on.

- <u>some</u> animals can be <u>both primary</u> and <u>secondary consumers</u>, e.g. fruit bats eat the fruit of banana trees, but they also eat mice, which have in turn eaten grass.

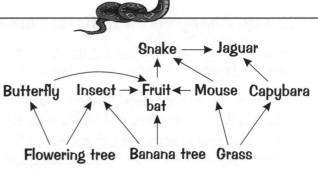

Rainforests are like my brother's hair — dense with lots of biodiversity...

Wot's all this biology malarky creepin' in to my beautiful geography book. Euugh. Still, you need to know it so I'm afraid you're going to have to read it again and then probably again. In a nutshell, you need to know why high rates of nutrient cycling lead to high biodiversity and complex food webs. Right, I'm off to consume some tea and cake...

Threats to Tropical Rainforests

Removal of trees from forests is called deforestation. It's happening on a huge scale in many tropical rainforests. And the threats to rainforests don't stop there — it's tough being a tree, I'm telling you.

Deforestation is a Direct Threat to Tropical Rainforests

There are lots of reasons why areas of tropical rainforest are destroyed:

Local demand for fuel wood — local people chop down trees to use as fuel for cooking or to burn to make charcoal.

Mineral resources — minerals (e.g. gold, copper and iron ore) are often found in tropical rainforests. Explosives are sometimes used to clear earth or deep pits are dug to reach the deposits.

Electricity (HEP) — many tropical rainforests have large rivers. Building dams to generate hydroelectric power (HEP) floods large areas of forest behind the dams.

Commercial hardwood logging — trees are felled to make furniture and for construction. Road building for logging also requires more tree clearance.

Commercial farming — forest is cleared to make space for cattle grazing, or for huge palm oil or soya plantations.

Subsistence farming — forest is cleared so farmers can grow food for themselves and their families.

Demand for biofuels — biofuels are fuels made from plants. Growing the crops needed to make biofuels takes up large amounts of land — trees have to be cut down to make space for them.

Deforestation has environmental impacts:

1) With no trees to hold the soil together, heavy rain washes it away (soil erosion). This can lead to landslides and flooding.

2) Without a tree canopy to intercept (catch) rainfall and tree roots to absorb it, more water reaches the soil. This reduces soil fertility as nutrients in the soil are washed away, out of reach of plants.

3) Trees remove CO_2 from the atmosphere. Also, burning vegetation to clear forest produces CO_2. So deforestation means more CO_2 in the atmosphere, which adds to the greenhouse effect.

Climate Change is an Indirect Threat to Tropical Rainforests

Tropical rainforests also face indirect threats — things that don't involve deliberately chopping down trees but still lead to damage to the ecosystem. One of the main indirect threats is climate change (see pages 6-7):

- Climate change can severely impact tropical rainforests. In some areas temperature is increasing and rainfall is decreasing, which leads to drought.
- Droughts lead to ecosystem stress — plants and animals living in tropical rainforests are adapted to moist conditions, so many species die in dry weather. Frequent or long periods of drought could lead to extinction of some species.
- Drought can also lead to forest fires, which can destroy large areas of forest.

The deforestation revision page — it's a cut above the rest...

Time to see if you really know this page as well as (deep down inside) you know you should:

1) Explain why climate change is a threat to tropical rainforests. [4]

Tropical Rainforests — Conservation

Whether you're a tree lover or not, the rainforests are pretty valuable — they provides us with loads of goods, e.g. medicines and chocolate, as well as looking after our climate and regulating the global water cycle.

The Rate of Deforestation Varies Globally

1) The rate of rainforest deforestation is very high — roughly 130 000 km² per year.

2) Deforestation rates are rising in some areas, e.g. Borneo and Nigeria. This is largely a result of:
   - Poverty — population growth and poverty mean there are many more small-scale subsistence farmers, e.g. in Borneo, and greater use of fuel wood (as other fuels are expensive), e.g. in Nigeria.
   - Foreign debt — there is a huge market for goods from tropical rainforests, so it's an easy way for poor countries to make money to pay back the debt they owe to richer countries.
   - Economic development — road and rail projects to promote development open up areas of the rainforest to logging, mining and farming, e.g. Borneo has huge palm plantations for biofuels.

3) However, some areas, e.g. Costa Rica and Brazil, are reducing deforestation rates as a result of:
   - Government policies — e.g. the Costa Rican government has invested in ecotourism (see next page) and pays landowners to reforest areas. Now, forest cover is increasing.
   - International condemnation — puts pressure on companies by naming and shaming those that are involved in deforestation. Many companies have pledged zero-deforestation as a result.
   - Monitoring systems — e.g. Global Forest Watch (GFW) provides satellite data to track forest loss. This means authorities can act more quickly to stop illegal logging etc.

REDD and CITES are Global Actions to Protect Tropical Rainforests

1) The threats to tropical rainforests involve the whole world — the goods from rainforests are traded internationally and all countries contribute to climate change.

2) This means that global actions are needed to try to protect rainforest plants and animals. For example:

	REDD	CITES
Overview	REDD (Reduced Emissions from Deforestation and forest Degradation) is a scheme that aims to reward forest owners in poorer countries for keeping forests instead of cutting them down.	CITES (Convention on International Trade in Endangered Species of Wild Fauna and Flora) is an agreement to tightly control trade in wild animals and plants.
Advantages	• Deals with the cause of climate change as well as direct impacts of deforestation. • The forest is protected so remains a habitat for species — biodiversity is not lost. • Everyone benefits from reducing emissions and it's a relatively cheap option for doing so.	• The issue is tackled at a global level, which means the trade of endangered species is controlled all over the world and not just in a handful of countries. • Raises awareness of threats to biodiversity through education.
Disadvantages	• Deforestation may continue in another area. • Aspects of REDD are not clear, meaning that it may be possible to cut down rainforests, but still receive the rewards if they are replaced with other types of forest, e.g. with palm oil plantations, which are low in biodiversity. • Preventing activities, e.g. agriculture and mining, may affect local communities who depend on the income from them.	• Although individual species are protected from poaching but it doesn't protect their habitat — they could still go extinct, e.g. due to the impacts of climate change. • Some rules are unclear, e.g. on the trade of ivory. • Not all countries are members — some countries even promote the trade of materials from endangered species.

Make sure you've REDD this page before you hit the webCITES...

...well, that's what I suggest anyway cos it has lots of important stuff you'll need for your exam. As always, nothing's simple — deforestation rates vary and global schemes have both pros and cons, but stick at it 'til you've got it all.

Tropical Rainforests — Conservation

When it comes to <u>conservation</u> you <u>don't</u> have to go <u>global</u> — a <u>little</u> can go a long way, or so they say...

Achieving *Sustainable Forest Management is a Challenge*

1) <u>Sustainable forest management</u> is when a forest is used in a way that <u>prevents</u> long-term damage, whilst allowing <u>people</u> to <u>benefit</u> from the <u>resources</u> it provides in the <u>present</u> and in the <u>future</u>.

2) Techniques include <u>selective logging</u> (where only <u>certain</u> trees are <u>removed</u>, rather than <u>large areas</u> being <u>cleared</u>) and <u>replanting</u> (where the trees that have been <u>removed</u> are <u>replaced</u>).

3) There are lots of <u>challenges</u> involved in <u>successful</u> sustainable forest management:

Economic
1) The <u>economic benefits</u> of sustainable management are only seen in the <u>long-term</u> — this affects <u>poorer</u> countries who need income <u>immediately</u>.
2) Sustainable forestry is usually <u>more expensive</u>, so it can be <u>difficult</u> to persuade <u>private companies</u> to adopt <u>sustainable</u> methods.
3) Many sustainable forestry schemes are <u>funded</u> by <u>government departments</u> and <u>NGOs</u> (see p.28). If the <u>priorities</u> of these organisations <u>change</u>, <u>funding</u> could <u>stop</u> quite quickly.

Environmental
1) If trees are <u>replanted</u>, the new forest may not resemble the <u>natural</u> forest — the <u>trees</u> are <u>replaced</u> but the entire <u>ecosystem</u> may <u>not</u> be <u>restored</u>.
2) Trees that are <u>replanted</u> for <u>logging</u> in the future can be very <u>slow growing</u> — companies may <u>chop down</u> more <u>natural forest</u> whilst they are waiting for the <u>new</u> trees to <u>mature</u>.
3) Even <u>selective logging</u> can <u>damage</u> lots of trees in the process of <u>removing</u> the <u>target trees</u>.

Social
1) Sustainable forest management generally provides <u>fewer jobs</u> for <u>local people</u> than conventional forestry, so many locals <u>won't</u> see the <u>benefits</u>. Some may turn to illegal logging, which is <u>difficult</u> to police.
2) If the <u>population</u> of a forest area <u>increases</u>, the <u>demand</u> for <u>wood</u> and <u>land</u> from the forest <u>increases</u>. Sustainable forestry is <u>unlikely</u> to provide enough resources to match the <u>increasing demand</u>.

Alternative Livelihoods *Might be a Better Long-Term* Option

The best way to <u>protect</u> tropical rainforests may be to encourage <u>alternative</u> ways of making a <u>living</u> from the rainforest that <u>don't</u> involve <u>large-scale deforestation</u>. For example:

Ecotourism

1) Ecotourism is <u>tourism</u> that <u>minimises damage</u> to the <u>environment</u> and <u>benefits</u> the <u>local people</u>.
2) Only a <u>small number</u> of visitors are allowed into an area at a time. <u>Environmental impacts</u> are minimised, e.g. by making sure <u>waste</u> and <u>litter</u> are <u>disposed</u> of <u>properly</u> to prevent land and water <u>contamination</u>.
3) Ecotourism provides a source of <u>income</u> for <u>local people</u>, e.g. they act as <u>guides</u> and <u>provide accommodation</u> and <u>transport</u>. It can also raise <u>awareness</u> of <u>conservation issues</u> and bring in more <u>money</u> for rainforest conservation.
4) If <u>local people</u> are employed in tourism, they don't have to <u>log</u> or <u>farm</u> to <u>make money</u>, meaning fewer trees are <u>cut down</u>. If a country's economy <u>relies</u> on <u>ecotourism</u>, there's an <u>incentive</u> to conserve the environment.

Sustainable Farming

Sustainable farming techniques <u>protect</u> the <u>soil</u> so that the land <u>remains productive</u> — there is no need to <u>clear new land</u> every few years. They include:

- <u>Agro-forestry</u> — <u>trees</u> and <u>crops</u> are planted at the <u>same time</u>, so that the tree roots <u>bind</u> the <u>soil</u> and the <u>leaves</u> protect it from <u>heavy rain</u>.
- <u>Green manure</u> — plants which <u>add nutrients</u> to the soil as they grow are planted to maintain <u>soil fertility</u>.
- <u>Crop rotation</u> — crops are <u>moved</u> between different fields each year with one <u>left empty</u>, so the soil has time to <u>recover</u>.

Sustainable management of revision — exam success now and forever...

And that's about it for rainforests. Make sure you understand how the rainforest ecosystem works, the negative effects of cutting down trees, and how it can be managed sustainably. Now make like a tree and get out of here...

Taiga Forests

You may've thought you were <u>out of the woods</u>, but you're most definitely not. Mwah hah hah. It's time to head north to the <u>cold</u>, <u>dark taiga forests</u>. Probs gonna need a <u>woolly hat</u> and <u>gloves</u> for this one.

Taiga Forests are Interdependent Ecosystems

<u>All</u> the parts of taiga forests (climate, soils, water, plants, animals and people) are <u>dependent</u> on one another — if any one of them <u>changes</u>, <u>everything</u> else is <u>affected</u>. For example:

> *Taiga (boreal) forests are part of the boreal biome — the climate is cool, dry and highly seasonal (see page 88).*

1) <u>Plants</u> gain their <u>nutrients</u> from the <u>soil</u>, and <u>provide</u> nutrients to the animals that eat them. In turn, animals spread <u>seeds</u> through their <u>dung</u>, helping the plants to <u>reproduce</u>.

2) The cold climate causes plants to <u>grow slowly</u> and also to <u>decompose</u> very slowly. This means that the soil is relatively <u>low in nutrients</u> — further <u>reducing</u> the ability of plants to <u>grow</u>.

3) <u>Herbivores</u> like reindeer that rely on plants like <u>mosses</u> to survive must migrate to areas where plants are <u>able to grow</u> to find food. <u>Carnivores</u> like wolves have to <u>follow</u> the <u>herbivores</u>.

> *Permafrost is permanently frozen ground.*

4) In <u>summer</u>, the trees <u>absorb heat</u> from the sun and shade the ground below — this prevents the permafrost below from <u>thawing</u>. The permafrost provides <u>water</u> for plants.

5) Changes to components of the ecosystem, such as <u>chopping down trees</u>, can have <u>knock-on effects</u> on the <u>whole ecosystem</u>, e.g. by causing permafrost to <u>melt</u>. Melting permafrost can <u>flood land</u>, preventing plants from growing. It also <u>releases</u> trapped <u>greenhouse gases</u> — leading to increased <u>global warming</u>, and changes to the <u>climate</u> of cold environments, threatening <u>plants</u> and <u>animals</u>.

Plants and Animals are Adapted to the Cool, Dry Climate

1) Taiga forests have a much <u>simpler structure</u> than tropical rainforests (see p.95) — lots of <u>tall trees</u> growing quite <u>close together</u> and not much else.

2) There aren't many plants on the <u>forest floor</u> because the <u>soils</u> are <u>poor</u> and very <u>little light</u> gets through the <u>dense canopy</u>. Plants that do survive include <u>mosses</u> and <u>lichens</u>.

3) Most of the trees are <u>conifers</u>, which are <u>adapted</u> to the cold, dry climate:

> - They are <u>evergreen</u> (they don't drop their leaves in a particular season), so they can make best use of the <u>available light</u>.
> - They have <u>needles</u> instead of flat leaves — this reduces <u>water loss</u> from strong, cold winds because it reduces the <u>surface area</u>.
> - They are <u>cone-shaped</u> — this means that <u>heavy winter snowfall</u> can <u>slide</u> straight off the <u>branches</u> without <u>breaking them</u>. The branches are also quite <u>bendy</u> so they're less likely to snap.

4) <u>Animals</u> in the taiga forest need to find ways to <u>survive</u> the <u>long</u>, <u>cold winters</u>. They also need to be able to find <u>enough food</u> and <u>escape</u> from <u>predators</u>.

> - Many of the <u>larger mammals</u>, e.g. caribou, are <u>migratory</u> — they move <u>long distances</u> through the forest in order to <u>find food</u>.

Caribou

> - Many animals are <u>well-insulated</u> against the winter cold, e.g. wolves have <u>thick fur</u>, and birds, e.g. ptarmigan, have <u>thick layers</u> of <u>downy feathers</u>.
> - Some animals <u>hibernate</u> to conserve energy and survive the <u>winter</u>, e.g. brown bears and marmots.
> - Some animals, e.g. snowshoe hares, have <u>white coats</u> in the <u>winter</u>, so they are <u>camouflaged</u> against the winter <u>snow</u> — this helps them <u>hide</u> from predators. Camouflage also helps predators to <u>sneak up</u> on prey <u>undetected</u>.

Taiga forest — orange-and-black-striped, roaring trees...

OK, I'm done. I promise I won't make any more taiga-tiger jokes. There are real taiga tigers though — check 'em out. Learning how plants and animals are adapted to survive in taiga forests will help you survive the exam. So, get to it.

Taiga Forests

Brrr. Dunno about you, but I'm feeling <u>chilly</u> already. Once you've <u>defrosted</u> your fingers and removed that <u>icicle</u> from the end of your nose I'll try and explain the effect of the <u>cold</u> on <u>nutrient cycling</u> and <u>biodiversity</u>.

Slow Nutrient Cycling *Leads to Slow Plant Growth*

1) In taiga forests, <u>few nutrients</u> are added through <u>precipitation</u> or <u>weathering</u>. Quite a lot of the nutrients that are added are <u>lost</u> through <u>runoff</u> and <u>leaching</u>.

2) <u>Most</u> of the nutrients are <u>stored</u> in dead organic material (<u>litter</u>), e.g. the layer of <u>fallen needles</u> on the forest floor.

3) The <u>cold</u>, <u>dry climate</u> means that nutrient cycling is much <u>slower</u> in taiga forests than in tropical rainforests.

① Trees are <u>evergreen</u>, so drop their needles <u>all year round</u>.

② Despite the constant leaf fall, <u>low temperatures</u> mean that it takes a <u>long time</u> for the litter to be <u>broken down</u> (<u>decomposed</u>) and added to the <u>soil</u> — conditions are <u>too harsh</u> for many <u>decomposers</u>. This means the soil <u>isn't very fertile</u>.

③ The <u>cold climate</u> also means that <u>plants grow slowly</u> — the <u>rate</u> of <u>transfer</u> of nutrients from soil to plants is <u>low</u>.

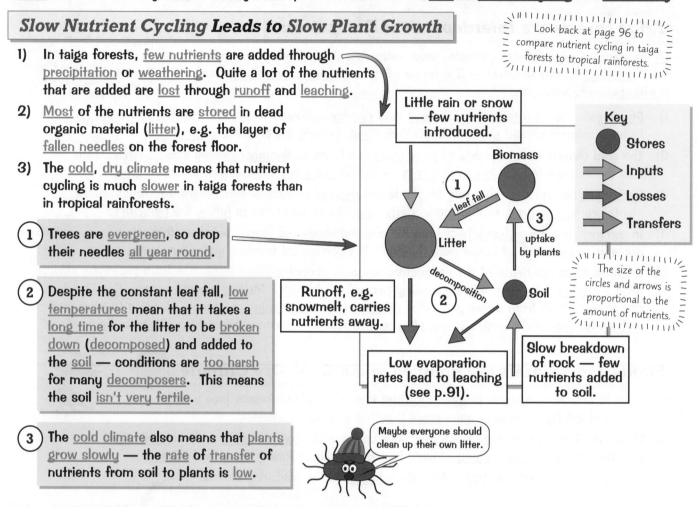

Look back at page 96 to compare nutrient cycling in taiga forests to tropical rainforests.

Little rain or snow — few nutrients introduced.

Biomass

leaf fall

Litter

uptake by plants

decomposition

Soil

Runoff, e.g. snowmelt, carries nutrients away.

Low evaporation rates lead to leaching (see p.91).

Slow breakdown of rock — few nutrients added to soil.

Key
● Stores
→ Inputs
→ Losses
→ Transfers

The size of the circles and arrows is proportional to the amount of nutrients.

Maybe everyone should clean up their own litter.

Taiga Forests have *Low Biodiversity*

Taiga forests have much <u>lower</u> biodiversity than tropical rainforests — many areas of forest contain a <u>single type</u> of tree, e.g. spruce, fir or pine. This is because:

1) The <u>land</u> was much colder and covered by <u>ice</u> until around 15 000 years ago. Species have had relatively <u>little time</u> to <u>adapt</u> to the current climate.

2) The <u>simple structure</u> means there aren't many different <u>habitats</u> — there are <u>fewer ecological niches</u> (see page 97) for organisms to fill, so <u>fewer</u> varieties of <u>species</u>.

3) Taiga forests are much <u>less productive</u> than tropical rainforests (plants grow <u>slowly</u>, so there's less biomass) and <u>nutrients</u> take a long time to be <u>returned</u> to the <u>soil</u> because it's so <u>cold</u>. The <u>growing season</u> is also <u>very short</u> — just a few months in the summer. This means there's <u>not much food</u> available, so there is a constant <u>struggle</u> for <u>survival</u>.

4) Some groups of animals are <u>under-represented</u> — there aren't many <u>amphibians</u> or <u>reptiles</u> because they <u>can't cope</u> with the <u>cold</u> climate (e.g. reptiles can't regulate their own body temperature and depend on the <u>sun</u> to stay warm).

Slow cycling and low productivity — yup, it's Monday morning...

Phew. Nutrient cycles may look complicated but just go through it one arrow at a time and you'll be fine. The arrows are mostly smaller for taiga forests than rainforests — basically cos everything goes slower.

1) State two reasons why taiga forests have low biodiversity. [2]

Threats to Taiga Forests

Advance warning — distressing page coming up. You've still got to read it though. Chin up, brave face...

The Exploitation of Resources is Threatening Taiga Forests

Taiga forests are exploited to make money — trees are deliberately chopped down for wood and paper, in the search for minerals and to satisfy the world's increasing demand for energy.

Logging for softwood — trees are cut down so that they can be made into housing, furniture and matches.

Pulp and paper production — felled trees are mashed into a pulp and used to make paper.

Exploitation of fossil fuels — trees are cleared to extract gas and oil from the ground.

HEP — dams to generate hydroelectric power from rivers in taiga forests flood large areas of land.

Exploitation of minerals — many taiga forests are rich in minerals, e.g. iron ore, gold, copper and silver. Lots of trees are chopped down to make way for mines as well as access roads.

Example: Tar sands

1) Tar sand is earth containing a thick, black oil, which can be processed into fossil fuels (e.g. petrol). Tar sands are found underneath taiga forests, e.g. in Canada.

2) Extraction of the tar sands often involves open pit mining or strip mining — digging up the land surface in strips to get to the sands beneath. This causes large-scale deforestation.

Acid Rain, Fire, Pests and Disease are Causing Loss of Biodiversity

Acid Precipitation

1) Burning fossil fuels releases gases, such as sulfur dioxide and nitrogen oxides. These dissolve in water in the atmosphere to form acids. When it rains or snows, the acids are deposited on plants and soils.

2) Acid rain damages plants' leaves and makes it harder for them to cope with the cold. It can also make the soils too acidic to support growth and kills organisms in lakes and streams.

Pests & Diseases

1) Pests and diseases cause damage to organisms.

2) Many pests and diseases are specific to one species, e.g. Spruce Bark Beetles attack spruce trees. As there is often a single tree species in a particular area in taiga forests, it's easy for the pests and diseases to spread and multiply — they can do a lot of damage.

3) It is thought that warming caused by climate change is making it easier for pests and disease-causing pathogens to survive — new pests and diseases are arriving and the frequency of attack is increasing.

Forest Fires

1) Wildfires are a natural part of the ecosystem — they allow new growth and regenerate the forest.

2) However, it's thought that climate change is leading to warmer, drier conditions in taiga forests. This is increasing the frequency of fires and making the fire season longer.

3) Forest fires can destroy huge numbers of trees and may change the distribution of species as some species are better at recolonising burnt areas. They may also break forests up into smaller sections, which makes it hard for migratory animals that need a lot of space to find enough food.

Oily, acidic and full of gas — sounds like my Uncle Tony...

If you're looking for the ultimate thrill, cover the page and jot down the causes of deforestation in taiga forests. And if you truly believe that you can handle more, you may as well finish up with the rest of the threats. Right, breathe...

Taiga Forests — Conservation

Taiga forests are under threat but it's not all bad news — here are some ways they can be conserved...

Conservation Methods Include Protected Areas and Sustainable Forestry

1) Taiga forests cover a huge area — a lot of them are inaccessible and very remote.
   However, human activity is expanding into these wilderness areas, particularly in Canada and Russia.

2) The forests can be conserved by setting up protected areas or by controlling the way that they are used.

Method	Overview	Strengths	Challenges
Creating a Wilderness Area	An area that is undisturbed by human activity that is managed with the aim of protecting the landscape.	Has the highest level of protection — most human activity is banned. The area is kept as pristine (untouched by humans) as possible. Usually covers a very large area so large-scale processes can still take place, e.g. animal migrations.	The large, remote areas are hard to police. There is economic pressure on governments from logging, mining and energy companies who want to use the resources. There is pressure from companies and tourists to build roads to allow greater access.
Creating a National Park	An area that is mostly in its natural state that is managed to protect biodiversity and promote recreation.	May be established to protect particular species, e.g. wood bison. Often cover a large area. Unsustainable human activity such as logging and mining is not permitted. There is good access for tourists and recreational users.	National parks must take into account the needs of indigenous communities, who may use the land for hunting etc. Tourism may be required to pay for the conservation, but access roads, infrastructure and pollution from tourists can harm the ecosystem.
Sustainable Forestry	Ways of harvesting the timber from the forest without damaging it in the long-term.	Limits can be placed on the number of trees felled or the size of clear-cut areas to allow the forest to regenerate. Companies may be required to regenerate the area after logging. Selective logging means some trees remain to become part of the new forest.	Some countries struggle to enforce the restrictions, e.g. Russia — lots of illegal logging takes place. There may be a lack of clear management or information about the ecosystem. Different groups may not agree with the rules and restrictions, e.g. indigenous people, loggers, government, environmentalists.

There are Conflicting Views on Managing Taiga Forests

Some people think that taiga forests should be protected. Other people think that the forest and its natural resources should be exploited. You need to know the reasons for each view point.

Protection

1) Taiga forests store lots of carbon — deforestation will release some of this as CO_2, which causes global warming.

2) Some species are only found in taiga forests. Because they are adapted to the conditions, the destruction of the habitat could lead to their extinction.

3) Many indigenous people, e.g. the Sami people of Scandinavia, depend on the forest for their traditional way of life.

Exploitation

1) The demand for resources is increasing — people need the wood, fuel and minerals that the forests provide.

2) Forest industries, e.g. logging and mining, provide a lot of jobs (e.g. forestry and logging employ 25 thousand people in Canada).

3) The exploitation of the forest generates a lot of wealth for the countries involved (e.g. the forestry industry in Sweden is worth nearly US $15 billion each year).

I have conflicting views — on whether to revise this page or go party...

Well, pain is temporary but glory is forever. So plunge yourself into the deep, dark forests once more and don't emerge 'til you can explain the challenges for sustainable management and why not everyone agrees they should be protected.

Revision Summary

Well I thought that section was a real tree-t and I bet it has left you wanting more. Luckily for you, here's a page full of revision questions. Threats to your exam grade include not being able to answer these questions, so I suggest you conserve your sanity by leafing back through anything you can't answer first time.

Tropical Rainforests (p.95-97) ☑

1) Give one example of interdependence in the tropical rainforest ecosystem.
2) What are stratified layers?
3) Name the four stratified layers in a tropical rainforest.
4) Why do some trees in the rainforest have buttress roots.
5) What are 'drip tips'?
6) Name the three nutrient stores in the tropical rainforest ecosystem.
7) Why are nutrients cycled quickly in tropical rainforests?
8) Why does the layered structure of tropical rainforests increase biodiversity there?

Tropical Rainforests — Threats and Conservation (p.98-100) ☑

9) True or false: chopping down trees is an indirect threat to rainforests.
10) Give three reasons why rainforests are being destroyed.
11) Give two environmental impacts of chopping down tropical rainforests.
12) Give two reasons why the rate of deforestation of tropical rainforests is decreasing in some areas.
13) What is the purpose of REDD?
14) Give one advantage of using REDD as a method of conservation.
15) What is CITES?
16) Give one disadvantage of using CITES as a method of conservation.
17) What is sustainable forest management?
18) Suggest three challenges to the success of sustainable forest management schemes.
19) What is ecotourism?
20) How does sustainable farming help protect tropical rainforests?

Taiga Forests (p.101-102) ☑

21) Give one example of interdependence in the taiga forest ecosystem.
22) True or false: taiga forests have a more complex structure than tropical rainforests.
23) Why do trees in taiga forests have needles rather than leaves?
24) Why are trees in taiga forests cone-shaped?
25) Give two ways that animals have adapted to survive in the taiga forest ecosystem.
26) How does the cold, dry climate affect the rate of nutrient cycling in taiga forests?

Taiga Forests — Threats and Conservation (p.103-104) ☑

27) How does the generation of hydroelectric power (HEP) threaten taiga forests?
28) Name two other human activities that are threatening taiga forests.
29) What is acid rain?
30) How do forest fires threaten the biodiversity of taiga forests?
31) What is a wilderness area?
32) Give two benefits of protecting taiga forests by creating wilderness areas.
33) Give two challenges of protecting taiga forests by creating national parks.
34) Why do some people want to protect taiga forests?
35) Give one reason why some people want to exploit taiga forests.

Energy Resources

What with the <u>palaver</u> over <u>climate change</u>, energy is a <u>hot topic</u> these days. So here's a whole section devoted to it, <u>just for you</u>, to help you do <u>stunningly well</u> in your exams.

Energy Sources can be Split into Three Categories

1) Energy sources can be <u>renewable</u>, <u>non-renewable</u> or <u>recyclable</u>.

2) An energy source is <u>renewable</u> if it can be <u>replenished</u> on a very short timescale. They're also known as <u>flow resources</u> because the planet has an <u>endless</u> supply of each one.

3) <u>Wind energy</u>, <u>solar energy</u> and <u>hydroelectric power (HEP)</u> are all renewable resources.

Renewable

- WIND ENERGY — Turbines use the energy of the <u>wind</u> to <u>generate electricity</u>, either <u>on land</u> or <u>out at sea</u>. Turbines are often built in <u>large windfarms</u>.

- SOLAR ENERGY — Energy from the Sun is used to <u>heat water</u> and <u>solar cookers</u> or to generate <u>electricity</u> using <u>photovoltaic cells</u>.

- HYDROELECTRIC POWER (HEP) — HEP uses the energy of <u>falling water</u>. Water is <u>trapped</u> by a <u>dam</u> and allowed to <u>fall</u> through tunnels, where the <u>pressure</u> of the falling water turns turbines to generate <u>electricity</u>.

4) <u>Non-renewable</u> energy sources <u>can't</u> be replenished quickly — they take <u>millions of years</u> to form. This means that they can <u>run out</u>.

5) They're also known as <u>stock resources</u> as the planet has a <u>limited</u> supply (stock) of each one.

6) <u>Fossil fuels</u> (<u>coal</u>, <u>oil</u> and <u>natural gas</u>) are non-renewable resources.

Non-Renewable

FOSSIL FUELS — Fossil fuels formed <u>millions of years ago</u> from the remains of dead organisms. They can be extracted from the <u>ground</u> and <u>seabed</u>. As technology <u>develops</u>, it has become possible to <u>extract resources</u> that were previously too <u>difficult</u> or <u>costly</u> to use, e.g. by fracking (see page 110).

7) <u>Recyclable</u> energy sources are those made from <u>waste products</u> or whose waste products can be <u>used</u> to generate <u>more</u> energy.

8) <u>Nuclear energy</u> and <u>biofuels</u> are recyclable sources of energy because they have <u>usable</u> waste products.

Recyclable

- NUCLEAR ENERGY — This uses uranium <u>atoms</u> — when they <u>split</u> lots of <u>heat</u> is produced, which is used to <u>boil water</u>. The <u>steam</u> turns a <u>turbine</u>, <u>generating electricity</u>. New <u>breeder reactors</u> can generate <u>more fuel</u> during the splitting process, making nuclear energy more like a <u>renewable</u> energy source. <u>Radioactive waste</u> can also be <u>processed</u> so it can be used to generate more energy.

- BIOMASS — Biomass (<u>wood</u>, <u>plants</u> or <u>animal waste</u>) can be <u>burnt</u> to <u>release energy</u> or used to produce <u>biofuels</u>. It's <u>easy</u> to produce biomass because living organisms <u>grow quickly</u>. Sometimes, biomass is <u>already available</u> as a <u>waste product</u> from other processes, e.g. farming. Sometimes the waste products from the <u>production</u> of <u>biofuels</u> can also be used as a <u>fuel</u>. For example, <u>sugar cane</u> is <u>fermented</u> to produce ethanol, a biofuel often used in <u>transport</u>. The leftover cane is then <u>burnt</u> to produce <u>more energy</u>, e.g. for heating.

If only my favourite energy supply was renewable — mmm, infinite pie...

I know, I know — it was a bad idea to mention pie so early on. The idea of 'flow' and 'stock' resources might seem a bit confusing, but it's actually really simple. We have a **constant flow** of renewables, but a **limited stock** of fossil fuels.

Impacts of Energy Production

Producing energy can cause <u>all sorts of problems</u> — particularly for the <u>environment</u>.

Mining and Drilling have Impacts on the Environment...

1) The <u>extraction</u> of fossil fuels, e.g. by <u>mining</u> and <u>drilling</u>, can damage the environment.

2) Mining has <u>several</u> environmental impacts:

- <u>Surface mining</u> strips away large areas of <u>soil</u>, <u>rock</u> and <u>vegetation</u> so that miners can reach the materials they want. This can <u>permanently scar</u> the landscape.
- Habitats are <u>destroyed</u> to make way for mines, e.g. through <u>clearing forests</u>, leading to <u>loss of biodiversity</u>.
- Clearing forests also affects the <u>water cycle</u> (see p.91) because there are <u>fewer</u> trees to <u>take up</u> water from the ground. This can lead to increased <u>soil erosion</u>.
- Mining processes can release <u>greenhouse gases</u>, e.g. <u>carbon dioxide</u> (CO_2) and <u>methane</u> (CH_4), into the atmosphere. These gases contribute to <u>global warming</u> (see p.6).

3) Extracting <u>oil</u> and <u>gas</u> involves <u>drilling</u> into <u>underground</u> reserves. It can be done <u>inland</u> (onshore) and <u>at sea</u> (offshore).

4) Drilling has negative <u>impacts</u> on the <u>environment</u>:

- Onshore drilling requires land to be <u>stripped</u> of vegetation to make space for the <u>drills</u> and <u>roads</u> to access the sites.
- <u>Oil spills</u> cause major damage to the environment — especially <u>out at sea</u>. The <u>Deepwater Horizon oil spill</u> in 2010 leaked around <u>4 million barrels of oil</u> into the <u>Gulf of Mexico</u>. Oil <u>coats</u> the <u>feathers</u> and <u>fur</u> of animals, which <u>reduces</u> their ability to <u>move freely</u> or <u>feed</u>.
- Extracting <u>natural gas</u> from underground reserves can cause methane to <u>leak</u> into the <u>atmosphere</u>, making the <u>greenhouse effect stronger</u> and contributing to <u>global warming</u>.

...and so do Some Forms of Renewable Energy

Although it has <u>fewer</u> impacts than non-renewable energy, generating <u>renewable energy</u> can still <u>affect</u> the environment:

Wind Energy

1) <u>Large numbers</u> of wind turbines are needed to produce significant amounts of electricity and they need to be set quite far apart. This means they take up <u>lots of space</u>.

2) Wind farms produce a <u>constant humming noise</u> — some people living close to wind farms have complained about this <u>noise pollution</u>.

3) The <u>spinning blades</u> on turbines can <u>kill</u> or <u>injure birds</u> and <u>bats</u>.

SHHHH!

Solar Energy

1) Some <u>solar farms</u> use <u>ground</u> and <u>surface water</u> to <u>clean</u> their <u>solar panels</u>. This can lead to water shortages in arid areas, which <u>disrupts ecosystems</u>.

2) The <u>heat</u> reflected from <u>mirrors</u> in solar farms can <u>kill</u> wildlife, e.g. birds.

3) Solar panels built on the <u>ground</u> can <u>disturb</u> and <u>damage habitats</u>.

Hydroelectric Power (HEP)

1) HEP plants use <u>dams</u> to <u>trap</u> water for energy production — this creates a <u>reservoir</u>, which <u>floods</u> a large area of land.

2) The <u>river</u> on which the dam is built can be affected by <u>changes in water flow</u>, e.g. <u>sediment</u> is deposited in the reservoir instead of <u>further downstream</u>.

3) A <u>build-up</u> of sediment can <u>block sunlight</u>, causing <u>plants</u> and <u>algae</u> in the river to <u>die</u>.

Get a job as a wind farmer — it's a breeze...

Most types of energy production have some form of environmental impact, but it's more severe for non-renewable energy.

Access to Energy

With more than 7 billion people in the world, supplying everyone with energy is no walk in the park...

Access to Energy is Affected by Many Factors

1) Energy resources are unevenly distributed — some countries naturally have more resources than others. E.g. Russia has almost 25% of the world's natural gas reserves, whereas Algeria only has around 2%.

2) There are also other factors that have an impact on a country's access to energy:

TECHNOLOGY — some countries are not able to exploit their energy resources as the technology required is unavailable or too expensive. For example, Niger has large uranium reserves but does not have the technology to develop nuclear power plants. Developed countries can exploit more renewable energy supplies, e.g. solar and wind power, but developing countries often have to rely more on fossil fuels.

GEOLOGY — fossil fuels are found in sedimentary rocks, where impermeable rocks have trapped the oil and gas in the permeable rocks below. Countries located on plate boundaries (see p.14) may be able to access geothermal energy (using the earth's heat to generate power).

ACCESSIBILITY — an area might have large energy resources but be unable to access them. For example, permafrost (permanently frozen ground) makes it very difficult to access fossil fuels. Some resources are also found in protected areas, e.g. Antarctica, and can't be exploited.

CLIMATE — solar power requires large amounts of sunlight to generate energy. Countries with sunny climates, e.g. Spain, can use solar power more effectively than countries with duller climates, e.g. the UK.

LANDSCAPE — wind turbines are most efficient in areas with a steady and reliable source of wind, e.g. on high ground or along the coast. Hydroelectric power usually requires lots of water to generate energy, and steep-sided valleys to use as reservoirs.

Global Energy Consumption is Unevenly Distributed

1) This map shows the energy consumption per person across the world in 2014.

2) There's a strong relationship between development and energy consumption:

- Developed countries, e.g. Australia, Norway and USA, tend to consume lots of energy per person because they can afford to. Most people in these countries have access to electricity and heating, and use energy-intensive devices like cars.

- Economic development is increasing wealth in emerging countries, e.g. China. People are buying more things that use energy, e.g. cars, fridges and televisions.

Energy consumption per person (tonnes oil equivalent)
6.0 and over | 3.0 – 4.5 | 0 – 1.5
4.5 – 6.0 | 1.5 – 3.0

- Developing countries, e.g. Chad and Mongolia, consume less energy per person as they are less able to afford it. Less energy is available and lifestyles are less dependent on high energy consumption.

3) Some regions rely on traditional fuel sources. For example, in sub-Saharan Africa, energy networks are poorly connected, which means people have to rely on biomass such as wood for cooking and heating. There's very little development, so countries can't afford to exploit their own energy reserves or improve existing infrastructure.

4) Industrial activities require large amounts of energy, e.g. to power machinery or for transport:

- Manufacturing industries in developed and emerging countries use huge amounts of energy.

- Developing countries have more primary industry (e.g. agriculture), which uses very little energy.

Exam mark supplies are affected by quantity of revision...

You need to understand how access to energy will have an impact on people. It's pretty hard for a country to develop if it's struggling to get the energy it needs — this is the situation in many developing countries.

Topic 9 — Consuming Energy Resources

Oil Supply and Demand

Oil is one of the world's main energy sources. It's constantly in demand, which means it's pretty vital that you learn about it. So find that comfy spot on the sofa, put your feet up, and 'oil' tell you all about it (sorry)...

Oil Reserves and Oil Production are Unevenly Distributed

1) Oil reserves are the amount of recoverable oil — oil that can be extracted using today's technology. Oil production is the process of extracting and refining crude (unrefined) oil.

2) The world's major oil reserves are found in a handful of countries — most of these are in the Middle East.

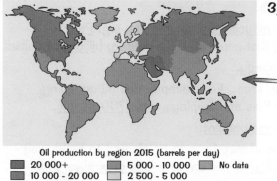

Oil production by region 2015 (barrels per day)
- ■ 20 000+
- ■ 10 000 - 20 000
- ■ 5 000 - 10 000
- ■ 2 500 - 5 000
- □ No data

3) Oil production doesn't just depend on a country's oil reserves — there are several factors that affect it:

- Infrastructure — in order to produce oil, a country needs the right equipment and technology. Russia, Saudi Arabia and the USA are the world's biggest oil producers.

- Domestic demand — Saudi Arabia relies on oil to meet its own energy needs.

- Shrinking reserves — oil production from North Sea reserves has been declining as reserves are used up.

4) Global oil consumption is increasing as countries develop. Between 2015 and 2016, the amount of oil consumed worldwide rose by 1.4 million barrels a day.

- As GDP per capita (see p.21) increases, so does oil consumption. People in wealthier countries have more energy-intensive goods, e.g. cars. Around 65% of all oil is used to fuel vehicles.

- Rapid industrialisation in emerging economies, e.g. China and India, also increases oil consumption. The combination of a growing population, a boom in industry and the expansion of cities leads to higher consumption of oil.

Oil Supply and Oil Prices are Affected by Different Factors

1) Oil supply and oil prices are closely linked and can fluctuate for a number of reasons.

2) Generally, periods of oversupply cause oil prices to fall and periods of undersupply cause prices to increase.

- CONFLICTS (e.g. those in the Middle East in the 1970s) can disrupt oil production, which leads to a decrease in oil supply. Shortages of oil cause prices to increase.

- DIPLOMATIC RELATIONS — oil prices may increase because of tensions between oil-producing countries. For example, relations between Saudi Arabia and Iran have led to uncertainty about oil production in the region.

- RECESSIONS (e.g. the global financial crisis in 2008) lower the demand for oil because industrial activities and economic growth slow down. This causes prices to fall.

- ECONOMIC BOOMS — oil prices increase during periods of rapid economic growth because of increased consumption and demand.

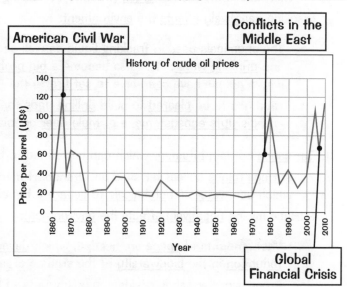

Crude oil — it's always making smutty comments...

Scientists have no idea when oil reserves will run out, but if we all keep consuming oil at the rate we are today, it won't be long before we need to look at exploiting new reserves. Or pressing the panic button.

1) Explain how changes in international relations can affect the price of oil. [4]

Increasing Energy Supply

If we're going to <u>keep up</u> with the world's <u>energy needs</u>, we'll need to start thinking about <u>increasing</u> our <u>supplies</u>.

Conventional Oil and Gas Reserves are being Exploited in Sensitive Areas

1) Despite the development of <u>renewable energy</u>, we still rely heavily on <u>fossil fuels</u>.

2) The <u>pressure</u> of meeting <u>growing</u> energy demands means new, <u>ecologically-sensitive areas</u> are being explored for conventional energy reserves, e.g. the Arctic circle and the Amazon rainforest.

> Conventional energy reserves are easily exploited, e.g. through drilling. Extracting oil or gas from them is quick and cheap.

3) Exploiting new oil and gas reserves brings <u>economic benefits</u>:

   • Countries with oil and gas reserves can save money by <u>reducing energy imports</u>, e.g. <u>Peru</u> is exploiting natural gas reserves in the <u>Amazon rainforest</u> that could save the country <u>billions</u> of dollars.

   • These countries can also <u>make money</u> from <u>exporting</u> energy.

   • Oil and gas companies bring <u>investment</u> and <u>jobs</u> to an area. For example, one oil company in Alaska has invested <u>4.5 million dollars</u> into communities and employs over <u>1700 people</u>.

4) However, these economic benefits come at a <u>cost</u> to the <u>environment</u>:

   • In order to reach new reserves (e.g. in the Amazon), land may have to be <u>cleared</u> to make way for <u>pipelines</u> and <u>roads</u>. This can disrupt <u>fragile ecosystems</u> and cause a <u>loss of biodiversity</u>.

   • Exploring <u>offshore</u> oil and gas reserves, e.g. in the Arctic Ocean, can have a big impact on <u>marine life</u>. <u>Noise</u> and <u>vibrations</u> from drills can <u>confuse whales</u> and other <u>marine mammals</u> that rely on <u>sound</u> to communicate, navigate and find food.

   > Told you we should've asked for directions.

   • <u>Opening up</u> isolated areas with <u>roads</u> and <u>industry</u> increases <u>air pollution</u> and can pollute <u>soils</u> and <u>water</u>.

Shale Gas and Tar Sands are Unconventional Gas and Oil Reserves

1) <u>Unconventional</u> energy reserves are exploited using more <u>expensive methods</u>, e.g. <u>hydraulic fracking</u>, that need <u>specialist technology</u>. Extraction takes a lot <u>longer</u> than from conventional reserves.

2) <u>Shale gas</u> is a form of <u>natural gas</u> that is trapped in <u>shale rock</u> underground. It's extracted by <u>fracking</u>:

   • <u>Liquid</u> is <u>pumped</u> into the shale rock at <u>high pressure</u>.

   • This causes the rock to <u>crack</u> (fracture), releasing the <u>gas</u>, which is collected as it comes out of the well.

   Fracking <u>negatively affects</u> the <u>environment</u>:

   • The <u>chemicals</u> used in <u>fracking liquid</u> as well as the shale gas itself can <u>pollute groundwater</u> and <u>drinking water</u>. This has become a <u>big problem</u> in some fracking areas in the <u>USA</u>, where people have been able to <u>set fire</u> to their <u>tap water</u>.

   • Land has to be <u>cleared</u> to build <u>drilling pads</u> for fracking — this <u>destroys</u> animal <u>habitats</u> and <u>disrupts ecosystems</u>, e.g. <u>mule deer</u> populations have been affected in <u>Wyoming</u>.

3) <u>Tar sands</u> contain <u>bitumen</u>, which can be refined to produce oil. It's mainly extracted by <u>mining</u>:

   • <u>Surface mines</u> collect tar sand and transport it to <u>processing plants</u>, which use <u>water</u> and <u>chemicals</u> to <u>separate</u> the bitumen from the sands.

   Surface mining <u>negatively affects</u> the <u>environment</u>:

   • Vast amounts of <u>space</u> are needed, which <u>devastates habitats</u> (see p.103). This can cause a <u>reduction</u> in the <u>biodiversity</u> of the area as organisms have <u>less space</u> to <u>live</u> and find <u>food</u>.

   • Processing tar sands creates huge amounts of <u>liquid waste</u> full of <u>harmful chemicals</u>. These can <u>pollute</u> water supplies if they aren't <u>managed</u> properly.

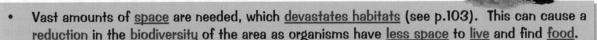

Who'd have thought it — ██████ with a ████████ ████████...*

Make sure you understand how fracking and tar sand mining work. They're both very controversial issues at the moment and I wouldn't be surprised if you get given a nice juicy question about them in your exam...

---

* this gag was exploiting sensitive areas and has therefore been censored for your protection.

Sustainable Energy Use

Sustainable energy is a big deal these days, which makes the next two pages pretty darn important...

The Demand for Energy can be Reduced

1) The demand for energy can be reduced by conserving energy and making energy use more efficient:
   - Energy conservation — conserving energy is about changing our behaviour as consumers.
     E.g. driving less, drying clothes on a washing line instead of in a dryer.
   - Energy efficiency — if something is energy-efficient, it does the same job but using less energy.
     E.g. a low-energy lightbulb.

2) Energy efficiency and conservation also make energy supplies last longer and reduce carbon emissions.

3) Transport and the home environment are two areas where the demand for energy can be effectively reduced:

Home

1) Insulation — by insulating walls, roofs and floors, less energy is required to heat homes.

2) Modern boilers — new boilers are more efficient than older models, so will use less energy in homes.

3) Solar panels can be fitted to the roofs of homes providing renewable, low-carbon energy.

Transport

1) Hybrid cars, vans and trains combine diesel and electric power to increase efficiency. They use electricity when possible, and recharge their batteries using diesel power.

2) Regenerative braking — road vehicles and trains can be fitted with devices to store the energy lost under braking, either to be used later or returned to the national grid.

3) Engine manufacturers are making more efficient engines in response to laws and rising fuel costs.

4) Improving public transport and encouraging walking or cycling reduces demand for energy used for transport.

Reducing the Use of Fossil Fuels has Lots of Advantages

There are three main advantages to reducing the use of fossil fuels:

1 Reducing carbon footprints

1) Burning fossil fuels releases greenhouse gases into the atmosphere, contributing to global warming (see p.6).

2) The greenhouse gas emissions are measured as people's carbon footprints (see p.114).

3) Carbon footprints include direct emissions (those produced from things that use energy) as well as indirect emissions (those produced making things that we buy).

4) By reducing their use of energy generated by using fossil fuels, people can shrink their carbon footprints.

2 Improving energy security

1) Energy security means having a reliable, uninterrupted and affordable supply of energy available.

2) Switching to renewable sources of energy will make sure energy is still available when the supply of fossil fuels runs out.

3 Diversifying the energy mix

1) Reducing reliance on finite fossil fuels and increasing the amount of energy generated by alternative methods will diversify the energy mix.

2) Having a diverse energy mix reduces a country's reliance on a single source of energy.

3) This increases energy security because countries are less affected by shortages of one energy source, reducing the risk of energy deficits — where the amount of energy produced isn't enough to meet a population's needs.

4) Using renewable energy sources instead of fossil fuels will also make non-renewable energy sources last longer.

Sustainable Energy Use

Alternatives to Fossil Fuels have Costs and Benefits

1) There are many <u>alternatives</u> to burning <u>fossil fuels</u>, including <u>renewable</u> and <u>recyclable sources</u> of <u>energy</u>.

2) These can help to <u>reduce carbon footprints</u>, <u>improve energy security</u> and <u>diversify the energy mix</u> (see previous page).

3) Each has <u>costs</u> and <u>benefits</u>:

See page 106 for how energy is generated from these fuels.

ENERGY SOURCE	COSTS	BENEFITS
BIOFUELS	• <u>Sources</u> of biomass have to be <u>managed sustainably</u> to make sure that they don't run out. • Growing crops for biofuels <u>reduces</u> the amount of <u>food crops</u> that can be grown and <u>lots</u> of <u>water</u> is needed. • Growing crops for biofuels is leading to <u>deforestation</u> in some areas (see p.98).	• Biofuels cause <u>less pollution</u> than fossil fuels when they're burned. • Some biofuels are made from <u>waste products</u> (see p.106), so they <u>reduce</u> the total amount of waste produced.
WIND ENERGY	• Wind is <u>unpredictable</u>, so the <u>amount</u> of electricity produced <u>varies</u>. • Wind turbines can cause <u>environmental issues</u> (see p.107). • It's <u>expensive</u> to <u>transport</u> the electricity produced from <u>offshore</u> wind farms to where it's needed.	• After the turbines have been made and transported to a suitable area, they don't release any <u>greenhouse gas emissions</u>. • It's a relatively <u>cheap</u> source of renewable energy.
SOLAR ENERGY	• <u>Sunny climates</u> are needed to produce <u>large amounts</u> of electricity, so it's <u>not</u> a reliable energy source in places where there's very <u>little sun</u>. • <u>Toxic</u> metals, e.g. mercury, are used in the <u>construction</u> of solar panels. • Solar panels can affect <u>habitats</u> and <u>ecosystems</u> (see p.107).	• Once the panels have been made and fitted, <u>no emissions</u> are produced. • Solar panels don't require much <u>maintenance</u> once they've been installed. • The technology is <u>widely available</u>.
HYDROELECTRIC POWER (HEP)	• Hydroelectric power plants are <u>expensive</u> to build and require <u>lots</u> of <u>water</u> and <u>land</u>. • <u>Methane</u> (a greenhouse gas) may be released from <u>rotting organic matter</u> in the <u>reservoirs</u> created behind the dams. • Hydroelectric power plants can cause other <u>environmental issues</u> (see p.107).	• <u>No emissions</u> are produced when hydroelectric power plants are used to generate electricity. • The <u>flow</u> of water through the turbines can be <u>controlled</u>, so the supply of energy is <u>reliable</u>.
HYDROGEN FUEL	• <u>Hydrogen</u> rarely exists <u>by itself</u> on Earth — energy is required to <u>extract</u> it, e.g. from <u>water</u>. The energy often comes from burning <u>fossil fuels</u>, releasing <u>greenhouse gases</u>. • The technology is <u>expensive</u> and <u>not widely available</u>, meaning that it is currently <u>unlikely</u> to be able to increase <u>energy security</u>. • <u>Storing</u> hydrogen is <u>dangerous</u> — it's <u>flammable</u>.	• Burning hydrogen doesn't release any <u>harmful emissions</u> — the only by-product is <u>water</u>. • Hydrogen is usually extracted from <u>water</u>, so it's <u>not limited</u> to particular areas.

Hydrogen fuel cells are currently only used on a small-scale but it is hoped they could be used to provide clean power for transport in the future.

Hybrid brains — increasing revision efficiency...

Examiners love getting you to weigh up different options — learn the pros and cons of each energy source.

1) Explain how reducing the use of fossil fuels can increase energy security. [2]

Energy Futures

The <u>future</u> of <u>global energy use</u> is uncertain. Some people think we need to make <u>significant changes</u> to make sure we have enough energy in the future, but others are quite happy to <u>carry on as usual</u>...

There are Contrasting Views about Energy Futures

1) There are two main <u>energy futures</u> to remember:

- **BUSINESS AS USUAL** — Everything <u>carries on as normal</u>. We go on getting most of our energy from <u>fossil fuels</u> and <u>don't</u> increase the use of <u>renewable energy sources</u>.

- **MOVE TO SUSTAINABILITY** — We <u>reduce</u> the amount of fossil fuels we use and increase our use of <u>renewable energy sources</u>.

2) <u>Different groups</u> have different <u>attitudes</u> towards energy futures:

1 Consumers

1) Consumers want <u>secure</u> energy supplies that won't be <u>disrupted</u> in the future.

2) When <u>fossil fuels</u> start to <u>run out</u>, <u>energy security</u> will decrease, increasing the risk of energy <u>shortages</u>.

3) Consumers also want <u>cheap</u> power — sustainable energy requires <u>investment</u>, which can <u>increase the price</u>.

4) Many consumers currently favour <u>business as usual</u>, as it provides a <u>cheap</u>, <u>secure</u> supply of energy. However, as supplies of fossil fuels <u>run out</u>, and <u>environmental awareness increases</u>, some consumers are beginning to favour a <u>move</u> to <u>sustainability</u> (see next page).

2 TNCs (Transnational Corporations)

1) Many TNCs, e.g. Shell, are involved in <u>extracting</u> and <u>refining</u> fossil fuels and <u>invest</u> a lot of money into the <u>energy sector</u>.

2) Controlling <u>oil reserves</u> gives TNCs lots of <u>power</u> and <u>wealth</u>, which means they may <u>lose</u> money if there is a shift towards using more <u>renewable</u> energy sources.

3) Sustainable energy needs <u>more investment</u> than fossil fuels, so these TNCs would have <u>higher costs</u> and potentially <u>lower gains</u> — this means they may <u>favour</u> the <u>business as usual</u> scenario.

4) TNCs <u>not</u> involved in the fossil fuel industry may also favour <u>business as usual</u> as <u>sustainable energy</u> is more <u>expensive</u> and would be likely to increase their <u>energy costs</u>.

3 Governments

1) Governments want to <u>secure</u> future energy supplies — fossil fuels are a <u>cheap</u> and <u>reliable</u> way of supplying energy in the <u>short-term</u>, but a more <u>sustainable</u> approach will be needed in the <u>long-term</u>.

2) In <u>developed countries</u>, governments are starting to come <u>under pressure</u> from some <u>consumers</u> to <u>protect the environment</u> — this means they want to start using more <u>sustainable energy</u>.

3) Fossil fuels have helped countries to <u>develop</u> and the <u>governments</u> of many <u>emerging</u> countries have <u>concerns</u> about whether sustainable energy sources will <u>continue</u> to help them <u>develop</u>.

4 Climate Scientists

1) <u>Climate scientists</u> study climate and how <u>human activities</u> are affecting it. The IPCC's <u>climate change scenarios</u> (see p.8) predict a temperature increase of up to 4 °C by the year 2100 under the <u>business as usual</u> scenario.

2) They want to reduce <u>reliance</u> on fossil fuels in order to lessen the <u>consequences</u> of climate change, e.g. <u>serious temperature increases</u> and <u>rising sea levels</u>.

5 Environmental Groups

1) <u>Environmental groups</u>, e.g. Greenpeace, want to <u>stop</u> people relying on fossil fuels for energy because their extraction and use <u>damages the environment</u>.

2) They want people to <u>reduce</u> their use of <u>fossil fuels</u> and <u>switch</u> to <u>renewable</u> energy sources in line with the <u>move to sustainability</u> scenario.

Energy Futures

Attitudes to Energy Futures are Changing

1) In <u>recent years</u>, many people have become <u>more aware</u> of the need to make energy use <u>sustainable</u> and <u>reduce</u> their <u>carbon footprint</u> (see below).

2) This is especially true in <u>developed countries</u>:

Rising Affluence

1) People with <u>more money</u> can afford to make a <u>choice</u> about <u>energy use</u>, e.g. buying <u>newer</u> cars that are more <u>fuel-efficient</u> or investing in <u>solar panels</u> for their <u>homes</u>.

2) <u>Governments</u> in <u>developed countries</u> have more money to invest in <u>public transport</u> and <u>renewable energy</u>.

Education

1) People in developed countries have <u>better access</u> to <u>education</u> through <u>school</u> and the <u>media</u> — this means they have a better <u>understanding</u> of the <u>consequences</u> of <u>unsustainable energy use</u> and <u>increasing emissions</u>.

2) People learn how to <u>reduce</u> their <u>carbon footprint</u>, which means there's more interest in using <u>cleaner energy sources</u> and <u>reducing energy consumption</u>.

Environmental Concerns

1) <u>Increased access</u> to <u>education</u> means people are more <u>worried</u> about <u>permanently damaging</u> the <u>environment</u> — they're <u>more likely</u> to try to <u>reduce</u> their <u>carbon footprint</u>.

2) Developed countries can afford to <u>invest</u> in <u>research</u> into the <u>environmental impacts</u> of different <u>energy sources</u> — this creates more <u>awareness</u> about <u>energy consumption</u> and how to reduce carbon footprints.

3) In <u>developing</u> countries, <u>economic development</u> can overshadow <u>environmental concerns</u>. As a country <u>develops</u>, the environment can become a <u>higher priority</u>.

Carbon and Ecological Footprints are Calculated Using Several Factors

1) A <u>carbon footprint</u> is a measure of the <u>amount</u> of <u>greenhouse gases</u> generated by the activities of an <u>individual</u> or <u>organisation</u>, or by a <u>product</u> over its lifetime.

2) An <u>ecological footprint</u> is a measure of how much <u>land</u> is needed to <u>support</u> an individual's lifestyle. It can also be used on a <u>larger scale</u> to calculate the impact of <u>cities</u>, <u>countries</u> or the <u>world population</u>.

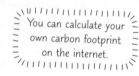
You can calculate your own carbon footprint on the internet.

3) Both are calculated from these key areas:

- <u>FOOD</u> — e.g. how much <u>meat</u> you eat (the process of meat production produces huge amounts of <u>greenhouse gases</u> and takes up <u>lots</u> of <u>land</u>), <u>food wastage</u> and whether you eat <u>locally produced food</u>.

- <u>HOME</u> — e.g. the <u>size</u> of your house and <u>how many people</u> live in it. It also looks at the type of energy you use to heat your home and whether your home has <u>energy-saving features</u>.

- <u>TRAVEL</u> — this is do to with <u>air travel</u>, <u>commuting</u> and what sort of <u>transport</u> you use.

- <u>LIFESTYLE</u> — this is to do with how much you spend on <u>clothes</u> and <u>electrical devices</u> in a <u>year</u> and how much <u>recycling</u> you do.

Carbon footprints — what Santa left on my beige carpet...

Well that's another section almost done and dusted — just a handful of revision questions, then you can get stuck into some geographical decision making. Calm down now. Please contain your excitement.

Revision Summary

Congratulations — you've made it to the end of the topic. Hope you're still full of energy, because here's a lovely page of revision summary questions. As always, all the answers you need are on the pages you (should) have just learnt — if you get stuck on a question, go back and revise the page again.

Energy Resources and Production (p.106-107) ☑

1) Define renewable energy.

2) Give an example of a non-renewable energy resource.

3) Describe a recyclable energy resource.

4) Give two ways that mining can affect ecosystems.

5) What impact does onshore drilling have on the environment?

6) Describe the environmental impacts of using solar energy.

Access to Energy (p.108-110) ☑

7) Briefly describe three factors that affect access to energy.

8) Give one way that development affects energy consumption.

9) What is an oil reserve?

10) Briefly describe three factors that affect oil production.

11) Give two reasons why oil consumption is increasing.

12) a) How might diplomatic relations affect the supply of oil?
    b) What effect do recessions have on oil prices?

13) What is a conventional energy reserve?

14) a) Give two economic benefits of exploiting conventional energy reserves in isolated areas.
    b) Give two environmental costs of exploiting conventional energy reserves in isolated areas.

15) What are unconventional energy reserves?

16) How does fracking affect the environment?

17) Describe the environmental impacts of extracting energy from tar sands in ecologically sensitive areas.

Sustainable Energy Use (p.111-112) ☑

18) What is the difference between energy conservation and energy efficiency.

19) a) Explain how homes can be made more energy-efficient.
    b) Describe two ways that transport can be designed to better conserve energy.

20) How does reducing fossil fuel use reduce carbon footprints?

21) Give two benefits of using biofuels instead of fossil fuels.

22) Give two disadvantages of wind energy.

23) Give one disadvantage of replacing fossil fuels with hydroelectric power.

24) Describe the advantages of hydrogen fuel.

Energy Futures (p.113-114) ☑

25) a) What is the 'business as usual' scenario for future energy use?
    b) What is the 'move to sustainability' scenario for future energy use?

26) Why might transnational corporations (TNCs) favour the business as usual scenario?

27) Give one reason why environmental groups support the move to sustainability.

28) How is rising affluence changing attitudes to energy futures?

29) a) What does a person's carbon footprint measure?
    b) What does a person's ecological footprint measure?

30) Give two factors used to calculate carbon and ecological footprints.

Making Geographical Decisions

Knowing all the <u>facts</u> isn't quite enough to get you through your exams — you'll also have to use what you've learnt to come to a <u>decision</u> about a geographical dilemma. Crumbs.

You'll Have to Make a Decision About a Geographical Issue

<u>Section D</u> of <u>Paper 3</u> asks you to make a <u>decision</u> about a geographical issue and <u>justify</u> your choice. You will be given <u>three</u> options to <u>choose</u> from and there will be <u>12 marks</u> available for your answer — plus <u>4 marks</u> for <u>SPaG</u> (spelling, punctuation and grammar).

1) The issue could be based <u>anywhere</u> in the world and could vary in scale from <u>local</u> to <u>international</u>.

2) It will relate to what you've learnt in <u>Topics 7, 8 and 9</u> — e.g. how to manage an area of forest or increase energy supply in an area.

3) It will involve elements of <u>physical</u> and <u>human</u> geography.

4) You'll need to link in what you've learnt from the <u>rest of the course</u> and it might extend into <u>new contexts</u> that you <u>haven't studied before</u>.

You'll Be Given a Resource Booklet to Help You

1) In the exam, you'll get a <u>resource booklet</u>. It will contain <u>loads</u> of <u>information</u> about the <u>issue</u>.

2) The booklet could include <u>several</u> different types of information, such as:

- Maps
- Graphs
- Photographs

- Diagrams
- Statistics
- Newspaper articles

- Quotes from people involved

> Make sure you can read all the common types of maps and graphs — see pages 118-126 for more on this.

3) You'll need to use <u>all</u> the information in the booklet to make your <u>decision</u>, but <u>don't worry</u> — you'll get to use the <u>sources</u> to answer questions in <u>Sections A, B and C</u>, which will help you to <u>understand</u> what they <u>show</u>.

Use All the Information to Form an Opinion About the Issue

1) You'll be asked to <u>argue</u> your <u>point of view</u> using the <u>information</u>, e.g. <u>suggesting</u> how an area could best be <u>managed</u> to meet the needs of <u>everyone</u> involved.

2) <u>There's no single right or wrong answer</u> — but you need to be able to <u>justify</u> your argument, so make sure you can use the <u>data</u> from the resource booklet to <u>support it</u>.

3) <u>Whatever</u> your view is, you need to give a <u>balanced argument</u>. Try to think of the potential <u>impacts</u> of the decision, both <u>positive</u> and <u>negative</u>, including:

- <u>Economic impacts</u> — e.g. will the decision bring more money to a country?
- <u>Political impacts</u> — e.g. are other countries likely to approve of the decision? If not, what effect might this have?
- <u>Social impacts</u> — e.g. will the decision improve quality of life for people in the area?
- <u>Environmental impacts</u> — e.g. is the decision likely to damage natural habitats?

You could also think about how any <u>negative impacts</u> could be <u>reduced</u>.

4) It's likely to be a <u>complex issue</u> with <u>lots</u> of <u>different parties involved</u>. So think about <u>possible conflicts</u> that your solution might cause <u>between different groups</u> of people, or between <u>people</u> and the <u>environment</u>, and how they could be <u>resolved</u>.

Shall I use a blue pencil for the sea? Geographical decisions are tricky...

It may sound a bit daunting, but the resource booklet will give you most of what you need to write a splendid answer. Just remember to back up your decision using facts and figures from the resource booklet, and the job's a good 'un.

Answering Questions

This section is filled with lots of lovely <u>techniques</u> and <u>skills</u> that you need for your <u>exams</u>. It's no good learning the <u>content</u> of this book if you don't bother learning the skills you need to pass your exam too. First up, answering questions properly...

Make Sure you Read the Question Properly

It's dead easy to <u>misread</u> the question and spend five minutes writing about the <u>wrong thing</u>.
Four simple tips can help you <u>avoid</u> this:

1) Figure out if it's a <u>case study question</u> — if the question wording includes 'using <u>named examples</u>' or 'for a <u>named</u> country' you need to include a case study or examples you've learnt about.

2) <u>Underline</u> the <u>command words</u> in the question (the ones that tell you <u>what to do</u>):

> Answers to questions with 'explain' in them often include the word '<u>because</u>' (or '<u>due to</u>').

> When writing about differences, '<u>whereas</u>' is a good word to use in your answers, e.g. 'Upland areas in the UK are often formed of igneous or metamorphic rocks, whereas lowland areas are often formed of sedimentary rocks.'

Command word	Means write about...
Describe	what it's <u>like</u>
Explain	<u>why</u> it's like that (i.e. give <u>reasons</u>)
Compare	the <u>similarities</u> AND <u>differences</u>
Suggest why	give <u>reasons</u> for
Assess	<u>weigh up</u> all factors
Evaluate	<u>judge</u> the <u>success</u> of something
Justify	give <u>reasons</u>

> If a question asks you to describe a <u>pattern</u> (e.g. from a map or graph), make sure you identify the <u>general pattern</u>, then refer to any <u>anomalies</u> (things that <u>don't</u> fit the general pattern).
> E.g. to answer 'describe the global distribution of volcanoes', <u>first</u> say that they're mostly on plate margins, <u>then</u> mention that a few aren't (e.g. in Hawaii).

3) <u>Underline</u> the <u>key words</u> (the ones that tell you what it's <u>about</u>), e.g. volcanoes, immigration, energy supply.

4) If the question says '<u>using Figure 2</u>', bloomin' well <u>make sure</u> you've talked about <u>what Figure 2 shows</u>. <u>Don't</u> just wheel out all of your <u>geographical knowledge</u> and forget all about the photo you're <u>supposed</u> to be <u>talking about</u>. <u>Re-read</u> the <u>question</u> and your <u>answer</u> when you've <u>finished</u>, just to check.

Some Questions are Level Marked

Questions worth <u>8 marks or more</u> with longer written answers are <u>level marked</u>, which means you need to do these <u>things</u> to get the <u>top level</u> and a <u>high mark</u>:

1) <u>Read</u> the question properly and figure out a <u>structure</u> for your answer before you start. Your answer needs to be well <u>organised</u> and <u>structured</u>, and written in a <u>logical</u> way.

2) If it's a <u>case study</u> question, include plenty of <u>relevant details</u>:

  • This includes things like <u>place names</u>, <u>dates</u>, <u>statistics</u>, names of <u>organisations</u> or <u>companies</u>.
  • Don't forget that they need to be <u>relevant</u> though — it's no good including the exact number of people killed in a flood when the question is about the <u>causes</u> of a flood.

3) Some questions have <u>4 extra marks</u> available for <u>spelling</u>, <u>punctuation</u> and <u>grammar</u>. To get <u>top marks</u> you need to:

  • Make sure your <u>spelling</u>, <u>punctuation</u> and <u>grammar</u> are <u>consistently correct</u>.
  • Write in a way that makes it <u>clear</u> what you mean.
  • Use a <u>wide range</u> of <u>geographical terms</u> (e.g. sustainable development) <u>correctly</u>.

Explain the similarities and differences between compare and assess...

It may all seem a bit simple to you, but it's really important to understand what you're being asked to do. This can be tricky — sometimes the differences between the meanings of the command words are quite subtle, so get learnin'.

Maps

Maps, glorious maps... there's nothing better. OS® maps are my personal favourite, but these aren't bad.

Latitude and Longitude are Used for Global Coordinates

1) The position of anywhere on Earth can be given using coordinates if you use latitude and longitude.

2) Lines of latitude run horizontally around the Earth. They measure how far north or south from the equator something is.

3) Lines of longitude run vertically around the Earth. They measure how far east or west from the Prime Meridian (a line of longitude running through Greenwich in London) something is.

4) Latitude and longitude are measured in degrees.

5) For example, the coordinates of London are 51° N, 0° W. New York is at 40° N, 74° W.

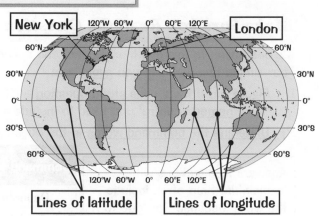

Describing Distributions on Maps — Describe the Pattern

1) In your exam you could get questions like, 'use the map to describe the distribution of volcanoes' and 'explain the distribution of deforestation'.

2) Describe the general pattern and any anomalies (things that don't fit the general pattern).

3) Make at least as many points as there are marks and use names of places and figures if they're given.

4) If you're asked to give a reason or explain, you need to describe the distribution first.

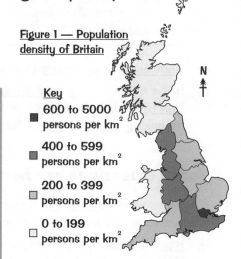

Figure 1 — Population density of Britain

Key
- 600 to 5000 persons per km^2
- 400 to 599 persons per km^2
- 200 to 399 persons per km^2
- 0 to 199 persons per km^2

Q: Use Figure 1 to explain the pattern of population density in Britain.

A: The London area has a very high population density (600 to 5000 per km^2). There are also areas of high population density (400 to 599 per km^2) in the south east, the Midlands and north west of England. These areas include major cities (e.g. Birmingham and Manchester). More people live in and around cities because there are better services and more job opportunities than in rural areas. Scotland and Wales have the lowest population densities in Britain (less than 199 per km^2)...

You could be given two maps to use for one question — link information from the two maps together.

Describing Locations on Maps — Include Details

1) In your exam you could get a question like, 'describe the location of cities in ...'.

2) When you're asked about the location of something say where it is, what it's near and use compass points.

3) If you're asked to give a reason or explain, you need to describe the location first.

Q: Use the maps to describe the location of the National Parks.

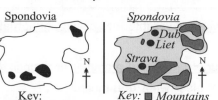

Spondovia

Key:
■ National Parks

Spondovia
• Dub
• Liet
Strava

Key: ■ Mountains
• Cities

A: The National Parks are found in the south west and north east of Spondovia. They are all located in mountainous areas. Three of the parks are located near to the city of Strava.

Describing maps — large, cumbersome, impossible to fold...

...but I love them really. Give me a paper map over some digital device — or worse, a GPS satnav type thing. Yuck. Make sure you're happy with latitude and longitude, then practise describing a map using lots of lovely details.

Geographical Skills

Maps

This page has more <u>dots</u> and <u>lines</u> than the Morse code highlights of the last footy match of the season...

Dot Maps *Show Distribution* and *Quantity Using Identical Symbols...*

1) Dot maps use <u>identical</u> <u>dots</u> to show how something is <u>distributed</u> across an <u>area</u>.

2) Use the <u>key</u> to find out what <u>quantity</u> each dot represents.

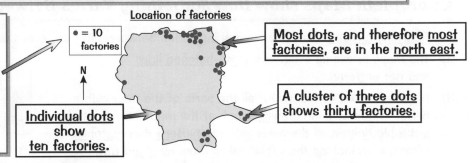

Location of factories

● = 10 factories

N

Individual dots show ten factories.

Most dots, and therefore most factories, are in the north east.

A cluster of three dots shows thirty factories.

...*Proportional Symbol Maps* use Symbols of Different Sizes

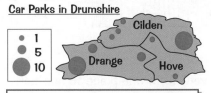

Car Parks in Drumshire

● 1
● 5
● 10

Cilden
Drange
Hove

Q: Which area of Drumshire has the most car parks?

A: Drange, with 20.

1) <u>Proportional symbol maps</u> use symbols of different <u>sizes</u> to represent different <u>quantities</u>.

2) A <u>key</u> shows the <u>quantity</u> each <u>different sized</u> symbol represents. The <u>bigger</u> the symbol, the <u>larger</u> the amount.

3) The symbols might be <u>circles</u>, <u>squares</u>, <u>semi-circles</u> or <u>bars</u>, but a <u>larger symbol</u> always means a <u>larger amount</u>.

Isolines on Maps Link up Places with *Something in Common*

1) <u>Isolines</u> are lines on a map <u>linking</u> up all the places where something's the <u>same</u>, for example:
   • <u>Contour lines</u> are isolines linking up places at the same <u>altitude</u>.
   • Isolines on a <u>weather map</u> (called <u>isobars</u>) link together all the places where the <u>pressure's</u> the same.

2) Isolines can be used to link up lots of things, e.g. <u>average temperature</u>, <u>wind speed</u> or <u>rainfall</u>.

3) Isolines are normally <u>labelled</u> with their <u>value</u>. The <u>closer together</u> the <u>lines</u> are, the <u>steeper</u> the <u>gradient</u> (how quickly the thing is changing) <u>at that point</u>.

1 Reading Isoline Maps

1) <u>Find</u> the place you're interested in on the map and if it's on a line just <u>read</u> off the value.

2) If it's <u>between</u> two lines, you have to <u>estimate</u> the value.

Q: Find the average annual rainfall in Port Portia and on Mt. Mavis.

A: Port Portia is between the lines for 200 mm and 400 mm so the rainfall is likely to be around 300 mm per year.
Mt. Mavis is on an isoline so the rainfall is 1000 mm per year.

Average annual rainfall on Itchy Island (mm per year)

N

600
500
1000
600
500
Mt. Mavis
800
Port Portia
600
400
200

2 Completing Isoline Maps

1) Drawing an isoline's like doing a <u>dot-to-dot</u> — you just join up all the dots with the <u>same numbers</u>.

2) Make sure you don't <u>cross</u> any <u>other isolines</u> though.

Q: Complete on the map the isoline showing an average rainfall of 600 mm per year.

A: See the red line on the map.

When it comes to maps, the key is, er, key...

No matter whether you've got identical dots, proportional symbols or wavy lines, the key to correctly interpreting the map is to understand what each symbol means. The title helps here, but you really need to check the key carefully.

Maps

Three more maps, with three more ludicrous names. Well the last two aren't that bad, but this first one — choropleth, sounds like a treatment at the dentist.

Choropleth Maps show How Something Varies Between Different Areas

1) Choropleth maps show how something varies between different areas using colours or patterns.

2) The maps in exams often use cross-hatched lines and dot patterns.

3) If you're asked to talk about all the parts of the map with a certain value or characteristic, look at the map carefully and put a big tick on all the parts with the pattern that matches what you're looking for. This makes them all stand out.

4) When you're asked to complete part of a map, first use the key to work out what type of pattern you need. Then carefully draw on the pattern, e.g. using a ruler.

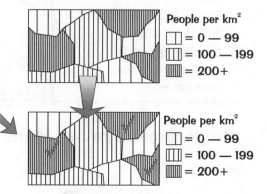

People per km²
☐ = 0 — 99
▦ = 100 — 199
▥ = 200+

People per km²
☐ = 0 — 99
▦ = 100 — 199
▥ = 200+

Flow Lines show Movement

1) Flow line maps have arrows on, showing how things move (or are moved) from one place to another.

2) They can also be proportional symbol maps — the width of the arrows show the quantity of things that are moving.

Q: From which area do the greatest number of people entering the UK come from?

A: USA, as this arrow is the largest.

Q: The number of people entering the UK from the Middle East is roughly half the number of people entering from the USA. Draw an arrow on the map to show this.

A: Make sure your arrow is going in the right direction and its size is appropriate (i.e. half the width of the USA arrow).

Some of the flows of people to the UK

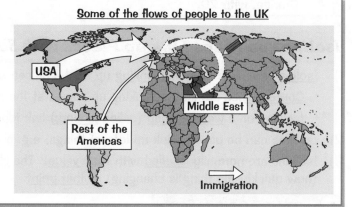

Desire Lines show Journeys

1) Desire line maps are a type of flow line as they show movement too.

2) They're straight lines that show journeys between two locations, but they don't follow roads or railway lines.

3) One line represents one journey.

4) They're used to show how far all the people have travelled to get to a place, e.g. a shop or a town centre, and where they've come from.

Desire lines showing journeys to Cheeseham

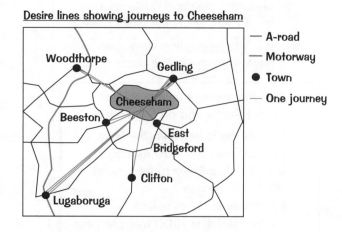

Desire lines — I'm sure my palm reader mentioned those...

...unfortunately I'm not as good at seeing the future as she is* so I can't predict if any of these maps are going to come up in your exam. They could do though, so make sure you know what they are and how to read them.

*If you're wondering, I'm going to meet a short, fair stranger very soon...

Ordnance Survey Maps

Next up, the dreaded <u>Ordnance Survey</u>® <u>maps</u>. Don't worry, they're easy once you know how to use 'em.

Learn These Common Symbols

Ordnance Survey (OS®) maps use lots of <u>symbols</u>. It's a good idea to learn some of the most <u>common ones</u> — like these:

- ▬ Motorway
- ▬ Main (A) road
- ▬ Secondary (B) road
- ⌣ Bridge
- ▬ Railway
- –·–· County boundary
- ▨ National Park boundaries
- ▨ Building
- ⬤ Bus station
- ⫶⫶⫶ Footpaths
- ⚕ Viewpoint
- **i** Tourist information centre
- **P** Parking
- +⊞⚫ Places of worship

You have to be able to Understand Grid References

You need to be able to use <u>four figure</u> and <u>six figure</u> grid references for your exam.

Q: Give the four figure and six figure grid reference for the place of worship.

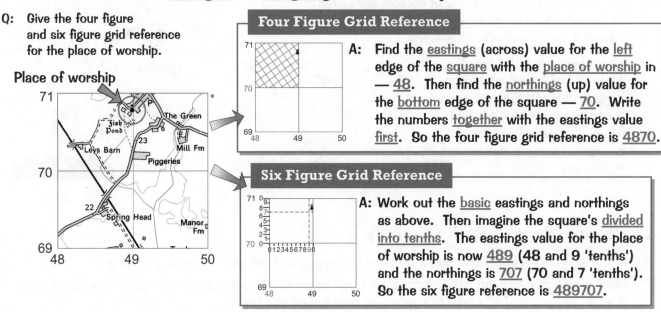

Four Figure Grid Reference

A: Find the <u>eastings</u> (across) value for the <u>left</u> edge of the <u>square</u> with the <u>place of worship</u> in — <u>48</u>. Then find the <u>northings</u> (up) value for the <u>bottom</u> edge of the square — <u>70</u>. Write the numbers <u>together</u> with the eastings value <u>first</u>. So the four figure grid reference is <u>4870</u>.

Six Figure Grid Reference

A: Work out the <u>basic</u> eastings and northings as above. Then imagine the square's <u>divided into tenths</u>. The eastings value for the place of worship is now <u>489</u> (48 and 9 'tenths') and the northings is <u>707</u> (70 and 7 'tenths'). So the six figure reference is <u>489707</u>.

You need to Know your Compass Points

You've got to know the compass — for giving <u>directions</u>, saying <u>which way</u> a <u>river's flowing</u>, or knowing what they mean if they say 'look at the river in the <u>NW</u> of the map' in the exam. Read it <u>out loud</u> to yourself, going <u>clockwise</u>.

North, East, South, West **OR** Never Eat Soggy Wheat

You Might have to Work Out the Distance Between Two Places

To work out the <u>distance</u> between <u>two places</u> on a <u>map</u>, use a <u>ruler</u> to measure the <u>distance</u> in <u>cm</u> then <u>compare</u> it to the scale to find the distance in <u>km</u>.

Q: What's the distance from the bridge (482703) to the place of worship (489707)?

A: They're 2.2 cm apart on the map...

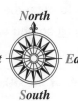
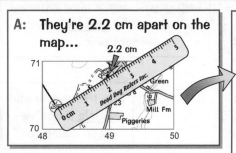

...which means they're 1.1 km apart in real life.

Scale 1:50 000
2 centimetres to 1 kilometre (one grid square)
Kilometres

2.2 cm x 50 000 = 110 000 cm = 1.1 km

Learn the common cymbals — and really annoy your neighbours...

I told you OS maps aren't as bad as you thought. If a bedraggled walker who's been out in the rain for five hours with only a cup of tea to keep them going can read them, then so can you. Get ready for some more map fun...

Ordnance Survey Maps

Almost done with map skills now. Just this final page looking at contour lines and sketching from Ordnance Survey® maps or photographs to deal with then you're free, free I tell you... (well, free from maps anyway).

The Relief of an Area is Shown by Contours and Spot Heights

1) Contour lines are the browny-orange lines drawn on maps — they join points of equal height above sea level (altitude).

2) They tell you about the relief of the land, e.g. whether it's hilly, flat or steep.

3) They show the height of the land by the numbers marked on them. They also show the steepness of the land by how close together they are (the closer they are, the steeper the slope).

4) For example, if a map has lots of contour lines on it, it's probably hilly or mountainous. If there are only a few it'll be flat and often low-lying.

5) A spot height is a dot giving the height of a particular place. A trigonometrical point (trig point) is a blue triangle plus a height value. They usually show the highest point in that area (in metres).

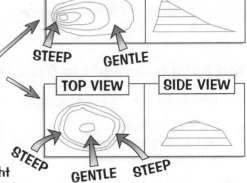

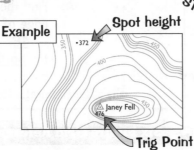

Sketching Maps — Do it Carefully

1) In the exam, they could give you a map or photograph and tell you to sketch part of it.

2) Make sure you figure out what bit they want you to sketch out, and double check you've got it right. It might be only part of a lake or a wood, or only one of the roads.

3) If you're sketching an OS® map, it's a good idea to copy the grid from the map onto your sketch paper — this helps you to copy the map accurately.

4) Draw your sketch in pencil so you can rub it out if it's wrong.

5) Look at how much time you have and how many marks it's worth to decide how much detail to add.

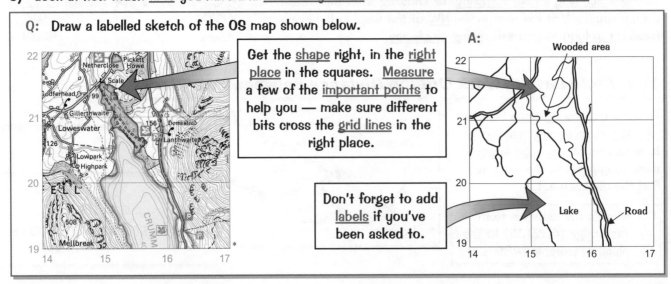

Q: Draw a labelled sketch of the OS map shown below.

Get the shape right, in the right place in the squares. Measure a few of the important points to help you — make sure different bits cross the grid lines in the right place.

Don't forget to add labels if you've been asked to.

A:

What a relief that's over...

When you're sketching a copy of a map or photo see if you can lay the paper over it — then you can trace it (sneaky). Anyway, that may be it for maps, but you're not quite free yet... It's time to rock the charts and graphs. Oh yeah.

Geographical Skills

Charts and Graphs

Stand by for <u>charts</u> and <u>graphs</u>. Make sure you can <u>interpret</u> (read) and <u>construct</u> (draw) each of them...

Describing *what Graphs Show — Include Figures from the Graph*

1) When <u>describing</u> graphs make sure you mention:

2) The general pattern — when it's <u>going up</u> and <u>down</u>, and any <u>peaks</u> (highest bits) and <u>troughs</u> (lowest bits).

3) Any <u>anomalies</u> (odd results).

4) Specific <u>data points</u>.

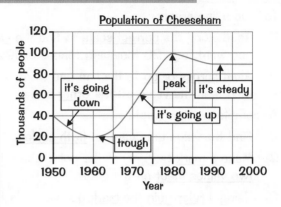

Population of Cheeseham

Q: Use the graph to describe population change in Cheeseham.

A: The population halved between 1950 and 1960 from 40 thousand people to 20 thousand people. It then increased to 100 thousand by 1980, before falling slightly and staying steady at 90 thousand from 1990 to 2000.

Bar Charts — *Draw the Bars Straight and Neat*

To <u>read</u> a bar chart:

1) Read along the <u>bottom</u> to find the <u>bar</u> you want.

2) To find out the <u>value</u> of a bar in a <u>normal</u> bar chart — go from the <u>top</u> of the bar <u>across</u> to the <u>scale</u>, and <u>read off</u> the number.

3) To find out the <u>value</u> of <u>part</u> of the bar in a <u>divided</u> bar chart — find the <u>number at the top</u> of the part of the bar you're interested in, and <u>take away</u> the <u>number at the bottom</u> of it (see example below).

To <u>complete</u> a bar chart:

1) First find the number you want on the <u>vertical scale</u>.

2) Then <u>trace</u> a line across to where the <u>top</u> of the bar will be with a <u>ruler</u>.

3) Draw in a bar of the <u>right size</u> using a <u>ruler</u>.

Oil production

Q: How many barrels of oil did Hoxo Plc. produce per day in 2015?

A: 500 000 – 350 000 = <u>150 000 barrels</u> per day

Q: Complete the chart to show that Froxo Inc. produced 200 000 barrels of oil per day in 2015.

A: 150 thousand (2014) + 200 thousand = <u>350 000 barrels</u>. So draw the bar up to this point.

Histograms *are a Lot Like Bar Charts*

1) <u>Histograms</u> are very <u>similar</u> to <u>bar charts</u>, but they have a <u>continuous scale</u> of <u>numbers</u> on the <u>bottom</u> and there <u>can't</u> be any <u>gaps between the bars</u>.

2) You can use <u>histograms</u> when your <u>data</u> can be divided into <u>intervals</u>, like <u>this</u>:

3) You <u>draw</u> and <u>plot</u> them just like a <u>bar chart</u>, but you have to make sure that the bars are all the <u>correct width</u>, as well as the <u>correct height</u>.

Time	Cars
0700-0800	334
0800-0900	387
0900-1000	209
1000-1100	121
1100-1200	?

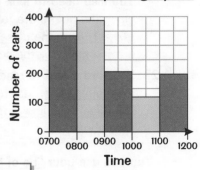

Number of cars passing a point

Q: How many cars were recorded between 1100 and 1200?

A: Trace a line from the top of the 1100-1200 bar and read the answer off — <u>200 cars</u>.

The top forty for sheep — the baaaaaaaaaaaaa chart...

Something to watch out for with bar charts (and line graphs on the next page) is reading the scale — check how much each division is worth before reading them or completing them. Don't assume each division is worth one...

Charts and Graphs

'More charts and graphs' I hear you cry — well OK, your weird wishes are my command.

Line Graphs — the Points are Joined by Lines

To read a line graph:

1) Read along the correct scale to find the value you want, e.g. 20 thousand tonnes or 1920.

2) Read across or up to the line you want, then read the value off the other scale.

To complete a line graph:

1) Find the value you want on both scales.

2) Make a mark (e.g. ×) at the point where the two values meet on the graph.

3) Using a ruler, join the mark you've made to the line that it should be connected to.

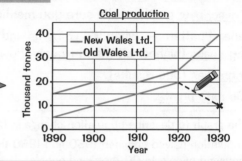

Coal production

Q: Complete the graph to show that Old Wales Ltd. produced 10 thousand tonnes of coal in 1930.

A: Find 1930 on the bottom scale, and 10 thousand tonnes on the vertical scale. Make a mark where they meet, then join it to the blue line with a ruler.

Scatter Graphs Show Relationships

Scatter graphs tell you how closely related two things are, e.g. altitude and air temperature. The fancy word for this is correlation. Strong correlation means the two things are closely related to each other. Weak correlation means they're not very closely related. The line of best fit is a line that goes roughly through the middle of the scatter of points and tells you about what type of correlation there is. Data can show three types of correlation:

1) Positive — as one thing increases the other increases.

2) Negative — as one thing increases the other decreases.

3) None — there's no relationship between the two things.

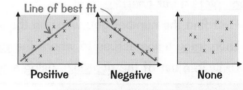

Positive   Negative   None

1 Reading Scatter Graphs

1) If you're asked to describe the relationship, look at the slope of the graph, e.g. if the line's moving upwards to the right it's a positive correlation. You also need to look at how close the points are to the line of best fit — the closer they are the stronger the correlation.

2) If you're asked to read off a specific point, just follow the rules for a line graph (see above).

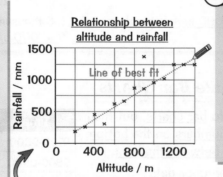

Relationship between altitude and rainfall

2 Completing Scatter Graphs

1) You could be asked to draw a line of best fit — just draw it roughly through the middle of the scatter of points.

2) If you're asked to add a point — just follow the rules for adding a point to a line graph (see above).

Q: Describe the relationship shown by the scatter graph.

A: Altitude and rainfall show a strong, positive correlation — as altitude increases, so does the amount of rainfall.

• You can use your line of best fit to make predictions by reading off values from the graph.

• If you're confident your best fit line will continue, you can extend it beyond the data you have collected. This means you can make predictions outside the range of data you collected.

Sorry darling, we've got no relationship — look at our scatter graph...

Line graphs and scatter graphs with a line of best fit are pretty similar, but don't get them confused — however much you might want to, it's not always ok to go around joining dots up. Study this page 'til you're seeing lines in your sleep.

Charts and Graphs

Chart or graph, tomayto or tomarto, Daddy or chips. I think I've lost it. Please continue as normal.

Pie Charts *Show Amounts* or *Percentages*

The important thing to remember with
pie charts is that <u>the whole pie = 360°</u>.

1 Reading Pie Charts

1) To work out the <u>%</u> for a wedge
   of the pie, use a <u>protractor</u>
   to find out how large it is
   in <u>degrees</u>.

2) Then <u>divide</u> that number
   by <u>360</u> and <u>times</u> by <u>100</u>.

3) To find the <u>amount</u> a wedge of
   the pie is <u>worth</u>, work out your
   <u>percentage</u> then turn it into a
   <u>decimal</u>. Then times the <u>decimal</u>
   by the <u>total amount</u> of the pie.

Pie Chart of Transport Type

(0°, 324°, 270°, 198°, 180°, 126°, 90° — Bicycle, Car, Pogostick)

Q: Out of 200 people, how many used a pogostick?
A: 126 – 90 = 36°, so (36 ÷ 360) × 200
    = 10%, so 0.1 × 200 = <u>20 people</u>.

2 Completing Pie Charts

1) To <u>draw</u> on a <u>new wedge</u> that you
   know the <u>%</u> for, turn the <u>%</u> into a
   <u>decimal</u> and <u>times</u> it by <u>360</u>. Then
   draw a wedge of that many <u>degrees</u>.

Q: Out of 200 people, 25% used a bicycle.
    Add this to the pie chart.
A: 25 ÷ 100 = 0.25, 0.25 × 360 = <u>90°</u>.

2) To add a <u>new wedge</u> that you know
   the <u>amount</u> for, <u>divide</u> your amount
   by the <u>total amount</u> of the pie and
   <u>times</u> the answer by <u>360</u>. Then <u>draw</u>
   on a wedge of that many <u>degrees</u>.

Q: Out of 200 people, 110 used a car,
    add this to the pie chart.
A: 110 ÷ 200 = 0.55, 0.55 × 360
    = <u>198°</u> (198° + 126° = <u>324°</u>).

Dispersion Diagrams *Show the Frequency* of Data

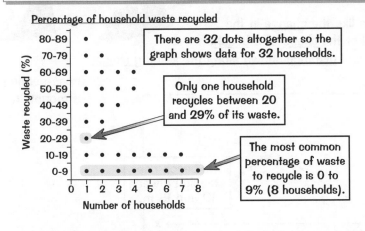

Percentage of household waste recycled

Waste recycled (%) / Number of households

There are 32 dots altogether so the graph shows data for 32 households.

Only one household recycles between 20 and 29% of its waste.

The most common percentage of waste to recycle is 0 to 9% (8 households).

1) Dispersion diagrams are a bit like a cross
   between a <u>tally chart</u> and a <u>bar chart</u>.

2) The <u>range</u> of <u>data that's measured</u> goes on one
   axis. <u>Frequency</u> goes on the other axis.

3) <u>Each dot</u> represents <u>one piece</u> of <u>information</u> —
   the <u>more dots</u> there are in a particular category,
   the <u>more frequently</u> that event has happened.

4) The dispersion diagram on the left shows the
   <u>percentage</u> of <u>household waste</u> that's <u>recycled</u>
   for <u>households</u> in a <u>particular village</u>.

Population Pyramids *Show the Structure* of a Population

1) <u>Population pyramids</u> are a bit
   like <u>two bar charts</u> on their <u>sides</u>.

2) It's way of showing the <u>population</u>
   of a country by <u>age</u> and <u>gender</u>.

3) The <u>number of people</u> goes on the <u>horizontal axis</u>, and
   the <u>age groups</u> go on the <u>vertical axis</u>. The <u>left side</u> is the
   <u>male population</u> and the <u>right side</u> is the <u>female population</u>.

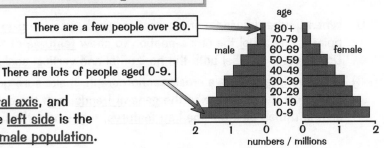

There are a few people over 80.

There are lots of people aged 0-9.

age / male / female / numbers / millions

Pie charts aren't bad, but I prefer cake...

Hmm, who'd have thought pie could be so complicated. Don't panic though, a bit of practice and you'll be fine. And
don't worry, there are only three more pages to go in the whole book. Congratulations — I'm so proud of you, sniff.

Charts and Graphs

Yep, you guessed it — there are <u>even more</u> charts and graphs to learn. These are the <u>last ones</u>, I <u>promise</u>.

Pictograms Use Pictures to Show Quantities

1) <u>Pictograms</u> use <u>symbols</u> instead of <u>numbers</u> to show frequency.

2) In a pictogram each <u>picture</u> or <u>symbol</u> represents a <u>certain number of items</u>. The <u>pictogram</u> below shows the <u>number of new houses</u> built in Bogdon from 2010-2015:

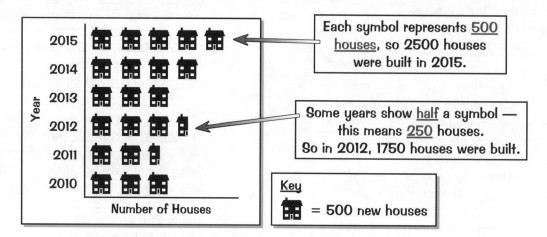

Each symbol represents <u>500</u> houses, so 2500 houses were built in 2015.

Some years show <u>half</u> a symbol — this means <u>250</u> houses. So in 2012, 1750 houses were built.

<u>Key</u>
🏠 = 500 new houses

Cross-Sections show the Land from Sideways on

1) <u>Cross-sections</u> show what the landscape looks like if it's <u>chopped</u> down the <u>middle</u> and <u>viewed</u> from the <u>side</u>.

2) In geography, they're useful for showing things like the <u>change</u> in the <u>height</u> of the land, the <u>shape</u> of a <u>river channel</u> or the <u>shape</u> of a <u>beach</u>. They're often presented in a <u>graph</u> with <u>height</u> and <u>distance</u> shown along the <u>x</u> and <u>y axes</u>. For example:

cross-section of mountain

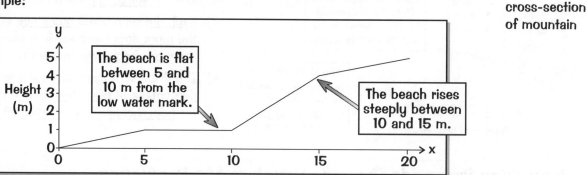

The beach is flat between 5 and 10 m from the low water mark.

The beach rises steeply between 10 and 15 m.

3) When you're <u>drawing</u> a cross-section graph, use the <u>y-axis</u> to plot the contour heights. <u>Join</u> all the points, then <u>label</u> the cross-section to show <u>features</u> of the landscape (e.g. valley sides, hilltops etc.) Don't forget to label both the <u>horizontal</u> and <u>vertical scales</u> (the x and y axes).

4) If you're <u>interpreting</u> a cross-section graph, make sure you look at both the <u>horizontal</u> and <u>vertical scales</u> carefully. Describe the <u>general trends</u>, e.g. the beach generally slopes upwards away from the sea, and then pick out the <u>key features</u>, e.g. where the land is <u>steepest</u> and where it is <u>flatter</u>.

A bit of revision helps to avoid cross sections in exams...

...or so I heard. Still, it can't hurt to be a little more prepared, so go back and learn this page 'til you can't see for pictograms and you're dreaming in cross-sections. Then direct yourself to the next page.

Statistics

EEEK, it's a page about <u>maths</u>. In a <u>geography</u> book. Still, it should all be <u>very familiar</u> from <u>maths lessons</u>...

Learn the Definitions for *Mode, Median, Mean and Range*...

<u>Mode</u>, <u>median</u> and <u>mean</u> are measures of <u>average</u> and the <u>range</u> is how <u>spread out</u> the values are:

<u>MODE</u> = <u>MOST</u> common
<u>MEDIAN</u> = <u>MIDDLE</u> value (when values are in order of size)
<u>MEAN</u> = <u>TOTAL</u> of items ÷ <u>NUMBER</u> of items
<u>RANGE</u> = <u>DIFFERENCE</u> between highest and lowest

REMEMBER:

<u>Mode</u> = <u>mo</u>st (emphasise the 'mo' in each when you say them)

<u>Median</u> = <u>mid</u> (emphasise the m*d in each when you say them)

<u>Mean</u> is just the <u>average</u>, but it's <u>mean</u> 'cos you have to work it out.

Sample	1	2	3	4	5	6	7
River discharge (cumecs)	184	90	159	142	64	64	95

Q: Calculate the mean, median, mode and range for the river discharge data shown in the table above.

A: • The mode is the most common value = <u>64</u>.

When there are two middle numbers, the median is halfway between the two.

• To find the median, put all the numbers in order and find the middle value:
 64, 64, 90, <u>95</u>, 142, 159, 184. So the median is <u>95</u>.

• Mean = $\dfrac{\text{total of items}}{\text{number of items}}$ = $\dfrac{184 + 90 + 159 + 142 + 64 + 64 + 95}{7}$ = $\dfrac{798}{7}$ = <u>114</u>

• The range is the difference between highest and lowest value, i.e. 184 − 64 = <u>120</u>

1) Each of these methods has <u>weaknesses</u>. The <u>mean</u> and the <u>range</u> are affected by any <u>outliers</u> (values that are a lot <u>bigger</u> or <u>smaller</u> than most of the other values) — this reduces their <u>accuracy</u>.

2) In some data sets, there might be <u>more than one mode</u> — or each value might be <u>different</u>, meaning there <u>isn't</u> a mode.

3) If you have a <u>large</u> set of data, it takes <u>longer</u> to calculate the <u>median</u>.

As well as finding the <u>median</u> (the middle value in a list), you can also find the <u>upper</u> and <u>lower quartiles</u> — the values a <u>quarter</u> (25%) and <u>three-quarters</u> (75%) of the way through the <u>ordered data</u>.

Q: The number of shoppers in each shop in a village were counted. Find the median and the quartiles of the data set.

A: 2, 3, **6**, 6, 7, **9**, 13, 14, **17**, 22, 22

| Lower quartile | Median | Upper quartile |

1) The <u>interquartile range</u> is the <u>difference between</u> the <u>upper quartile</u> and the <u>lower quartile</u>.

2) It contains the middle <u>50%</u> of values — this is one of its <u>weaknesses</u> because it <u>doesn't</u> take <u>all</u> the values into account.

Q: Find the interquartile range of the number of shoppers.

A: 17 − 6 = <u>11</u>

You also Need to Know How to Find the Modal Class

If your data is <u>grouped</u> you might need to find the <u>modal class</u>. This is just the <u>group</u> with the <u>most values</u> in.

Q: Find the modal class of the population data shown in the table.

A: Modal class = <u>20-39 years</u>

Age	Number of people
0-19	21
20-39	37
40-59	27
60+	15

Remember, the modal class will be the group — not how many items are in that group.

This page is mean — wish I was still on those maps pages...

Sheesh, I wasn't expecting so much stats in a geography book. But here it is, so you might as well learn it before it comes up in your exam. Anyway, this is the penultimate page in the book so once you've cracked it, you're on the home straight.

Statistics

Phew, you've made it to the <u>last page</u> — just a few more <u>statistics</u> to look at, then it's time for a <u>nap</u>.

You Need to be Able to Calculate Percentages and Percentage Change...

To give the amount X as a <u>percentage</u> of a sample Y, you need to <u>divide</u> X by Y and <u>multiply by 100</u>.

> Q: This year, 35 out of the 270 houses in Foxedapolice were burgled.
> Calculate the percentage of houses burgled in Foxedapolice.
>
> A: $35 \div 270 \times 100$
> $= \underline{13\%}$

Calculating <u>percentage change</u> lets you work out <u>how much</u> something has <u>increased</u> or <u>decreased</u>.
You use this <u>formula</u>:

$$\text{Percentage change} = \frac{\text{final value} - \text{original value}}{\text{original value}} \times 100$$

A <u>positive</u> value shows an <u>increase</u> and a <u>negative</u> value shows a <u>decrease</u>.

> Q: Last year in Foxedapolice, only 24 houses were burgled.
> Calculate the percentage change in burglaries in Foxedapolice.
>
> A: $\dfrac{35 - 24}{24} \times 100 = \underline{46\% \text{ increase}}$ in the number
> of burglaries in Foxedapolice.

Percentiles Tell You Where in Your Data Set a Data Point Lies

1) Percentiles are useful if you want to compare the value of <u>one data point</u> to the <u>rest</u> of your data.

2) To find a percentile, you <u>rank</u> your data from smallest to largest, then <u>divide</u> it into <u>one hundred equal chunks</u>. Each chunk is <u>one percentile</u>.

3) This means that each percentile represents <u>one percent</u> of the data, and so the <u>value of a percentile</u> tells you what <u>percentage</u> of the data has a value <u>lower than</u> the data points in that percentile.

> E.g. Sid the Stone is in the <u>90th percentile</u> for <u>weight</u> in his section of the river bed. This means that <u>90%</u> of the stones are <u>lighter</u> than Sid.

4) Percentiles can be used to give a more realistic idea of the <u>spread</u> of data than the <u>range</u> — by finding the range between the <u>10th</u> and <u>90th percentiles</u> in a data set (the middle 80% of the data), you can look at the spread of the data while ignoring any <u>outlying</u> results.

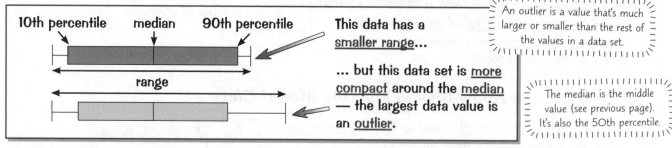

10th percentile   median   90th percentile

range

This data has a <u>smaller range</u>...

... but this data set is <u>more compact</u> around the <u>median</u> — the largest data value is an <u>outlier</u>.

> An outlier is a value that's much larger or smaller than the rest of the values in a data set.

> The median is the middle value (see previous page). It's also the 50th percentile.

5) Percentiles have a couple of <u>weaknesses</u>:
   - Any <u>outliers</u> in the data set are given the <u>highest</u> or <u>lowest percentile</u>.
   - If a lot of the data is <u>very close</u> to the mean, any <u>differences</u> are <u>exaggerated</u> by percentiles.

Percentiles — found in every mathematician's bathroom...

Well, that's your lot for skills. I know this has been a big ol' section, but it's all important stuff, so there's no excuse for not learning it. Now it's officially time for that nap — you should have nothing but sweet geographical dreams.

Acknowledgements

Estimated temperature variations for Central England (1000-2000) on page 5 based on Palaeogeography, Paiaeoclimatol., Palaeoecol., 1 (1965) 13-37, H. H. Lamb, The early medieval warm epoch and its sequel, p25, Copyright © 1965, with permission from Elsevier.

Photograph on p.7 (UK flooding) © Rose and Trev Clough/p.44 (Grampian Mountains) © Trevor Littlewood/p.44 (Cheshire Plain) © Peter Styles/p.44 (Snowdonia) © Bill Boaden/p.44 (The Weald) © Peter Jeffery/p.46 (Limestone Pavement) © Martyn Gorman/p.47 (Llyn Idwal) © Dudley Smith/p.47 (Dry Valley) © Colin Smith/p.51 (Old Harry) © Raymond Knapman/p.54 (tractor in field) © Roger Lombard/p.54 (coastal town) © Lewis Clarke/p.54 (quarry) © Mike Faherty/p.54 (industry) © David Dixon/p.54 (groyne) © N Chadwick/p.55 (rock groyne) © J Thomas/p.60 (Hell Gill Force) © Roger Templeman/p.60 (Eden at Salkeld) © Greg Fitchett/p.60 (Eden floodplain) © Rose and Trev Clough/p.60 (Eden at Appleby) © Steve Daniels/p.62 (interlocking spurs) © Bob Bowyer/p.66 (River Kent) © Karl and Ali/p.69 (Flooding in Carlisle and flood aftermath) © Rose and Trev Clough/p.70 (flood wall in Edinburgh) © Robin Scott/p.70 (embankment) © Chris Denny/p.70 (Thames Barrier) © John M/p.70 (Demountable flood barrier) © Chris Whippet/p.70 (grasslands) © Richard Croft/p.79 (Central London) © Philip Halling/p.79 (Bluewater shopping centre) © Ken Brown/p.81 (Converted oast house) © Oast House Archive. Licensed under the Creative Commons Attribution-Share Alike 2.0 Generic Licence. http://creativecommons.org/licenses/by-sa/2.0/

Graphs showing future temperature and sea level rise on page 8 adapted from Figure SPM.6 Climate Change 2014: Synthesis Report. Contribution of Working Groups I, II and III to the Fifth Assessment Report of the Intergovernmental Panel on Climate Change [Core Writing Team, Pachauri, R.K. and Meyer, L. (eds.)]. IPCC, Geneva, Switzerland.

Satellite image on page 9: Jeff Schmaltz, MODIS Rapid Response Team, NASA/GSFC

HDI data on page 22 and page 29 from 2015 Human Development Report, United Nations Development Programme from hdr.undp.org. Licensed for re-use under the Creative Commons Attribution 3.0 IGO license (https://creativecommons.org/licenses/by/3.0/igo/)

Data used to compile table (except HDI) and create pyramids on p.22 from The World Factbook. Washington, DC: Central Intelligence Agency, 2017.

Data for quintiles diagram on page 24 and graph of % urban population 1980-2015 on page 33 from the World Bank: World Development Indicators.

India GDP and GNI per capita on page 29: The World Bank: India: World Bank national accounts data, and OECD National Accounts data files.

India industrial sector data on page 29: The World Bank: Employment in agriculture and industry (% of total employment): International Labour Organization, Key Indicators of the Labour Market database.

Primary education data on page 29: UNESCO Institute for Statistics (UIS), http://uis.unesco.org

India development data on page 30: The World Bank: India: Life expectancy at birth, total (years)/ Fertility rate, total (births per woman)/ Urban population (% of total): United Nations Population Division. World Population Prospects

GDP per capita data for Bihar and Maharashta on page 30 from statisticstimes.com.

Urban Population & Literacy rate data for Bihar and Maharashta on page 30 © Office of the Registrar General & Census Commissioner, India.

HDI data for Bihar and Maharashta on page 30 © Copyright 2016 United Nations Development Programme.

Female literecy rate data on page 30 from The World Bank: India: Literacy rate, adult female (% of females ages 15 and above): United Nations Educational, Scientific, and Cultural Organization (UNESCO) Institute for Statistics.

Projection of future urban population % and map of countries by categorised by HDI on page 33 © Copyright 2016 United Nations Development Programme.

Satellite images on pages 38 and 39: USGS/NASA Landsat

Extent of Lagos by 1920, 1960, 1990 (overlays on satellite image on page 38) adapted from Planning, Anti-planning and the Infrastructure Crisis Facing Metropolitan Lagos, page 373, by Matthew Gandy and Piecemeal Urbanisation at the Peripheries of Lagos, page 5, by Lindsay Sawyer.

Birth and death rates in Nigeria on page 39: The World Bank: Nigeria: Death rate, crude (per 1,000 people)

Photo of Makoko slum on page 39 © Heinrich-Böll-Stiftung. Licensed under the Creative Commons Attribution-Share Alike 2.0 Generic license. (https://creativecommons.org/licenses/by-sa/2.0/deed.en)

Topographic map of the United Kingdom on page 44 by Captain Blood, Licensed under the Creative Commons Attribution-Share Alike 3.0 Unported license. (https://creativecommons.org/licenses/by-sa/3.0/deed.en)

Geological map of the UK on page 45 contains British Geological Survey materials © NERC 2017

Map extracts on pages 47, 48, 53, 65, 121 and 122 reproduced with permission by Ordnance Survey ® © Crown copyright 2017 OS 100034841

Data used to construct maps on page 72 and graphs on page 74, ethnicity data on page 74, UK industrial data on page 75, FDI and infrastructure data on page 76, housing deprivation data on page 82: Office for National Statistics licensed under the Open Government Licence v.3.0. http://www.nationalarchives.gov.uk/doc/open-government-licence/version/3/

Data used to construct graph on page 75: Office for National Statistics licensed under the Open Government Licence v.2.0. http://www.nationalarchives.gov.uk/doc/open-government-licence/version/2/

Satellite image of London on page 77 courtesy NASA/GSFC/MITI/ERSDAC/JAROS, and U.S./Japan ASTER Science Team

Outline map of London boroughs on page 78: Contains National Statistics data © Crown copyright and database right [2012] and Contains Ordnance Survey data © Crown copyright and database right [2012]. http://data.london.gov.uk/documents/Geography-licensing.pdf

IMD data and ethnicity statistic on page 78, Docklands employment data and London recycling data on page 80: Contains public sector information licensed under the Open Government Licence v3.0. http://www.nationalarchives.gov.uk/doc/open-government-licence/version/3/

Population projection graph on page 92: from World Population to 2300, by Department of Economic and Social Affairs, Population Division, © 2004 United Nations. Reprinted with the permission of the United Nations.

Global Energy Consumption map on page 108 and graph showing history of crude oil price on page 109 © BP Statistical Review of World Energy 2016

Data used to create map of global oil production page 109 from OPEC Annual Statistical Bulletin 2016

Oil consumption data on page 109 source: U.S. Energy Information Administration (Jan 2017)

Data relating to oil industry investment and employment in Alaska on page 110 © BP in Alaska Statistical Review 2016.

Data used to construct the Population density of the UK map on page 118 and flow map of immigration on page 120 — Source Office for National Statistics © Crown Copyright used under the terms of the Open Government Licence

Index

A

abiotic components 89
abrasion 49, 61
accuracy 86
acid rain 103
agriculture 6, 48, 54
agro-forestry 100
air pollution 31, 41
analysing data 86
arches 51, 53
asteroid collisions 5
asthenosphere 13
atmosphere 6
attrition 49, 61
averages 127

B

backwash 50, 52
bar charts 123
bars 52
bays 51, 55
beaches 52, 53
  replenishment 57
biodiversity 97
biofuels 98, 106, 112
biological weathering 49
biomes 87-89
biosphere 90
biotic components 89
birth rates 21, 22
boreal forests 88
Boserup's theory 93
bottom-up strategies (development)
        27, 42

C

carbon dioxide 6
carbon footprints 111, 114
carboniferous limestone 45, 46
caves 51, 53
CBD (Central Business District) 37
chalk 45, 46
channels 59
chemical weathering 49
choropleth maps 120
CITES (Convention on International
    Trade in Endangered Species
    of Wild Fauna and Flora) 99
clay 45, 46, 55
cliffs
  coastal 53
  river 63

climate change 4-8

climate change 4-8
  effect on coastal flooding 56
  effect on tropical storms 9
  threat to taiga forests 103
  threat to tropical rainforests 98
coastal landforms 50-53
coastal management 54, 55, 57
coasts 49-57
colonisation 23
command words 117
Common Agricultural Policy (CAP) 73
compass points 121
composite volcanoes 15
conclusions 86
concordant coastlines 50
conservative plate boundaries 14, 16
constructive waves 52
consumerism 26
continental crust 13
contour lines 65, 119, 122
convection currents 13
convergent plate boundaries 14-16
core (of the Earth) 13
correlation 124
corries 47
counter-urbanisation 36
crops 7
cross profiles 59
cross-sections 126
crust (of the Earth) 13
Cyclone Nargis 12

D

dams 98
death rates 21, 22
decomposers 97
deforestation 67
  taiga forests 103
  tropical rainforests 98
de-industrialisation 34, 36, 79
deltas 64
deposition (in rivers) 61
deserts 88
desire line maps 120
destructive waves 50
developed countries 22, 34, 35
developing countries 22, 34, 35
discharge 67
discordant coastlines 50
dispersion diagrams 125
divergent plate boundaries 14-16
dot maps 119
drilling (for oil) 107
dry valleys 47

E

earthquakes 16-19
Earth's structure 13
ecological footprints 114
economic sectors 35, 75
ecosystems 87-89
ecotourism 100
embankments 70
emerging countries 22, 34, 35
employment (types of) 35
energy
  consumption 108
  security 111
energy sources
  conventional 110
  non-renewable 106
  recyclable 106
  renewable 106
  unconventional 110
enterprise zones 73
environmental groups 113
ERDF (European Regional
        Development Fund) 73
erosion 47
  by waves 49, 51, 55
  in rivers 59, 61
European Union (EU) 31, 73, 74, 76
eustatic sea level rise 7
evacuations 11, 12
evaluations 86

F

FDI (foreign direct investment)
        29, 31, 76
Ferrel cells 2, 3
fertility rates 22, 30
fieldwork 84-86
flood defences 11, 12, 70
flooding
  coastal 56
  river 68-70
flood plains 64
  retention 70
flow line maps 120
flow resources 106
food chains 97
food webs 97
forest fires 103
forestry 48
fossil fuels 106-108
fracking 110
Frank's dependency theory 25
free trade 26, 76
freeze-thaw weathering 47, 61

Index

Index